W9-BFG-351

March 20, 2002

Dear Joey and Sid,

I am extremely proud to be included in the "Winners Circle" and I thought you might enjoy a copy.

Thank you both for the confidence you have placed with me over the years.

Air Force buddies and good friends...

Looking forward to the wedding.

Sincerely,
John

161

The WINNER'S

How 30 Financial Advisors Became the Best in the Business

CIRCLE

Foreword by Launny Steffens
Former Vice Chairman, Merrill Lynch
Managing Director, Spring Mountain Capital

R.J. Shook

Cahners

Library of Congress Cataloguing-in-Publication Data
Shook, R.J. (Robert James)
        The Winner's Circle: How 30 Financial Advisors Became the Best
    in the Business / R. J. Shook
        p. cm.
    ISBN 1-58862-086-7
        1. Financial Advisors—United States.   2. Success in business.
    I. Shook, Robert J.,   II. Title.
    338.7 --dc21   2002

This publication is designed to provide accurate and authoritative information in regard to the subject matter covered. It is sold with the understanding that neither the publisher nor the author is engaged in rendering legal, accounting, or other professional services. If legal advice or other expert assistance is required, the services of a competent professional person should be sought.

From a Declaration of Principles
Jointly Adopted by
a Committee of the American Bar Association
and a Committee of Publishers and Associations

© 2002 by R. J. Shook

ISBN 1-58862-086-7

All rights reserved. No part of this book may be reproduced in any form or by any means without permission in writing from the author.

Published by
Cahners Business Information
A Division of Reed Elsevier Inc.

Printed in China

10 9 8 7 6 5 4 3 2 1

Acclaim for *The Winner's Circle*

"Open access to financial markets and information may be important, but relationships still matter the most. By profiling thirty of the most successful financial advisors in the business, Shook captures the essence of the industry's best practices and offers comprehensive insight into attracting the 'right' clients and building lifelong relationships. Whether reading this book for business or for pleasure, readers will be enthralled by financial advisors' stories of sacrifices they made on their way to the top, and captivated by their never-ending supply of anecdotes. This book is a winner!"

Wick Simmons
CEO, The Nasdaq Stock Market

"With the profiles in this volume, R.J. Shook again offers readers an engaging opportunity to examine the character and spirit of the nation's most successful financial advisors. For those who aspire to succeed in an industry as dynamic and competitive as ours, the insight gained by reading this book has never been more important or more valuable."

Danny Ludeman
CEO, First Union Securities

"A great read! *The Winner's Circle* is a comprehensive view of how America's top financial advisors win and serve clients, and constantly raise the bar of excellence. Read this book for fresh perspectives on the age-old challenge of building a book of loyal clients; innovative insights relating to managing wealth and investment philosophies; building a world-class team; and giving back to the community. Whether you're in the business, in a related sales profession, or you're an entrepreneur, you'll find ideas and styles that are right for you. Investors will be equally enlightened with fascinating stories and insights on how these top financial advisors successfully manage billions of dollars."

Jamie Price
President, Prudential Securities

"A compelling look at how the industry's most successful financial advisors climbed their way to the top. Shook provides up-close-and-personal insight into how these superstars built a business, established lifelong customer relationships, and effectively manage assets. Additionally, their passion to become the best at what they do and to exceed client expectations is very inspirational. If you're striving for excellence in any business, if you're an investor reading for pleasure, or if you're looking for wealth-management ideas, you should read this book."

Jim Brinkley
President, Legg Mason

"Shook superbly captures—and draws insights from—the best financial advisors in the business. These individuals offer roadmaps for developing a successful practice—from building a winning team and investing in your business, to enhancing skills and taking customer service to higher levels. This book is a must read for financial advisors."

Jim Cannon
President, Sentra Spelman and Sun America Securities

"R. J. Shook's narrative of how thirty successful financial advisors developed their business and appealed to their customers is a well-written and extremely interesting saga. It enthralls the reader by revealing how these people achieved success and continue to enhance their businesses throughout their careers. I found quite remarkable some of the ways in which they have redefined their objectives as well as the manner in which many of these people gave back to the communities in which they serve."

Gilbert Harrison
Chairman, Financo

"*The Winner's Circle* is a fascinating read for anyone within the industry or for those considering financial services as a profession. The insights and strategies discussed can clearly serve as a roadmap for becoming a successful financial advisor."

Rich Santos
Publisher, Registered Representative Magazine and Trusts & Estates

"Top financial advisors always have a distinctive style of doing business, yet common threads run among their diverse styles. R.J. Shook captures this invaluable information and delivers it to his readers in a swift and exhilarating read."

Bernie Madoff
Chairman, Bernard L. Madoff Investment Securities

"R.J. Shook has written a book every financial advisor should read, perhaps several times. Part of the way a person becomes better at something is by closely studying the people who are already the best at that activity. What do they do differently than I do? Do they think differently? Focus differently? The author has been granted unique access to people who certainly could not take time to share what they do with everyone who might individually ask. His book is certainly the next best thing to being right there in the office with these highly successful professionals."

Bill Good
Chairman, Bill Good Marketing, Inc.

"*The Winner's Circle* proves that the American dream is alive and well. This book is full of invaluable insights into how America's financial elite made it to the top of their profession. Every financial advisor who wants to join this elite group will find *The Winner's Circle* a gold mine of secrets for professional success. And every investor who wishes to become better informed about his or her financial future should read it as well."

Britt Beemer
Chairman, America's Research Group

Dedication

To my wife Elisabeth and my son Jacob,
for the love they give and, more importantly,
for the love they receive.

CONTENTS

ACKNOWLEDGEMENTS

Hundreds of people contributed to the creation of *The Winner's Circle*, and I am extremely appreciative to all of them. First, I would like to express how honored I am that Launny Steffens agreed to write my foreword. With his leadership and ideas, Wall Street—and investors around the world—have benefited from his innovations and foresight. I am also honored to count him as a friend, because we created a terrific relationship during the production of this book. Special gratitude is due to members of *The Winner's Circle*, all of whom I have come to admire and respect. I deeply value the friendships that have developed along the way. These financial advisors need not seek publicity, for their immense success keeps them busy managing hundreds of billions of dollars for hundreds of thousands of accounts. In virtually all cases, their motives for participating were altruistic and magnanimous. For example, as Tom Gau, Oregon Pacific Financial Advisors put it, "I like to see others do well; if I can give one financial a single idea as a result of this, then it's worth it."

Or as Augie Cenname of Merrill Lynch stated, "Why not do something positive for the industry, and share our knowledge? It's our way of helping to promote best practices."

Similarly, Joe Montgomery at First Union Securities said, "It's important to give back to the industry." And John Cooke, of Prudential Securities says: "When I was starting out, I sought to learn from the best. Unfortunately, *The Winner's Circle* didn't exist back then." I received comments like these from all financial advisors profiled in this book.

Special thanks are due to members of the securities industry for their involvement in facilitating the creation of *The Winner's Circle*, and their dedication to establishing the highest standards for the industry (listed alphabetically by company): Laura Schreiner at Bear Stearns; Maureen Gillespie at CIBC World Markets; Tony Mattera at First Union Securities; Laura Lang at Legg Mason; Michael Goldman at Lehman Brothers; Joe Cohen at Merrill Lynch; Megan Ochampaugh and Melissa Stonberg at Morgan Stanley; Deborah Grieves at Oregon Pacific Financial Advisors; Susan Atran at Prudential Securities; Christy Spilsted and Lynne Morrill at Salomon Smith Barney; Dave Fischer at Sentra Spelman; and Susan Wentworth at UBS PaineWebber. And a special thank you to Chad Smith for going the extra mile, especially during his days off.

Thanks to Erik Niermeyer, Jim Madden, Brad Zucker, Jim Clauss, and Diane Niermeyer for their endless support and advice. More gratitude to my editor Jeanne Flagg, contributions from Dom Delprete, and, of course, the talented team at Cahner's, particularly Kelly Keane for her expertise and guidance, Jacqui Dawson for design and Maura Brown for editorial support.

FOREWORD

BY LAUNNY STEFFENS

The industry that we have come to know as financial services has experienced more change during the last three decades than it has in the previous 100 years. It's true, change is common in all industries, but few have seen such an impact on all aspects of a business—the core structure, products, technology, distribution, and client relationships. These changes have fundamentally altered both the capital-raising process and, more significantly, the client service model.

In the past, the structure was simple. The financial needs of both individuals and corporations were served by three separate sectors: banks, insurance companies, and securities firms. Due to regulatory barriers, clients had to utilize these separate structures to complete their financial needs. Corporations used banks for short-term borrowing needs, securities firms for equity capital, and the insurance industry for asset protection. Individuals also used banks for mostly short-term services such as checking and credit; they used securities firms for investing in common stock and insurance companies for the protection of assets. Many of these service providers had no way to integrate these offerings into a cohesive whole. Each organization provided its own product solution, and even if it wasn't a perfect fit, that was all it was able to offer. Clients were faced with the difficult task of putting this puzzle together in a way that would meet their needs.

For decades, this worked, because financial complexity was not a major concern for most Americans. However, as the U.S. economy grew and general wealth increased (along with exposure to the securities markets), this lack of an integrated choice put pressure on the regulators to change the system. When this lacked any timely focus, innovation took over.

Today, of course, banks, insurance companies, and securities firms each ubiquitously offer financial-service packages to compete for their clients' total financial needs. Nowhere has the impact of structural change been more significant than with the client service model, which remained relatively static from 1930 through the 1970s. The private banker, the financial advisor, and the do-it-yourself investor are all focused on integrating the pieces of the financial puzzle and understanding the implications of each.

The financial advisors profiled in this book, while different in many ways, have all been able to adjust to the changes around them while maintaining a singular focus: serving the needs of their clients. This means much more than understanding their clients' complete financial picture. It means understanding some of the softer issues, such as knowing how clients feel about providing for their children, what dreams they have for the future, what causes they would like to support. Creating strong, long-term, personal relationships with clients is one of the most rewarding aspects of these advisors' careers.

In my opinion, whether or not one is running a company or a personal business, to be successful, one must have the drive to learn everything it takes to be the best, the ability to recognize the implications of change and even to embrace it, and the firm commitment to serving clients' needs, even to exceed their highest expectations. And the last piece to achieving an outstanding and rewarding career is dedication to the industry and a sincere desire to give back to one's community.

I invite you to meet the men and women who exemplify the highest level of professionalism and dedication in the financial-services industry.

ABOUT LAUNNY STEFFENS

John "Launny" Steffens served as president, then chairman, of Merrill Lynch's Private Client Group and vice chairman of Merrill Lynch until his retirement in 2001. Under his leadership, client assets at Merrill rose from $189 billion to about $1.6 trillion.

Known as a "living legend" in the business, Launny's movements are closely followed by industry observers. Pursuing his vision for the future of the securities industry, he led Merrill into several new areas, such as insurance, mortgage lending, and banking. He also worked to help Merrill become one of the first securities firms to link customers' brokerage accounts to government-guaranteed bank deposits. He was a chief lobbyist for the Roth IRA. He led Merrill to offer low-cost online trading to its clients, and the firm's Unlimited Advantage program has been emulated throughout the industry.

In 1998, during the online trading boom, Launny faced criticism for this controversial remark: "The do-it-yourself model of investing, centered on Internet trading, should be regarded as a serious threat to Americans' financial lives." He was proven right when the markets corrected and many individual investors returned to their full-service relationships for guidance.

In June 2001, Launny celebrated his retirement from Merrill Lynch by ringing The Closing Bell at the New York Stock Exchange. He then launched Spring Mountain Capital, an investment management firm providing alternative investment management and advice that covers a full spectrum of hedge funds and private equity investing.

INTRODUCTION

MY OWN STORY

After graduating from Babson College in Wellesley, Massachusetts in 1987, I landed a job as a stockbroker with a major securities firm. Armed with a business degree, I was eager to apply what I had learned in the classroom to the real world.

As a rookie broker in the 1980s, the secret to a stockbroker's success was: "Make 100 phone contacts a day, generate ten solid prospects, close one account—and trade those accounts."

After one year of cold calling—and almost making it through the G's in the phone book—I was the local office's number one account opener, but I wasn't meeting my earnings expectations.

I was frustrated because I knew there had to be a better way, yet I only wanted to learn from the best. I spent many sleepless nights wondering what the industry's top producers did to become so successful. I wasn't interested in reinventing the wheel; I only wanted to emulate proven techniques practiced by the best stockbrokers.

Since those early days in the investment field, my career has taken me in several directions. I come from a family of writers; my father, sister, brother and I have authored more than 50 published books, known as "Shook Books" in the industry. In 1990, I wrote a book titled *The Winner's Circle: How Ten Stockbrokers Became the Best in the Business*. I did it because I wanted to fill the need I had as a young, neophyte broker. To research the book, I spent countless hours interviewing America's leading stockbrokers, picking their brains, uncovering what they attributed to their success. As a young stockbroker, I ordinarily would not have been able to meet with these remarkable individuals. Yet, after meeting with them, I recognized a common trait: they were all willing to give back to an industry that had treated them so well. They willingly shared their secrets with me. Consequently, I was able to write unprecedented, detailed profiles on these extraordinary people. It came as no surprise to me that *The Winner's Circle* became an instant bestseller among stockbrokers. The book's success verified my belief that there were many other rookies and established brokers who shared my interest in finding out what the industry's star performers were doing.

The same year that *The Winner's Circle* was published, I transferred to my firm's Wall Street headquarters where I assumed a position as a senior research analyst. Writing in the evenings and on weekends, five years later I delivered *The Winner's Circle II* to my publisher. In 1999, I left Wall Street to pursue writing on a full-time basis.

Two years later, as the sixth book I've written, I am tackling a more ambitious project. This time, I have sought out the top 30 financial advisors in the securities industry.

THE NOMINATION PROCESS

In the beginning, it was easy to identify superstars. That's because a handful were so obvious. For example, there was Lehman Brothers' Martin Shafiroff. His legendary record-breaking commissions volume over the past two decades had established him as the number one financial advisor in the country, and most likely, the world. Likewise, there were others like Mark Curtis, Managing Director—Investments, at Salomon Smith Barney, the acknowledged top producer in stock-option business with many of the *Fortune 50* companies as clients, and Ace Greenberg at Bear Stearns, with a client list that reads as a *Who's Who*. These were easy choices.

In searching for America's most successful brokers, now known more eloquently, and appropriately, as financial advisors, I developed a system that I deemed fair and suitable. First, I narrowed a lengthy list of firms to somewhere over a hundred; I qualified these entities based on acceptable compliance records. Following discussions with these firms that identified their top sales-people, my list was reduced to 46 firms.

At each of these firms, my research process required me to speak with several representatives in multiple departments, including public relations, national sales, divisional and regional managers, compliance/legal departments, and often CEOs and Presidents. Each firm provided me with recommendations, based on my criteria, that they considered their most successful financial advisors. At this point, my list was comprised of approximately 300 candidates, each of whom qualified as a strong role model for industry professionals and as an excellent representative of his or her firm.

My selections were based on the following weighted criteria:

- *Consistently high production numbers.* While I encountered phenomenal stories about many financial advisors, I wasn't interested in superstars without tenure. Flash-in-the-pans and Johnny-come-latelys were not acceptable.

- *Acceptable compliance and legal records.* Only brokers with the highest ethical standards and integrity would be considered. In fact, in an industry where every formal complaint, whether justified or unfounded, is archived forever, many of *The Winner's Circle* brokers—such as Prudential's Alan Jusko and Morgan Stanley's Ira Walker—have never had a formal client complaint; what's more, virtually all are in the top echelons in terms of client-loss records.

- *Community involvement.* Interestingly, this was the easiest criterion. It was almost a given that the 300 financial advisors on my initial list were active role models in their community and in the industry. This was a common thread throughout the interviews. Ace Greenberg at Bear Stearns said it best: "The more I give, the more money I seem to make."

Over the course of two months, I pre-interviewed these top 300 financial advisors. My ultimate decisions were primarily based on my objective approach in utilizing my criteria, as well as a lighter subjective approach, consisting of identifying individuals from a variety of firms, and a cross-section of the country. In the end, I was able to select 30 financial advisors from 13 brokerage firms, and I felt comfortable that as a composite, they were indeed the most successful in the business.

CONTENTS OF BOOK

Since I've written the first two *Winner's Circle* books, I've had the opportunity to speak at hundreds of industry engagements, ranging from training classes and incentive trips to seminars and conferences. After talking individually to thousands of brokers, I decided to change the format of the third edition of *The Winner's Circle*. First, instead of ten, I profiled 30 financial advisors in order to provide broader perspectives. Second, I segmented the book thematically by dividing the book into 14 sections, with each financial advisor profiled in at least one chapter within one or more sections. Hence, each individual appears in a section that best represents his or her strengths.

The obvious benefit of organizing the book in this format is that a reader who is interested in becoming more involved in his or her community, for example, will find Deborah Frazier's approach to building a book of business to be of particular interest. This Merrill broker began her career by educating and offering financial advice to lower-income families and church groups. Proving Greenberg's theory, in what seems to defy logic, Frazier became successful by giving to the community first.

CHARACTERISTICS OF *WINNER'S CIRCLE* FINANCIAL ADVISORS

Interestingly, no individual in this book resembles another; I find no archetypical personality that lends itself to being a successful financial advisor. So, for the record, the myth that a top producer in the securities field must possess a gift of gag is just that: a myth. While some of these 30 individuals do have strong, outgoing personalities, others do not. Some even border on being introverted. One, for example, may come across as a hard sell, while another is low-keyed and shy. Of course, some common denominators are apparent, but all financial advisors share some similarities to others. Surprisingly, there appears to be no special aptitude. So much for the aptitude tests, perhaps they're most appropriate for weeding out those obviously ill suited for the business. Still, qualities such as tenacity, conscientiousness, and commitment play a key role in determining long-term success. But these attributes are applicable for attaining success in every field.

There is no apparent cut-and-dry formula for the successes illustrated in this book. While some, for example, may have spent long hours concentrating on cold calls during the beginning of their careers, others refused to use shotgun telephone approaches to prospecting. Similarly, there are a variety of investment strategies that these individuals apply. So, if you're a financial advisor, you can choose what works best for you. And, if you're not in the securities field, you're now presented with a wonderful opportunity to get an inside view of 30 of the best professionals in the business.

Each of these financial advisors is a dedicated professional who is certainly qualified to serve as a role model to others in the investment field. I hope that many existing and future financial advisors will pattern themselves after one or more of the 30 people profiled in this book. If so, my writing will have made a valuable contribution to the investment community around the world.

CHAPTER 1:
WEALTH MANAGEMENT

Joseph W. Montgomery, CFP™
Wealth Management "All Star"

Optimal Service Group of First Union Securities
First Union Securities
Williamsburg, Virginia

Joe Montgomery may no longer be a football star, but his clients certainly consider him their hero. Joe credits his fierce competitiveness, willingness to jump hurdles, and diligent focus on a winning strategy for his success in the securities industry. Maybe it comes as no surprise that, as an early adopter of the wealth-management model; Joe has built his own all-star team.

Joe recalls what it was like growing up as a star athlete in Lynchburg, Virginia. "My parents were very smart people," he says, "good at supporting me and not pushy. I was under a lot of pressure to play college football. Recruiters were following me trying to get me to sign. My parents sat me down in the living room and said, 'We think it's great if you want to play football in college, but if you don't want to, we'll figure out how to pay for your college education without the scholarships.' That took off so much pressure. 'We want you to do what's right for you, right for your future,' my parents told me." This message would resonate in Joe's mind for the rest of his life.

Joe decided to give college football a try. He was one of his high school's first-ever football scholarship winners. He chose the College of William and Mary so he could play for then-coach Lou Holtz, now famous as Notre Dame's legendary former head coach. Four years later, after earning a business degree, being elected co-captain of the football team, and winning a spot in the school's hall of fame and on the All-America Team, Joe was off to the big leagues.

That's when reality set in. "When I got to the pros, I was good enough to play, but not so outstanding that every team was willing to sign me." He joined the Philadelphia Eagles, but he was later cut. The next year he joined the Charlotte Hornets of the World Football League. He played part of the season, then hung up his helmet as the league folded. "In professional sports, you can be your best and still lose your job," he says. "But if you work hard and smart in the securities business, it's hard not to be successful."

He headed home for Lynchburg where he met Larry Phillips, the manager of Wheat First Securities, now part of First Union Securities, and applied for the training class. Once accepted, Joe established a new game plan.

The athlete's entrance into the business world consisted of extensive cold calling for municipal bond and equity business. Joe considered his first three years to be his training program. Just as a head coach must know all he can about every position in order to be a great leader, Joe believed that a financial advisor should learn and practice everything he can about the business before he shoots for big leagues. His training consisted of intensive studying and learning about investors' preferences. Eventually he earned his Certified Financial Planner™ designation.

The opinion that one makes more money as a heart surgeon than as a general practitioner never applied to Joe's practice. "Our approach is that we want to help anyone who wants our help," he says. "Find out what people need and seek to help them fill that need."

Perhaps Joe's biggest lesson came from what Lou Holtz showed him: "Don't be afraid to hire people who are smarter than yourself." Always a team player, Joe knew that with a winning team, he would carry the ball for his clients and lead them to their own Super Bowl.

Returning to Williamsburg in 1979, Joe created the Optimal Service Group of First Union Securities. His objectives were to meet the needs of affluent individuals nationwide, and to develop long-term relationships based on a high level of skill and service. The team members, says Joe, pride themselves on three principles they feel give them a competitive edge. According to Joe, these are: "sound financial advice, quality investments, and well-structured plan execution." He adds, "Our comprehensive financial-planning and wealth-management process really sets us apart in helping clients achieve their preferred future." Joe further offers clients the convenience of e-mail and on-line accessibility to account information to boost client relationships to a new level.

"When we consider clients' accounts, we're not referring just to their investments with us," Joe says. "We consider everything that they're involved in financially. For years, brokers have managed the asset side of the balance sheet. We can also include the liabilities side, and our trust capability is second to none." He credits the firm's alliance with First Union Corporation as a significant competitive edge in the important trust and lending businesses. "First Union is currently ranked fourth in the nation in personal trust assets, and our clients benefit from First Union's extensive Family Trust capabilities. For example, if you have aging parents anywhere in the country who need to be looked after daily, arrangements can be made for paying the bills, making sure they take their medicine on time, driving them to the doctor, and keeping their affairs in order.

"We want to be our clients' personal CFO," he continues. "You never give up control of your money, but like any good CEO, you need a good CFO. When you hire us, you don't have to go through all the details. We design our practice so that as CEO, our clients hire us as they would their CFO—it's just a management position."

A short time ago, Joe and team member Ed Bartlett flew to New York to meet with a potential client. She was referred by another New York client who realized she needed the advice of a financial advisor with expertise in trusts. Her situation was a bit unusual. Because of certain control measures she wanted to incorporate into a trust—in order to provide protection for inheritances—she was a candidate for a dynasty trust. This trust ensures that assets will be available to her children if they ever need them; to the extent that her children do not need them, the assets will be retained in trust, free of additional estate and gift taxes, for the benefit of the client's grandchildren and those who come after them. Unable to obtain the help of a financial advisor in the New York area with this capability, she was referred to Joe. "It was hard to believe that we were in the heart of the financial world and First Union had a better mousetrap!" he says.

Joe gives other examples of his group's access to special services for their clients. "What happens if a client wants to buy a beach house? Many brokers would only notice that money has been taken out of the account for the down payment. One client of ours previously had a 25-year relationship with a bank. Because she understands our approach to the business, she doesn't even consider going to the bank; we now handle her finances entirely. She asks us what would be the best route for her to obtain a loan.

"A $20-million client had his trustee contact us because he needed a bridge loan for a house out West. In less than one week, our team arranged the financing. Another client called about buying a farm. The client had already obtained an attractive rate from a Federal farm program, but because we could immediately see all his assets, we were able to obtain a very competitive rate to give him a choice."

Joe and his team send letters to clients informing them that this service is available to them. "One client, CEO of an industrial company, called after he received the letter and told me he loves the idea of having everything in one place, especially the convenience of not filling out 900 forms. He said, 'Please have someone contact me; I've never had a mortgage on my house, and I'd like to talk to you about the tax advantages.' Another client called to transfer all of her other accounts to us—including her entire relationship with a Florida bank—because she wanted to consolidate everything, including her loans."

One of Joe's favorite examples of his wealth-management concept involves a female client who had suffered an emotionally stressful divorce. A teacher who earned a modest paycheck, she received a small nest egg from the settlement. With two young children to raise and no experience with personal finance or investing, she sought Joe's help.

"We analyzed her financial situation and placed her on a strict spending and saving regime. We carefully allocated her assets and planned for many life events, including a college education for her children. She has remained disciplined about saving money on a monthly basis, taking full advantage of dollar-cost averaging in several investments. After sticking to her textbook financial planning schedule, she is now financially comfortable, with no problems paying for two college educations, her home, or her retirement. She has been an astute student, soaking up all the advice we've provided. In fact, since her father passed away she has been making some very sophisticated decisions about settling the estate."

Joe is proud that his team can "coach" clients, elevating them from uninformed to informed. "Our job is to have the knowledge so that we can conceptualize and 'contextualize' what should be done, and ensure that it is correctly applied toward their preferred future."

Joe acts as coach of the Optimal Service Group of First Union Securities—but unlike a football team, his team consists of two offenses because they're always carrying the ball.

The Wealth Management team, which includes Judy Halstead, Edward Bartlett, Sean Driscoll and Pamela Sardeson, helps clients identify investment objectives, set asset allocations, monitor strategies, and review portfolio performance; it also provides expertise in investments and financial products, portfolio analysis, financial planning, trust and estate analysis, and administration. Thomas "TC" Wilson, III, previously First Union's Director of Institutional Consulting, joined the team in 2001 to coordinate the team's efforts with institutions, such as endowments and corporations, and help with asset allocation and planning for high-net-worth clients. "We're essentially treating our high-net-worth clients the same as our institutional clients, with similar tools and resources," Joe says. "TC has been particularly instrumental in developing customized, detailed executive summaries that we're providing our clients." The group's reports now include aggregated assets, even those held outside First Union.

The group's Client Services team, which includes Pamela Malamphy, Ashley Parnell, and Christine Stiles, supervises operations and administrative projects and details. The Client Services team is available to assist with banking and investing issues and spends a great deal of time managing client relationships.

Joe is a great believer in the future of the team concept. "More and more affluent clients are looking for not only a comprehensive range of services but for expert advice that can address their total financial needs. Providing all of that—and doing it well—simply takes more time, energy, and knowledge than one person has."

The team concept also allows Joe to focus on his family and his community. He and Linda, his wife, are regulars in the schools and activities of Joseph, Jr. and Madeline, their children. "The team helps me maintain my priorities as they should be. This allows me greater clarity on what's important. Hopefully I can bring this perspective to benefit my clients."

Joe gives many hours each year to organizations like William and Mary's Endowment Association; he previously gave his time to the College's Society of the Alumni and Board of Visitors. He currently serves on the boards of Future of Hampton Roads, the Jamestown Yorktown Foundation Inc., the Williamsburg Community Health Foundation, the Greater Williamsburg Community Trust, and WHRO Public Television's foundation.

"The key word with Joe is *integrity*. Here is a guy who does everything the right way and does what's best for the client," says Marshall B. Wishnack, former president of Wheat First Union, predecessor to First Union Securities.

"I always try to do what's best for my clients and my community," Joe says. He recommends that all brokers spend time in their community and try to help others. "If you help others, you will surely benefit. I receive such fulfillment, giving back to the community," he continues. "I'm a big believer that what goes around, comes around. I've been very fortunate in this business; I'm thrilled to be so involved in giving back to the community."

HARRY M. FORD, JR.
TURNING SCHOOL TEACHERS INTO MILLIONAIRES

The Ford Team
Legg, Mason
Baltimore, Maryland

"Harry, thank you for helping me reach my retirement dreams," says a 65-year-old woman.

"I never ever imagined I would be a millionaire," another client, a 60-year-old schoolteacher, tells him.

"These comments are music to my ears," says Harry. "The greatest satisfaction I receive in this business is when clients thank me for helping them attain a financial goal. But of course, it's a two-way effort—it can't happen without the client's involvement and commitment."

These achievements—and countless others—are the result of a fine-tuned, well-disciplined approach to wealth management that Harry has mastered over the decades. In fact, Harry's method may seem old-fashioned considering the security industry's growing reliance on high-tech computer models. Yet his personal approach is proof that careful planning and execution, along with a full understanding of a client's needs, drive successful investing. Ford's formula can't be replicated by bits and bytes.

Before laying out an investment plan, Harry and his partners—sons Mac and Mitch—spend ample time getting to know the client. "My objective is simple: to discover all goals and objectives, to learn everything a client hopes to achieve with his or her investments," Harry explains. "I need to have a full understanding of clients' risk tolerance, their investments outside their account at Legg Mason—including other brokerage accounts, real estate, cars, etc.—and their investing experience. To arrive at a winning plan, I learn what the cash flow looks like for the foreseeable future. Then I get a good impression of the potential savings down the road," he says.

As a rule of thumb, Harry and team recommend that clients set aside 10% of everything they earn, and more if possible. "How much can you put away every month?" and "How can we cut down on expenses and pay yourself more?" are some of the first questions clients hear. "If you want to create wealth for yourself, you've got to be your number one bill," Mitch explains. "Pay yourself before you consider other expenditures."

"We believe we have a plan by which we can take any young adult and transform them into millionaires if they follow our recommendations," Harry expounds.

"At 15% your money doubles around every five years," Mitch explains. "So, if you start with $145.00 per month in your first year, at age 25, then before you turn 55, you'll have accumulated around $1 million. Of course, if you increase that amount as your paychecks increase, you would hit that million-dollar mark much sooner.

Ten years ago, for example, a 22-year-old client pledged to contribute 10% of his gross income each year. The first year he contributed a fixed dollar amount every month, then increased that amount as he received pay raises. The money is transferred automatically, electronically, to his Legg Mason account where it's designated to one of the firm's growth mutual funds. Today, that account is worth around $400,000. "Assuming the client continues his monthly contributions, and a healthy market prevails, he'll be another million-dollar success story in five or six years," Harry says.

Harry then describes "touchable" and "untouchable" money by shuffling a stack of papers into two stacks. "This untouchable stack is for my financial independence, and I won't touch this come hell or high water. The untouchable money stack," he says, pointing, "includes security money, such as IRA and 401(k) money that the government will penalize you for withdrawing before age 59, but it also includes money that is put into an escrow account that can grow to support you before you are 59. Although you can legally withdraw this money without penalty, mentally you have to discipline yourself to think, 'I can't touch this.'"

The "touchable" account is money that a client has access to. "Within that account, we will set up separate accounts for, say, buying a house and buying a car. We may use mutual funds, such as a value fund, for the portion of the account that is allocated to the house; a growth fund might be used for the car account. But this touchable money is what the client is going to use to fulfill these needs." Harry then explains how setting financial objectives such as buying a car can serve as ways to receive discounts in the future. "If I contribute $15,000 to my car fund, eventually it's going to hit the $20,000 mark for the new car. This is also how we help clients pay for that dream vacation and the down payment on a home. Of course, we also plan for the taxes the client will be paying on any gains."

"We'll do the same thing for other special accounts, such as a custodial account or a 529 Plan for college education," Mitch adds.

After a savings plan is developed, Ford and team discuss their investment philosophy with the client. They begin with a brief story about equities, fixed-income securities, and risk. "The key to a successful plan," says Harry, "is making sure the client understands the benefits of investing in equities. Equities, we tell our clients, are the best investment to overcome taxation and inflation. Historically, equities' returns have far surpassed the returns of bonds. Even though most investors believe bonds are safer, over the long term they actually bear greater risk. That's because purchasing power erodes. In fact, stocks have outperformed bonds by a ratio of 53 to 1 since 1925. But for short-term safety, say an investment horizon of one or two years, then bonds are the way to go."

Once the client grasps this concept, the team explains the different risks involved in the stock market."The more conservative the investor, the less volatile the stocks will be that we recommend. If the investor requires income, we will place them in high-dividend-paying stocks, like utilities. For someone in their thirties or forties, for example, we would recommend high-growth equities. This is how we begin to tailor the portfolio."

Mac is quick to point out that many investors wrongly perceive retirement as an end goal, a time when their income-producing securities will do the job and see them through the years ahead. "The problem is," he says, "many of these people are living well into their nineties, but they've only prepared for sufficient income through their eighties. Within their 30 years or so of retirement, the cost of living will probably double twice."

Mitch steps in to explain with a story about a 70-year-old woman, widowed for 15 years, who was referred by another client."She was worried because the apartment complex in which she lived was raising her parking rate, and she was feeling poorer and poorer. When she showed me her account, I could see she was justifiably concerned; she was invested in certificates of deposit and government bonds, and had minimal exposure in utility stocks. She was also confused because her income varied dramatically; she was receiving periodic interest checks from different types of securities—some were paying quarterly, some semi-annually, and some monthly.

"I told her that we needed to plan for her to live to 105 years, which meant a time horizon of another 35 years. We restructured her portfolio so that she still had some exposure to bonds—mostly corporate bonds, which yield more than Treasuries and CDs. Other money was allocated to blue-chip mutual funds, and lesser amounts into mid- and small-cap funds. Now her financial future is diversified, and a much higher percentage of her wealth is in growth-oriented assets. We also established a systematic withdrawal program where money is transferred on a monthly basis to her checking account."

Mitch assured the woman that no matter how the market performed, she would still receive her monthly check. "Since then, four years ago," he says, "we've increased her monthly income three times and she has moved to Florida, and bought a new car, and her wealth has nearly doubled."What made the real difference, he firmly believes, is the amount of time he spent "re-educating"her about investing."This client continues to call us on our toll-free number just to check in."

Often, clients express their fear that the market may be headed for a correction, or worse, a bear market."We're able to outperform the market for our growth investors because we actively manage the account,"Mitch says."We prefer stocks that are out of favor but are still expected to perform in terms of earnings growth. Even if the market remains flat, we seek to buy during dips and sell at the peak. In this day and age, the institutions will dump a stock just because it missed projections by a penny. But the company that they dump could still be projected to display incredible growth. So we'll buy during this dip. Essentially, we buy when stocks are undervalued, and sell when they achieve fair valuations."

"I'm a value stock buyer," Harry explains. "I buy stock by the value theory of investing. I invest in companies with strong fundamental characteristics that are selling at price/earnings multiples less than what stocks historically trade in their industry. These will be stocks that are out of favor temporarily for one reason or another. I consider these stocks bargains in the market. It's like buying a car; you're not going to pay list price, you're going to shop around for the best price. That's what I look for in stocks. The undervalued stock that I buy I'll hold until it becomes fully valued or overvalued. If it's overvalued, I'll move out of it and into a better bargain."

Besides their own research, the Ford team relies on information from a variety of sources, but mostly counts on Legg Mason's resources, including star fund-manager Bill Miller, leader of the Legg Mason Value Trust. The team, conveniently located in the same building at Legg Mason's headquarters, keeps in close contact with Miller for new ideas.

Harry adds: "I get excited about stocks I buy that turn out to be big winners. But I'm looking for steady moves rather than big jumps. Babe Ruth had the home-run record in baseball. But did you know that he also held the record for the most strikeouts? I don't buy stocks looking for home runs. I look for singles, doubles, and maybe even triples."

The Fords extend their personalized wealth management services to their 401(k) participants. With thousands of participants at dozens of companies, the team is quick to answer their toll-free telephone number and make in-person visits to those requesting added service. "We typically begin with seminars, and we take them through the same type of consultation that we offer our clients, with more of a slant toward the longer time horizon. Most firms provide 'cookie-cutter' service to their plan participants," Mitch points out. "When we visit the account, we bring a Legg Mason retirement specialist to work closely with the company and their specific issues, and we visit any employee upon request."

Recently, the Fords received a 401(k) referral from a client. The Fords submitted a proposal and were asked to give a presentation. "We were one of many firms competing for the business of this manufacturing company," Mitch says. "To prepare, we learned everything we could about the company and about their employees, such as demographics." The team gave a well-prepared presentation and won the account.

The next step was meeting with the employees. "For a 401(k) to be truly successful, you need as much participation from the employees as possible," Mitch continues. "They should fully understand the benefits of accumulating wealth."

A large men's locker room served as a seminar room for some 75 manufacturing-assembly men, still dirty from work and some wearing hard hats. A projector was set up to provide visual reinforcements of the concepts introduced.

"I'm here for one simple reason," Mitch began. "I want to help create wealth for each one of you as individuals and for your families. I want to help you guys for the long term to become very, very wealthy." As Mitch explained his team's philosophy, the men sat up straighter in their chairs.

When he concluded, the employees barraged him with questions: "Can you sit down with me and talk this out?" many employees asked. "Can I have some time with you alone?"

"Overall," says Mitch, "the group was extremely appreciative that we took the time to explain—in terms they could relate to—the basics of building wealth. Most people think you need a lot of money to be in the market; people must realize this just isn't the case."

The team asked employees to schedule an appointment on a sheet of paper Mitch had prepared earlier. Over 20 employees signed up for a follow-up meeting. The majority of those individuals are now enrolled in the 401(k) plan.

The Fords are as committed to giving to their community as they are to doing their best for their clients. The team has served on numerous boards, including those of St. Paul's School for Girls, the Gilman School, the University of Maryland endowment funds for its medical school, and the Lacrosse Foundation. Additionally, they give considerable time to the Science Center, the Maryland Historical Society, and Genesis, an organization that helps unemployed individuals rejoin the workforce in the Baltimore area. "It's our nature to help wherever and whenever we can," Mac says.

"Whether it's financially or our time, it's important to us to get involved and give back," Harry says. "It's also been an excellent way to meet the leaders of our society."

CHAPTER 2:
PARTNERSHIPS AND TEAM BUILDING

AUGUST A. CENNAME
THE DREAM TEAM: "WE BUILD DREAMS"

Cenname & Team
Merrill Lynch
Columbus, Ohio

The sun was shining in Columbus, Ohio on a Monday morning, but the Cenname team's office was subdued. The team was still bereaved over the loss of a client.

"His son called us with the news," Beverly Davis tells me. "He said that his father wouldn't be calling anymore. He thanked us for making his father's financial affairs trouble-free and said, 'Your estate planning leaves us well prepared.'"

"We share tears and sadness with our clients," says August "Augie" Cenname in his deep, well-articulated voice. "But we laugh and celebrate with them, too. We go to their weddings, their bar mitzvahs, and their funerals, and sometimes we'll just stop by for a visit. We're like that cousin you can always rely on," he muses. "We're part of the family."

While Augie may be the senior member of the Cenname "Dream Team," he considers himself more a team member rather than the owner or manager. "With this approach," he says, "everyone feels free to speak up and share ideas—it builds collegiality.

"As a team," he continues, "we build solid, lifelong relationships. We build dreams. This calls for a group of dedicated and committed individuals who work in harmony and are totally focused on helping clients achieve success." Flexibility is also required. Says Augie, "We evolve as our clients' needs change."

And Augie has evolved plenty of times with his clients. At the outset of his career, in 1966, clients' goals were simple: to make money in the market. He admits this with a chuckle. "I truly was a stock broker. And there was only a small group of us in the industry. I had very few competitors."

Augie identifies the years 1973 and 1974 as a period of major secular decline in the market. It was then that he helped build one of the largest retail hedging businesses in the country. The markets continued to trade within a certain range with high volatility, and this allowed him to continue making money for clients. "The period was also marked by high inflation, which rose from the low single digits to around 15%. Interest rates spiked up to 21%. We were constantly adjusting our services to accommodate our clients' needs," he recalls.

"As we moved into the early 1980s, of course, all that changed," he continues. "In the summer of 1982, one of the great bull markets emerged—we had a whole new political situation, and corporate America began its restructuring.

We started coming off the high interest rates, and high inflation. That's when Paul Volker took over the Federal Reserve, beat inflation and high interest rates, and pulled us out of the recession. As the bull market of the 1980s took hold, people's concerns shifted from wealth accumulation to putting kids through college, creating financial independence, preserving and enhancing lifestyles, and defending against inflation and taxes."

In 1983, the Dream Team changed its focus once again to meet the needs of its clients. "In the 1980s," says Augie, "we and our clients witnessed the crash of the market in 1987, the fall of the Berlin wall in 1989, and a host of other events through the 1990s that continued to advance and change our business. Markets were unleashed in the 1980s, and they really took off in the '90s.

"As our world was being reshaped," he explains, "the demographics of our client base changed." He notes that borrowers became savers, and those savers became investors. "Add the acceleration of technology, the globalization of business, and the aging of the population of this country, and the result is a great deal of change. Investors' needs were becoming much more complex and demanding of professional attention."

Augie soon realized what he needed to do: build a team of experts with particular specialties. He called a meeting in 1983 with colleagues Beverly Davis, who joined Augie in 1977, and Julie Barnett, a newer team member at the time. "We understood that our clients' needs were changing, that we had to evolve into a financial planning-based business in order to succeed," Augie says. They emerged from the meeting with a redefined purpose—to exceed clients' expectations—and to expand the team.

First, Beverly acquired expertise in servicing high-net-worth clients, with products ranging from equities and mutual funds to all fixed-income products. Her know-how in fixed-income and liability-management services aided the team with its asset-management services. Julie became manager of all operational and administrative aspects of the business.

With several years of experience as a trust officer at a bank and as a member of Merrill Lynch's capital markets division, Kathy Tann was a prime candidate to oversee corporate services. The corporate services group is a resource for the relationship managers as it relates to corporate accounts. "Augie told me years before I joined the team that he was going to hire me away. Fortunately, he always keeps his word," she says.

With client associate Debbie Lance working beside her, Kathy made it possible for the Dream Team to provide employee-benefits services for over 250,000 customers worldwide. The team assists corporate clients by developing educational programs, conducting stock options seminars, promoting 401(k) enrollment, liability management services, endowment services, and more.

"For example, stock options confuse people, and many don't participate. So we developed a simple, non-threatening process for people to very easily get involved." As needed, Kathy meets with employees "to help them get comfortable with this service, one that could represent a great deal of their wealth."

Kathy and her team build relationships with the human resources departments, which are typically responsible for administering benefits locally within their corporation. "As markets move and stock prices rise, exercising options can occur quickly," Kathy says, "so we immediately service those who need our expertise." Kathy has spent a great deal of time training her teammates to act as she would. "They've gained so much experience that they can do it without me," she says proudly.

Recently, one of the team's corporate customers spun off—in a stock offering—a division that had built a strong brand and was highly profitable. The team helped the division build a new 401(k) from scratch in record-breaking time. "Fortunately, we always have access to the real power and resources of Merrill Lynch; they provided tremendous backing, including a total of 62 associates who helped us put this together," Kathy says. "We took the customer from 'What is a 401(k)?' all the way through the proposal process." The Dream Team went up against 25 competitors for this opportunity. "We just smothered them with service to help them meet their deadline—they never knew what hit them!"

"These are the types of deals that gave me gray hairs," Augie says with a laugh. "But it's worth it to see a happy customer."

Peter Motta is the "COO" of the team, in charge of day-to-day operations. He works closely with Beverly Davis and Augie to formulate all asset management strategies. Peter was the recipient of an Ohio State University scholarship funded by Augie for his involvement in a student investment program. Beginning in 1991, he interned for two summers and worked part time during the year, then joined the team when he graduated with his MBA in 1993. His specialty is asset management, with an emphasis in equities, managed money, research, and portfolio strategy. The team's financial planner, Charles Jarrett, aids the investment strategy he constructs.

Also a senior financial planner, with both Certified Financial Planner™ and Certified Financial Manager designations, Charles Jarrett focuses on all financial planning, estate planning, and retirement planning aspects of the client relationship. After meeting with clients to help identify their current situation, he spends considerable time evaluating their financial situation and needs, then designs a map of how they will reach their goals. When creating these solutions, he works side-by-side with other team members, as well as with accountants, lawyers and estate-planning professionals.

Augie is intent on providing customer service that exceeds each client's expectations. With that in mind, he hired Kim Gibson in 1990 to act as the team's customer-service leader. Focusing squarely on enhancing relationships with each and every client, Kim works closely with team members. She seeks perfection in internal and external communications, administrative efficiencies for clients, and is always prepared to act as back up for any timely issue. "Overall, her contributions have empowered the entire team to heightened levels of customer service," Augie says.

Angela Contini and Nicole Simpson are the first line of contact with the clients. Often, they alone answer clients' questions and satisfy their needs. If necessary, they direct the client to the appropriate team member or Merrill Lynch representative."This team approach ensures that there is always someone standing ready to act for any client, anytime," Augie says firmly. "We never spread ourselves so thin that if an individual is on vacation, the office can't function."

Using the latest technology, Angela and Nicole also maintain a sophisticated system that tracks client contacts and personal appointments—whether they're in the office or at the clients' home or office. Angela and Nicole also work closely with other team members, to help prepare clients for meetings by organizing any paperwork, ascertaining clients' meeting objectives, and establish the agenda. With high client exposure, they're also intimate with client preferences: "Some people like to be very involved, so we contact them frequently," Angela says. "Others want to be involved weekly, monthly, or even quarterly. We have a system that ensures all expectations are being met."

Client preferences are then articulated to Jane Lacoste, who manages the team's internal technology and systems effort, and seeks efficiencies using technology. The systems Jane supports detail clients' needs and expectations, maintains the team's calendar, and coordinates appointments with clients and appropriate team members.

Under Augie's leadership, the team successfully built a thriving 2,000-client practice, managing over $3 billion in assets. Even though the financial-planning business was flourishing, Augie was ready to identify the next evolutionary stage.

In the year 2000, Augie anticipated the changing needs of his clients. Two disparate groups of clients were forming. His larger base of clients still required the full asset-management and financial-planning services that he has provided for nearly two decades. This group was interested primarily in the creation and management of wealth. The second group is the emerging clientele—typically with assets starting at $5 to $10 million—that are interested in wealth management, with an emphasis on capital preservation."This really is a contin-uation of what we've been doing for the last 35 years," Augie begins."During the past five years or so, tremendous wealth was created. Realizing our goal to remain one step ahead of our clients' needs, we were required to restructure. We saw the need to build the infrastructure—including new solutions that cater to these needs—to help our clients manage and preserve their wealth."

To facilitate the changes, Augie and Peter felt strongly that two distinct teams—both sharing resources—would be needed to focus on these two distinct client groups, and "create something special," Augie says. Rather than hurriedly adding members to his team, they sought an established, successful team that was experienced in providing asset-management and financial-planning services to their clients."First, we thought it might be nearly impossible to find a team that would be in tune with our business, and able to provide the excellent service that our clients have come to expect." After performing a nation-wide search for a number of months, they found the ideal team. They struck an alliance with a successful six-person Merrill Lynch team across town in Dublin, constructed and led by long-time friend and colleague Tom Kelsey.

"I couldn't have written a better script," Augie exults. "They're even right here in Columbus!

"This partnership deepens our capabilities within the asset-management and financial-planning area," Augie says, carefully articulating his thoughts. "This outstanding team is needed to ramp up our resources to accommodate our growing client base."

The emerging clientele, focusing on private wealth advisory services and capital preservation, is based in the Dream Team's Columbus headquarters. The entire 14-person team is devoted to "wealth management in its purest sense," he says with pure conviction. "We are committed to the preservation and management of our client's wealth." He continues: "To make this transformation, we've raised our level of competency to become solution oriented for all the complexities and challenges that these successful people are facing.

"I really believe this is the next big thing," Augie says. "We are offering services far beyond asset management and financial planning; we're virtually an advocate for the client's family, a trusted advisor for all aspects of a client's finances. Our clients are comfortable knowing that all of their financial affairs are being handled properly. And our solutions run deep, from philanthropic planning—a prevalent service we offer with the wealth that's been created—to credit services. We're involved on both sides of the balance sheet. Our investors want a complete platform of services. They don't want to make 15 phone calls to make 15 things happen. They can make one phone call—to us. We are their advocates, an extension of their family."

Clearly, clients view the Dream Team as family. Why else would a client call them first when he realized his identification was stolen? "Our client didn't know who to turn to, so he instinctively called us," Augie says. "Just to be safe, we were in touch with the best resources in the country to help investigate and correct the situation." Due in part to the team pre-empting the situation, the imposter unsuccessfully attempted to withdraw funds from another financial institution. "Our client was ecstatic that we were able to help him so quickly and efficiently."

In addition to the team's experience in financial crisis management, the team added specialists in the areas of credit management, estate planning, and philanthropic services. They also employed sophisticated liquidity strategies related to concentrated stock positions and privately held businesses. This helps the team deliver solutions like exchange funds, costless collars, prepaid forwards, and numerous estate-planning techniques. Both offices support the team's growing corporate business.

This additional expertise—especially the estate-planning and philanthropic services—was particularly helpful when advising a client who wished to make a gift to a charitable organization. The client sought the team's advice on the best way to accomplish this. "We assessed the client's needs, on both a short-term and long-term basis, considered all the interests of all the family members, and reviewed tax considerations. Consequently, we created a plan for the client that far exceeded their income needs and expectations, and far exceeded each family member's needs and wealth transfer possibilities. In the end, our client contributed $10 million more than what he originally thought he could.

"Overall, it was a win-win for everyone: the charitable organization received far more money, the family members received more, the client received more income, and we had the satisfaction knowing that our client was well served. Additionally, the client is able to leave a very positive legacy. This was also an example of how we tend to think out of the box for our clients."

At the time of the transformation, team business manager Cindy Evans was brought on board. Cindy's task is to focus on current processes, and identify opportunities for enhancements and efficiencies within the team's systems. Previously a senior-level administrative director at a large bank, Cindy's responsibilities ranged from marketing and compliance to trading and client service. "Instead of creating new processes and efficiencies at a large firm and making a modest impact, Cindy is able to make a tremendous and immediate impact in our relatively small group," Augie says.

Cindy's ability to focus solely on client needs enables the team to proactively offer services and offer better tools to enhance communications with clients. For example, Cindy works with Jane to constantly review the latest technologies to improve communications within the group, and with clients. Once Cindy initiates a project, she employs the appropriate team members and manages the project from start to finish. Most the ideas she generates are from feedback at her weekly team meetings. "In an open-communications environment, we are able to really anticipate client needs, and thus evolve with our clients," she says.

One more change Augie pursues is multiple geographical locations. "This is really the result of two trends: the benefits we can reap from technology," he explains, "and, perhaps more importantly, the mobility of current clients and the addition of new clients. As a result, we commit to a great deal of travel to visit these clients. But to truly become an extension of their families, we are establishing associates in areas across the country. These areas include California, Florida, New York and several other locations."

Impressively, the team works as a well-rehearsed sports team. In this context, Augie, as head coach, provides the vision and works with every team member and client. The client may be thought of as the team owner who benefits from the winning team: "Clients don't have to be bothered with all the details," Peter says. "They need to be kept informed as their team works for them to create the winning game plan for their particular needs."

At the initial meeting, a client is assigned a "customer care" team, consisting of Augie, a relationship manager, and client service representative, either Angela or Nicole. "We've found that clients are more comfortable speaking to a few people than to a whole team," Augie explains. But he is quick to point out that if any team member is out of the office, there are ample team members who are familiar with any client's situation. "We are always covered."

At the initial meeting, the three-member team gathers background information, and then guides clients through an exploration of their lives—their needs, wants, and dreams. Needs come first. "We firmly believe that to achieve success is to satisfy needs," Augie says. "Then we move to the 'want' spectrum. We ask clients, 'What do you want to do with your life?' And 'What is it going to take to enable you to do that?'" He tells them to think in terms of job satisfaction and lifestyle, and transition of wealth.

"Then we talk about dreams," Augie continues. "We ask, 'what do you really want to do? Do you want to leave a legacy on this planet? A legacy for your children? What good do you want to do? How do you want people to look back upon you and your life? What do you want them to say about you? What do you want them to think about you?'"

Armed with the insights they've acquired into a client's interests, goals, aspirations, and temperament for risk, the team creates a professional wealth-management plan, complete with implementation of ideas and strategies. Over time, regular face-to-face meetings are scheduled—either monthly or quarterly, depending on the needs of the client—to ensure that the plan remains on track. "It's important to us to discuss with our clients their current situation relative to their goals and objectives," Augie says.

The team prefers to have meetings, says Augie, "at least quarterly to review the clients' total financial situation to make sure that all objectives and the means to obtain them are still intact." Clients are asked from time to time, "What are your needs?" and "How are your needs changing?"

Additionally, the team is always prepared to quickly respond to client inquiries of any financial kind: "We often get calls asking us for all sorts of financial advice, not just estate planning and tax-related questions," Charles says. "Often they're questions like, 'I want to buy a boat or car, how should I pay for it?' or 'Should I take out a home-equity loan or take cash from my account?'"

Communication within the group is so precise that if a client tells a Dream Team member that, for example, she is at home sick, everyone on the team is informed. "A client once asked if we posted his illness on a billboard because every time he called that day, everyone asked him how he was feeling," Nicole recalls.

What's Augie's secret to creating an award-winning team? After considering a prospective team member's credentials, rarely will he break his "two-year rule," Augie says. "In other words, you have to know somebody for a period of about two years before you really get to know them. Additionally, the candidate must have the world's greatest attitude, so not only do we have a team of highly qualified individuals who can effectively implement our strategy and our mission, we have a team with the world's greatest attitude.

"Teams are the future for everyone," he says thoughtfully. "I just don't see how you can deliver world-class services and solutions—and the complexities that are involved—without a team rich in resources. This is a trend that will continue, especially as the wealth-management business becomes more prevalent."

Speaking of shaping the future, in June of 2000, an event occurred that would forever change Augie's life. It would also help define the future of his business.

Driving to attend a client's board of directors meeting, a truck collided with the back of Augie's sedan. His car ran off the side of the road and over a hill. The truck landed on top of the car, trapping Augie. Augie was able to escape seconds before the car exploded in flames.

Miraculously, Augie escaped with cuts and bruises, but his life is inexorably altered: "I remember this event like it happened yesterday—and I never want to let go of this feeling," he explains emotionally, as he recounts his near-death experience. "I look at life very differently now." Then his look of disbelief turns to a smile: "I don't get upset about anything; in fact, I don't have bad days. I will enjoy every minute for the rest of my life. I have a new perspective on life. I am energized to a new level that is unimaginable."

Augie continues profoundly: "We look at life through the prism of our life experiences, and as our experiences evolve or change, or as events occur, we change our point of view. This event is my benchmark for every day that I live. Every day is wonderful. Other than finding my soul mate, Tina, and having my children, Spencer and Augie, this was the best gift ever given to me."

He then identifies his second passion, right after family: "This is one more reason why I'm going to create something really special here at Merrill Lynch. To be in a position to help so many families in so many unique ways is really quite special. This puts an added value on building clients' dreams."

Helping to build dreams isn't limited to the Dream Team's clients: They are literally building dreams in the community. Around the time of this interview, the team spent an entire weekend building a house for a deserving young family with the Habitat for Humanity organization. This is an annual ritual for the team, working together for a very worthy cause.

Says team-member Augie, "This is not just a super team. This is a team of super individuals."

Raj Sharma
The Financial Conductor

Merrill Lynch
Boston, MA

Nothing makes Raj Sharma happier than to see people do well. Whether it's his family, clients, colleagues, fellow financial advisors, or the needy, Raj is on a mission. Maybe that's why his individual and corporate clients entrust him and his team with over $2 billion.

It's easy to see where he got his kindness.

Growing up in India, Raj saw his share of poverty. In a country of a billion people, with an extreme polarization of wealth, Raj's family was one of the relatively few fortunates. But that's not to say he didn't have considerable exposure to the popular side; his father, after all, was the Robin Hood of India—only he gave from himself.

Raj's father was a chemist and family practitioner. He ran his practice based on philanthropy, rather than profitability. His mother, too, was his partner. They were passionate about caring for people. Together they established free drugs and medical attention in poor neighborhoods, and offered medical attention to those who were unable to pay.

The parents' first priorities, of course, were their five children. They believed that exposure to all cultures would help their children build character, and foster their dreams of opportunities and happiness.

Raj attended college and received his MBA in business management in India, then moved to the United States when he was 23. He knew he wanted to follow in his father's footsteps by building his own business, and helping people with his skills, but he hadn't yet found his passion. His skills were financial, not medical. His father hoped he would become a banker, though Raj decided that this career would distance him too much from individuals. His first job in the U.S. was as a financial analyst. He then obtained his masters in mass communications, and spent several years as a media consultant, making films and running ad campaigns for corporate clients.

In September 1987, Raj found his passion: Financial Advisor. He knew he wanted to join a leading firm, and determined Merrill Lynch as a leader in financial services. He contacted the Boston office, and landed an interview. His obvious intellect, poise and ideas easily won him over with management.

"It was good luck that I started in the business at the bottom of the market," Raj says with his friendly smile and articulate voice, referring to the crash that occurred one month after he started. "Though at the time, people were concerned about depression."

At the beginning, Raj followed the herd of new brokers in the securities industry by cold calling with product. "Although I was playing the numbers like ever other broker," he says, referring to the increased probability of converting prospects into clients as more cold calls are made, "this didn't seem like the best way for me to build my practice. With my media background, I wanted to essentially develop a segmentation strategy in the Boston area and surrounding areas to pursue sources of wealth. 'What kind of industries are prospering in this economy?' I asked myself. At that time, the answer was in the biotech and medical industries. Both are areas where I happened to feel very comfortable."

Raj spent considerable time studying this market segment, and determined that the professionals in these industries, from the executives at the corporations to the physicians at the hospitals, didn't have time to properly manage their money. These individuals, he determined, were highly likely to delegate this responsibility to a professional.

His tactic was to differentiate himself from the legions of other brokers by using unique and innovative prospecting and account management methods. His most successful work required him to use communications skills by networking, giving seminars, and—to a lesser extent—cold calling. To remain focused, he only cold called during selective times, and only to people within these businesses.

The first seminar he gave was at a local hospital. The topic: retirement planning. He offered the seminar every Friday for about seven weeks. Other topics included other educational discussions, such as stock selection and investment management. Raj became a familiar face at the hospital. "They thought I was a doctor there!" he says, laughing. "I got to know so many people through these seminars, I almost felt like I worked there." One by one, the accounts trickled in. Over time, with numerous referrals and increased credibility in the hospital, the new accounts came in more rapidly.

Raj's next step was to further embroil himself in the biotech industry. "I became a member of several Boston-oriented industry associations," Raj says. "As I learned more and more about the industry, I was able to contribute my thoughts to the meetings." He realized that the more insight and ideas he could contribute, the more they considered him an expert. "Most of the ideas I was contributing involved industry trends, especially those relating to finance."

Eventually, Raj became known in the Boston area as a financial specialist in biotech. "This point of differentiation lead to a lot of open doors," he says.

During his first eight months in the business, he attended a party and was introduced to a scientist. She worked at a medical devices company and expressed concern that her company didn't have a 401(k) plan. She arranged to introduce him to the firm's CFO, and Raj promptly called him. "The CFO overwhelmed me with questions that I wasn't prepared to answer at the time," he says. "So all I did was actively listen and ask him questions."

Raj was able to turn the swell of questions into a fact-finding session, which he later used as an excuse to call the CFO with precise answers. Over time, Raj, still a rookie, was able to better understand the company's needs and seek answers. In the process, he was able to build a relationship with the CFO, as well as other top executives. Finally, he was able to earn the company's business, only it wasn't the 401(k); it was their cash management and compensation plans. At that time, the company employed around 20 people. He soon earned most of the employees' accounts, as well as the accounts of many others in the industry. This extensively connected him to Boston's medical industry.

At the beginning of his career, Raj received a referral to a doctor. This medical professional kept around $15 million in each of several banks in the Boston area. Raj's reputation led the doctor to "test" Raj, but with only $10,000. "I spoke to him about building a portfolio of biotechnology stocks and that this could be a tremendous wave of the future. The biotech companies of today could become the pharmaceutical companies of tomorrow," Raj predicted. "He was concerned that this was speculation, which it was, but appropriate for at least a portion of a portfolio." As the doctor's confidence in Raj grew, he transferred more and more of his assets.

"It always paid to ask a new client, 'Who else do you know with similar questions and may not have the time to strategically answer them?'" he says. "People are receptive to providing names. Even today, I ask my clients."

Though Raj was becoming further entrenched in the biotech industry, he maintains that in order to properly prospect corporate business, you must take the time to completely understand the industry. "This is important because you want to fully understand a company's individual situation—it's products, constraints, etc. You need to genuinely show an interest in the company. Most important, once you fully understand the company's business and industry, including the inside competition, you can understand and emphasize and truly connect with clients. They see that you care and understand. They feel free to call you, and to rely on you.

"After all," Raj continues, "clients essentially hire you for your competence and knowledge." Raj has taken this "expert approach" to several other industries. "I took the time to understand every business that I targeted, not just biotech."

Becoming an expert has required a great deal of work. To this day, Raj begins his day at 4:30 a.m. by reading financial newspapers. He is consistently on the lookout for new company developments, searching for new investment ideas. At the beginning of his career, the workday ended around 7 p.m. These days, he is home in time for family dinner. At night, he is busy reading research and other business material. "There is an endless supply of reading material," Raj says. "I'm constantly seeking ways to broaden my knowledge. It requires a lot of work to stay on top of new developments, and to consistently offer a total financial planning package."

Raj describes his philosophy of managing money as a concept of total financial planning. "You must look at individuals' needs in their totality, not just from a narrow investment point of view. You must look at the short-term objectives they have, such as education needs, home-buying needs, and health—as well as their long-term aspirations, such as retirement and estate planning. People like to be financially independent; so we look at their liabilities, survival protection issues, even things like their home insurance to review their umbrella liability coverage. I like to add value by going beyond what's necessary. I think you really need to position yourself to fully understand the total financial situation."

Raj explains the various components of total financial planning. First, he identifies long-term, mid-term, and short-term goals and objectives. A client recently told him, "My principle goal over the next ten years is to accumulate enough money so that I can be financially independent. That is my goal. My other goal is to send my four kids to college. I also want to be very tax efficient."

At this point, Raj and team drafted a thorough document that explains the strategies. "Once you get a real consensus as to what the strategies are, the actual decision-making becomes the after part," he says. "It is key that the client knows that you fully understand these plans."

Raj will then meet with the client again, and—depending on their goals— ensure that they understand the basics of investing, the dynamics of the economy, the markets, and any risks. After the meeting, Raj will continue to educate the client by sending or e-mailing articles, and calling on the telephone. "One of the most important concepts we want clients to understand is risk," Raj explains. "Clients generally define risk as losing money. This is true, but there is much more involved. We define risk as the probability of loss, and volatility. We want clients to understand the difference, as well as understand their true tolerance for risk." Raj accomplishes the latter by asking clients to fill out a questionnaire designed to quantify their risk tolerance.

Once Raj understands the client's risk tolerance, he will customize an asset allocation model for the clients' profile. Raj's typical model is weighted towards equities at 65%, and the remaining 35% to bonds and cash. "Then we drill down and figure out how to invest those monies," Raj explains. Determining what types of equities or bonds requires knowledge about the client as well." Raj explains that besides diversifying and selecting securities within asset classes, such as stocks, clients may have their own preferences. "For instance, in the medical industry, many doctors think twice before buying the tobacco stocks, but may be interested in certain biotech or drug companies. If a client has a strong preference, you must respect that, even if a money manager is making the decisions."

Raj stresses the importance of asset allocation, and credits his team for their expertise within this area. "Of course, asset allocation is the most important variable in total return," Raj begins. "Our sophisticated process begins with the asset classes, followed by allocation within the different asset classes. We take this to the next level by altering this allocation as we monitor each money manager's total return performance, and risk exposure. Consequently, we rebalance the asset mix on a quarterly basis." Raj says that this strategy works particularly well when reducing risk as an asset class, say stocks, become expensive, and increasing exposure as stocks get cheap. "This discipline helps us to protect our client's principal."

This is when Raj's investment policy statement comes to play. "Every single client gets a policy statement," he says. "This is something that has been done on the institutional side for years, and we think it's important enough for our clients. It takes a lot of time and preparation, but in the long run it's beneficial to our clients." The statement includes information such as investment objectives, asset allocation mix, how the portfolio is to be managed or delegated, how often the portfolio will be rebalanced, and goals for managed investments.

The team relies on Merrill's open architecture model, which allows financial advisors to have the flexibility to leverage Merrill's extensive money-management resources, or seek outside assistance. "We have over 3,000 investment managers and 5,000 mutual funds to choose from," he says, shaking his head in disbelief. "As a result, we can select the best managers, while acting independently so we can find the best match for our clients."

Once the investment policy is instituted and placed into action, Raj's team evaluates and manages the portfolio according to the statement. The team also evaluates performance on an ongoing basis. "We essentially deliver value by providing an effective product," Raj says.

In order to provide the high level of expertise and quality service, Raj leverages his team and the vast resources available at Merrill Lynch.

"I'm a conductor," he admits, "and the reason for my team's is success is our structure. Our team is comprised of very motivated and proficient people, and everybody is fundamentally optimistic. Every team member is a part owner; they each share in the revenues. It's important to empower people and set up each individual for success.

"Because we're so focused on the entire area of financial planning, it must be a team effort," he continues. "There are so many distinct areas, we need experts that are extremely proficient in their areas." Raj explains that some of these areas include estate planning, money management, risk management and portfolio management, as well as corporate financial planning and compensation strategies.

This team consists of ten individuals, including Raj and his partners, Marcie Behman, Chris Kemp and Ken Sharma. The team's investment associate, Ellen Stebbins, supervises accounts and manages the quarterly portfolio analysis. The portfolio analysis is like a report card that grades investment returns and risk levels and offers comprehensive data in a client-friendly report. Raj adds that the team has received more referrals from the portfolio analysis service than any other service. The team maintains an additional, and separate, database from Merrill, which allows the team to customize the information and perform extensive analysis.

Deanna Riccitelli and Christina Caputo head the administrative team, with support from five individuals, including Jennifer Dejesus, Lauri Hartford and Visa Arumugham. Additionally, Raj employs up to four interns at any given time. "Their goal is to ensure the highest level of client satisfaction on all administrative matters," Raj says. In fact, team efforts recently led to a new client, the president of one of the world's largest companies. "This happened because of superior customer and administrative services," he says. "My team is merely offering to simplify clients' lives with ideas and services—such as account consolidation and superior order execution—clients tend to make us their primary financial advisor and refer business."

The team meets every Tuesday for up to four hours. "While each team member has a specific role, we all work together in a very unified manner to achieve the same goal: best-in-breed service for our clients."

Merrill's specialists, whom he lists on his marketing material, noticeably enhance the ten-person team. "As an extended part of the team," Raj explains, "They're fantastic. When we have client meetings, they join us and offer their expertise. Recently, Raj had a client meeting to discuss estate planning, and one of Merrill's specialists joined the meeting. They discussed a dynasty trust, a perpetual trust that allows the benefactor to grow money for future genera-tions, free of estate taxes. Raj has also been helping clients with philanthropic financial planning, using strategies such as private foundations, charitable lead trusts and charitable remainder trusts.

Additionally, the team takes advantage of the advanced coursework that Merrill offers. This way, they're able to keep in tip-top financial planning condition.

In the late 1980s, Raj opened a new account with a man who Raj considered an extremely aggressive investor. The client had heard that Raj was a great stock picker, and his million-dollar portfolio was invested solely in high-volatile equities. The client did not understand the need for financial planning. "To him, financial planning was making the most of his money in terms of fast growth."

Raj immediately realized that he had some needs that required careful planning, beyond aggressive capital appreciation. The team took the new client through the fact-finding process to develop the investment profile and state-ment. For example, the client supported his mother and required scheduled income. He also wanted to plan for his own financial independence, as well as education needs for his children.

After Raj had time to study the client analysis, he met with his new client. "Listen, you have some important objectives," Raj began. "You don't want to be constantly wondering whether or your kids will go to college. You want to make sure your mother is financially in good shape with no worries. And wouldn't it be nice to feel more secure about your retirement planning? What if an investment doesn't work out? You want to make sure you develop a program for these objectives." The client acquiesced, and followed Raj's advice. Money was apportioned according to Raj's customized investment policy and asset allocation model. A portion is professionally managed.

The client now appreciates being on track: his mother receives her monthly checks with little risk; money for his children's educations is allocated; and his retirement account is well funded. The current value of his holdings is $6 million.

Three years ago, a prospect was referred to Raj. The prospect was a successful executive with a $5 million portfolio, and had left his company. Around 80% of this portfolio was tied up in the company's stock, and he was unable to sell the stock due to lockout restrictions. "I always tell clients in this situation that it doesn't matter what stock you own. It could be the greatest stock in the world, but always think financial planning," Raj says. "This means you don't want any more than 10% or 20% in any single position." He and the client discussed the need to protect that position in a way that would enable diversification. For this particular situation, Raj recommended more exposure to large-cap stocks and international equities.

"We collared around 80% of this client's stock position," he says. Additionally, Raj's team helped with his total financial planning needs, including the establishment of trusts, insurance policies, and insurance policies to protect his kids from estate taxes. "He has been extremely satisfied with the results. We have received a tremendous amount of referrals from this client."

Raj is also a proponent of prepaid forward transactions. This is a transaction that enables an investor to collect a majority of the proceeds of stock position's value upfront, say 85 to 90%, while deferring the gain to a predetermined time several years later. The pre-paid forward eliminates an investor's downside risk in the stock position, while maintaining significant upside exposure. Raj recently arranged a pre-paid forward transaction for a client with a stock position worth $3 million. The investor realized 88% of the proceeds immediately with no tax consequence. There's no downside exposure, and the stock still has upside potential. The sale will be realized in two years.

Exchange funds are another vehicle that Raj recommends to investors who want to diversify large single holdings. Investors contribute their stock to the fund, and in exchange receive shares in the fund for the same value. That way, an investor is assured of diversification, and the gains are tax deferred until the positions are redeemed. There are many types of exchange funds, including those that specialize in mid caps or blue chips.

With investors who have large concentrated stock positions, Raj makes it clear that he manages risk. "Their wealth has been made by concentration," he says. "I tell them I'm a specialist in risk management. My objectives are to make sure I help them preserve their wealth, and to make sure we build upon it.

"I've always considered myself a financial consultant who specializes in risk management," he continues. "When I speak to entrepreneurs, I explain that a substantial amount of money locked in one position exposes them to a tremendous amount of risk. This is when I introduce the strategies available to them." Raj points out that he happens to have a meeting with eight executives of a company that is one month away from going public. The topic is concentrated stock position management. He will discuss risk, proper portfolio management, and financial planning. This was a referral from a client who is also an executive at a start-up company.

"I feel I'm able to differentiate myself from other financial advisors because of my understanding and interests in risk management," Raj says. "I strongly believe I offer products that few financial advisors even get close to. While most are focusing on traditional product, I offer something unique, and it's a service that's desperately needed by a large number of people."

Even though Raj receives a large number of referrals, he still seeks other sources for new business. For example, he has prospected many venture capitalists. "It's easy getting the appointment because they like conversing with someone who knows the language. They may not have had other calls from financial advisors, unlike all the cold calls they receive for the traditional business. This is a real specialized service that we at Merrill can offer; it's not a traditional, commoditized security.

Raj feels prospects and clients appreciate the fact that he is attuned to Merrill's investment strategist, which helps him determine proper asset allocations.

"This business is really all about helping people achieve dreams," he says in a caring voice. "I want to do more than just simply help clients make money. I want to help them retire more comfortably, get their kids an education, manage the risk of their stock position. This business isn't just about the performance aspect of a client's portfolio. We get deeply involved in our clients' financial situation."

Raj points out that once a year, members of the team meet with each client, along with outside professionals, such as lawyers and accounts, to help review the client's objectives. "We look at non-performance aspects. Has someone planned the estate properly? What are the client's charitable giving goals? Are they being met? Are the kids' educational needs being met?" Raj continues: "Investing is important, but it's only one aspect of an individual's financial plan.

"It's a business about individuals' futures; it's not a business about the past. To be successful in this business, you must be unnervingly optimistic. What investor would want to plan the rest of their financial future with a pessimist? Investors need a financial advisor that can help them dream, and plan how to get from point A to point B."

Raj believes that every action has a reaction. "When we do good things, then good things will happen to us," he explains. "This business has a direct impact on people's lives. People come to us and they trust us; they give us all their savings. There is a great fiduciary responsibility that I take very seriously. It's an obligation. We've got to make sure we treat their money with great diligence and do the right thing. Then things will happen to you; and that's a reaction. It's a cause and effect relationship. And if you treat somebody really well, and take care of him or her, they're going to become your spokesperson, your advocate. That's how you acquire more clients. Up to 70% of the clients we get today are from referrals." Raj and team open around 300 new accounts every year.

This caring approach extends well beyond Raj's business. Within the securities business, he believes that the more he contributes, the more of an impact he will have on business practices. "I want to give this business a great name," he says proudly. He lectures frequently to Merrill Lynch rookies and established financial advisors, and is part of the firm's national speaker's bureau. One point he makes is the transition from transaction-based business to one focused on strategic planning, investment management, and risk management business. He is particularly fond of the fee-based business model, where he is rewarded if the client is rewarded.

Raj then reflects on his upbringing in India, and the principles learned from his parents: "I strongly believe in people having opportunities," he says slowly. "Having come from India, I consider myself very fortunate. Now I have to give back to India." Raj funds educational activities for impoverished Indian children, and housing and books for homeless children.

Additionally, Raj contributes his time and expertise as board member to the Island Alliance, a group dedicated to preserving and raising the public awareness of the Greater Boston Harbor Islands.

He then reflects about his own pride: his loving wife, Nalini, and four beautiful children—Meara, Neil, Jay and Tara. "I give my wife a great deal of credit for my success," he says. "She is a great source of support and encouragement; additionally, she takes the time to understand my business and acts as a great coach.

"Family is everything," Raj adds, then looks up. "This is where I do my best conducting—this is my symphony," he says with a broad smile.

CHAPTER 3:
COMMUNITY INVOLVEMENT

ALAN "ACE" GREENBERG
ACE OF HEARTS

Bear Stearns
New York, NY

Some call him the heart of Wall Street. Others simply say he's the most generous man they've ever met. *Fortune* magazine named him "one of the fifty most fascinating people in business." He has been named Man of the Year by numerous organizations, including the National Conference of Christians and Jews, B'nai Birth Youth Services, and the United Jewish Appeal, and Philanthropist of the Year by the National Society of Fund Raising Executives.

Bear Stearns Chairman Alan "Ace" Greenberg makes a lot of money running a major investment-banking powerhouse and trading his clients' portfolios. And he gives a lot of it away. "The more I give away, the more I make," he says. "My wife and I have gotten much more out of it than we've given. Some of our most pleasurable moments are seeing results of certain gifts we've given. I encourage everyone else to try it—I think they'll like it."

The tens of millions of dollars and countless hours that Ace and his wife, Kathy, dedicate to nonprofit organizations do more than enrich dozens of causes. Ace has become a role model for business people on Wall Street and around the world. What has inspired him to give his money and his time to benefit others? How has it affected his business? And why does he feel that giving has been the greatest factor in his success?

Answers date back to over a century ago when a young Russian man immigrated to the United States to pursue a better way of life. After five years of saving, he sent money to his sister, brother and cousin so that they could make the same journey. "That cousin was my grandfather," Ace says. "I'm very lucky to live in this great country, and it's important for me to give back." He then recounts a promise he made to himself as a child: "I've always felt that if I made a lot of money, I wanted to give a lot of it away."

During his fight to land a job on Wall Street after college in 1949, Bear Stearns offered him a job he couldn't refuse. "They paid me $32.50 a week to serve as a clerk in their oil and gas department," he says. "My job was to put pins in maps of Texas and Canada where oil wells were being drilled. " His qualification for the job? He was a former resident of the state of Oklahoma. Once he got a foothold, Ace rocketed up the corporate ladder, which has been fortunate for his beneficiaries.

Ace worked relentlessly to learn the business. Within six months he became a risk arbitrage clerk, and by the time he was 25, he was running the department. He found his passion in trading and quickly built a book of business. In 1958, at the age of 30, he became a partner.

A year after making partnership, something happened that changed his life forever. Ace was diagnosed with colon cancer and was given a 25% chance of survival. His brother Maynard well remembers Ace's reaction: "Well, the odds aren't too bad, but the stakes are awfully high." Friends recall that Ace kept his sense of humor at the time, saying that he wasn't going to buy any long-term bonds. Ace defeated cancer, and after 12 years of semi-annual visits to the Mayo clinic, he believes he was given a second chance. "Ever since, I never put off something I want to do. I just do it," he says. "I was lucky—I think all of us are very, very lucky."

Though his cancer is long gone and his childhood promise to himself is just a memory, they've had lasting effects on Ace's career. He's admired for his poise under extreme pressure. His outlook is distinctly short-term. This attitude has clearly aided him in becoming one of the Street's greatest traders, and an advocate of helping others "like there's no tomorrow."

Take a tour of Bear Stearns and you'll quickly witness Ace's personality and the results of his personal philosophy. For example, he still enjoys managing this powerhouse and his clientele from the middle of the action on the firm's tremendous trading floor. And where else are all senior managers and directors required to give 4% of their gross income to charity? "We don't care who they give the money to," Ace says. "It could be a local hospital, a library, or a school. We find that once they do it, they become finer citizens, better known in the community, and I'm sure it helps the firm overall. Maybe we force them to get into the habit, but no one has ever resented it. In fact, most of them give much more."

Under Ace's leadership, Bear Stearns has become the largest per capita donor to the United Way and the United Jewish Appeal. Each year, just before the start of the UJA Federation campaign, Ace personally invites every managing director at the firm to come to a "kick-off" cocktail party. "I also tell them that those who don't come will be personally solicited by me. We get almost 100% attendance." Ace relies on the directors to relay the invitation to their staff. The UJA generates around $4 million from Bear Stearns employees each year.

"It's called peer pressure," the fund-raiser says cheerily. Is he concerned about being too pushy? "I'm not concerned with backlash," he says, "I'm interested in things that work."

Ace's philanthropic passion is truly boundless. This means putting in long hours for fund-raising. "What charitable organizations need are people who will call for money," he says. "I don't want to be on the boards or committees. I'm only interested in fund-raising." After all, who is better qualified than an individual with Ace's skills for selling ideas and raising money for investments?

Ace recommends that newcomers to the business get involved in their community not only as a means of contributing to society, but with the added benefit of meeting new people and networking. "It certainly helps to meet new people and network," he says. "Whether they'll get any business out of it, I don't know. I have never tried, but personally my wife and I have enjoyed this kind of work immensely."

While Ace credits the satisfaction he feels when receiving something in return from charity work, he does come in contact with important and wealthy people who may make major contributions. While such contact is not his motive, he admits that it helps generate good will. "Our goal still remains; a high return on equity with integrity." He adds: "Treat people right. They'll talk nicely about you and that feeds on itself. There's nothing like a recommendation from a happy client."

With a soft spot in his heart for children, Ace recently hosted a magic show for employees and their children at the company's headquarters in New York City. Ace astonished the onlookers with tricks using eggs, peanut butter and jelly. "A three-year-old once told me it was the best magic act he'd ever seen," Ace says with a broad smile.

Ace has clearly shown that he's not afraid to do things a little differently.

After reading that some insurance companies and state health programs are refusing to cover the anti-impotence drug Viagra, Ace turned more than a few heads when he announced a donation of $1 million to provide the drug to needy men.

"I saw an article saying that at $10 each, a lot of impotent men wouldn't be able to afford it. So I said, 'Kathy, let's help.' And by Tuesday we had it done. The public interest in Viagra says a lot about how many people have been suffering in silence.

"It's just a quality of life issue, that's all," he says about his Viagra donation, comparing it to his donation of swimming pools and soccer fields to children. "I was asked, 'Why not give to something more worthy like AIDS or cancer?' This doesn't wipe out our other giving, which we continue to take seriously. It's just as worthy and might be overlooked.

"Depending on demand, I might add to it," Ace says, then adds with his sly humor: "It can only go up, not down."

DON DEWEES
THE COMMUNITY IS OUR BEST INVESTMENT

First Union Securities
Wilmington, Delaware

In the summer of 1992, Don DeWees was diagnosed with acute myelogenous leukemia, a cancer of the bone marrow. He was given 90 days to nine months to live. If he didn't respond to chemotherapy and interferon, there would be nothing more the doctors could do for him.

Believing that each day could be his last, he cherished every moment with his family. He asked his son, Don, Jr., if he would join his team at Wheat First, predecessor to First Union Securities, so they could spend quality time together. This way, they could begin preparing his son to lead the nine-person team he had assembled over the years. Don, Jr., who has always had a special fondness for his father, sold his ophthalmology business in 1993 and changed careers.

While at Sloan-Kettering Hospital for treatment, the Mother Superior of the Sisters of Charity, Mother Theresa's foundation, asked DeWees to pray with her. They had met in the chapel, and she told him that she, too, was dying. Never a religious individual, a depressed DeWees told her bluntly, "It's not going to help, Mother. Besides, I'm not Catholic."

"This I can tell you," she said. "You're not going to die of leukemia."

"Mother, I've got a six-page bill for $35,000 which details exactly how I'm going to go," DeWees said with his usual dry humor.

"You must believe," she said. "You're going to get a call to do something."

DeWees dismissed the notion with a polite "thank-you" and handed the Mother Superior a check for a generous amount of money. Insulted, she tore it up.

Six months later, he received a call from an excited oncologist. "There's not a cancer cell in your body that you have to worry about!" he exclaimed.

"You mean I'm cured?" an incredulous DeWees replied.

"Let's just say we believe you'll end up dying from something else," the doctor said.

After a brief celebration with his wife, DeWees called Mother Superior; he hadn't communicated with her since that day in the chapel. "It's so good to hear from you, Mr. DeWees," she said. "I can only presume you're going to tell me you are now well. Remember, you're going to be called to do something. And if you fail, the leukemia's probably going to come back."

DeWees determined that his "calling" was to give back to the community, and subsequently he plunged himself into a slew of philanthropic projects. First, he joined the Leukemia Society of Delaware, where he is now a board member. Other organizations soon benefited from his professional know-how. Today he is active with the American Cancer Society, the Delaware Symphony, the Delaware Art Museum, the Boy Scouts, the Ingleside Nursing Home, and the Kalmar Nykle Foundation. He is a volunteer for the Make-a-Wish Foundation and an officer of the National Association of Christians and Jews. While maintaining their business at First Union Securities, DeWees and Don, Jr. together contribute nearly 400 hours every year on community-related activities. They are equally as generous with their monetary contributions.

Although the charity work they do is spiritually fulfilling, it can be emotionally challenging at times. "At the Make-a-Wish Foundation, we had one child who was diagnosed with amyotrophic lateral sclerosis, Lou Gehrig's disease," recalls DeWees. "It's heartbreaking to see somebody in that condition. Her dream was to meet the Pope. I could introduce her to just about anyone— a Hollywood celebrity, the President, a professional athlete—but how was I going to introduce her to the Pope?"

Through his web of contacts, however, DeWees was able to arrange a private 737 jet to fly the young girl and her family to visit His Holiness and spend a week in Italy at the luxurious Excelsior Hotel. Because the Make-A-Wish Foundation prohibits its members from meeting the children they help, DeWees never had the opportunity to speak to the girl. However, a touching letter that she sent to the foundation was forwarded to him. She was allowed to meet with the Pope for five minutes, she wrote, and he had given her a stuffed teddy bear. DeWees was greatly saddened to hear of her death almost a year later, but honored that he'd helped to make her dream come true.

DeWees, a native of Philadelphia, studied business at Bucknell University, then earned an MBA from the University of Pennsylvania in 1954. After a stint as a computer salesman he joined the brokerage community in the early 1960s. Fortunately, a talent for sales helped DeWees quickly establish himself in his new career. Since then he has seen tremendous success, and his son has followed in his footsteps. Not surprisingly, their charitable activities have helped them expand their business through an abundance of referrals. In fact, the duo estimate that most of their new business is a direct result of community involvement.

Both father and son can attribute several large accounts as a result of rolling up their sleeves with fellow community doers. For example, some years ago, DeWees was asked to contribute $1,000 to support a periodic appreciation luncheon for the staff of an inner-city planning commission. He continued to contribute this amount for five years. Then one day, the executive director of the foundation called to say he was retiring at the end of the year, and he'd like DeWees to manage his finances. "The next thing we know, we've got a couple of million dollars of his assets," DeWees says.

Another time, DeWees was asked to review the investment portfolio of a church. He had been an active board member there for five years, helping to raise money and to plan events. DeWees accepted the offer and made several recommendations. The board acted on all of them, and then rewarded him with the $2 million portfolio. "I had no idea they were even considering moving the account," says DeWees, who appreciates the thought more than he does the business. Some time later, the executive director moved to a larger establishment, and "we earned their $6 million account as well." He offers considerably discounted transaction costs to all of the non-profit organizations he works with. "It's really just one more way I can contribute," he adds.

All told, the DeWees duo credits their extensive community involvement for a good portion of the $3 million in assets they bring in every month. Father and son also encourage their team members to become active in the community. For example, Tamara Bowers, DeWees' right hand and a financial consultant, serves on the Daffodil Committee of the American Cancer Society. "It's been three years now, and it's very rewarding, but time-consuming," she says. Rather than expecting her to use her vacation time, the DeWees allow her to take time away from the office—about 30 hours a year—to work on the committee.

DeWees and Don, Jr. value the relationships they've built with fellow community leaders—Corporate executives, CPAs, lawyers, business owners, and other professionals—with whom they usually meet on boards and in finance committees. "Because we're all active members who also live and work in the community, there is a natural networking among us all," Don, Jr. says. "We all believe in helping out those who help others—the friendly banker, broker, lawyer—whoever.

"It's a great form of camaraderie," he continues. "We're out there rolling up our sleeves with the movers and shakers in the community. It's a high-visibility situation—you get to contribute your wisdom, guidance, and leadership, and you provide your professional financial advice. This definitely helps to elevate you to a level of much greater influence and stature than that of the average financial advisor. You still have to develop your business in the traditional ways—you can't rely on community involvement. But let's face it, anytime you can run with the movers and the shakers in the community, you've got a shot at earning their trust and confidence, and possibly their business."

The senior DeWees readily agrees: "We've never considered getting involved in a nonprofit for the purpose of earning business. We like to give back because we enjoy enriching the community, and helping people. Earning business as a result is a pure by-product; we're sitting there with the CFO or the CEO of every major corporation in town that gives time and money to these organizations. It does help us, absolutely. But our priority is our clients, who are entrusting us with their finances."

The DeWees team, who manage nearly $1 billion in client assets, insist they would provide even more of their time to the community if they weren't so committed to servicing their clients.

"If you don't take care of your clients, they won't take care of you," DeWees says. "We build lifetime relationships with our clients—we have clients going back nearly forty years. On the rare occasion that they leave, they typically come back within five years."

He reflects, "I've had a long successful career in the securities business. My leukemia didn't recur. And I would say that the best moves I've made have been community involvement related. In more ways than one, this has been my best investment!"

DEBORAH FRAZIER
A LEAGUE OF HER OWN

Merrill Lynch
New York, New York

Deborah Frazier has it all backwards. Most people become successful, then give back to the community; Deborah has become successful by giving back to the community.

She may be a financial advisor—in fact, *The Winner's Circle* ranks her as one of the most successful female African American financial advisors in the country—but she could just as easily be called a financial humanitarian. Her business was built from the ground up—literally. Although Deborah's business model consists of comprehensive wealth management for high-net worth individuals, remarkably, she began by providing financial advice to families with modest means and church groups. It may seem contradictory, but this financial advisor isn't in it only for the green. She hit Wall Street armed with "courage, spirit, and a sincere desire to give back to the community."

Listening to her tell her story is a joy. She's one of the kindest people you'll ever meet, and with her friendly smile, affable demeanor and genuine compassion, she evokes a sense of great faith. Indeed, her story is both inspirational and heartening. And it clearly shows that one can be rewarded many times over for giving to the community.

One reason Deborah will always give back is because she'll never forget where she came from, and how she was raised. And while many financial advisors seek industry leaders as role models, Deborah's mother has always been her mentor. The lessons Deborah learned from her mother weren't financial or sales related. In fact, Deborah's mother never invested a penny outside a small bank account. Yet Deborah learned some of the most valuable lessons of all: integrity, compassion, and benevolence. Her mother passed away in 2001, although, Deborah says, her lessons will live on. "She was the shining light in so many lives. She had a positive effect on everyone she came in contact with." Deborah has more in common with her mother than she thinks.

Deborah grew up with six siblings in the steel town of Gary, Indiana. "I grew up in the best environment—a loving and nurturing family, a great school system and a tight-knit community in which everyone looked after everyone else," she says, reflecting.

Her father held two jobs, days in a steel mill and off hours driving a cab; her mother worked at a laundry cleaner and cashiered at a retail store. With these incomes, they supported the family, living in a two-bedroom rented house.

Deborah was a track star until she almost lost her life from a ruptured appendix. Her dreams of becoming an Olympian were replaced by working for an assistant principal at her junior high school. Additionally, she earned money by baby sitting, tutoring, and later working for U.S. Steel. "Everyone in my family had a strong work ethic," she says. "We all worked and contributed what we could to the family. We had everything we ever needed," she says with her soft voice, with a smile. "We felt like we had it all, and we did." She attributes her track days and early work experience to her competitiveness, stamina and character.

After graduating from Indiana University in 1979 with high marks in marketing and business management, Deborah spent several years the ranks at U.S. Steel. When she decided she wanted to pursue a career in finance, her competitiveness sent her to the big league: Wall Street. "I left home nearly 20 years ago for Wall Street on a hope and a prayer to work at Merrill Lynch," she says.

After five years with Merrill Lynch and achieving the position of Department Supervisor, Deborah decided to pursue a career as a financial advisor. With little direction, and no business plan, she began the tedious process of cold calling—from 7 a.m. until 11 p.m.—obtaining leads from the telephone book. Her dedication to working with lower-income families added to her malaise. The type of investors Deborah focused on the most were not exactly the most sought-after target market by financial advisors.

Her work in the community led her to offer financial advice to families who were not investing or even planning for retirement. She offered free advice, spending as much time as needed, usually in the evenings after work, with people who really needed the help.

To this day, Deborah will not refuse to advise any individual, as long as they are serious about taking responsibility for their own financial future. "I will never turn an individual away, regardless of the size of their investable assets. I always try to be helpful to each person who seeks my help."

Her break in the business came from her community involvement. Through her association as a Board Member for the Brooklyn Chamber of Commerce, Deborah was asked to serve on an economic development committee at the time. She fostered a relationship with a committee member who later approached Deborah. He asked her about managing investments for his personal account and financial planning for his own family.

A number of years later, the board member—an executive for a medium-sized corporation—was so impressed with Deborah's investment performance and the financial advice she provided, he expressed an interest in transferring his corporate 401(k) plan to Merrill Lynch. After 18 months of presentations and proposals, Deborah won the account. "Of course, Merrill Lynch's state-of-the-art turnkey administrative services for mid-market retirement accounts was instrumental in helping win this business," she says.

Additionally, Deborah's commitment to educational investment seminars for company employees—and Deborah's ability to deliver these services—was also paramount in winning the account. Even the executive, who opened a personal investment account with Deborah, told her: "For the first time in 20 years, I'm actually making money with my investments." Later, Deborah earned some cash-management business from the company.

Adding to Deborah's pressure was her decision to adopt a son, Zachary, when he was an infant. Then, incredibly, as the single parent of a two-year old, Deborah took the pressure one step further; by attending the Executive MBA Program at Columbia University business school. For two years, Deborah struggled and juggled. She kept long hours, building a book of business, attending classes, working with her church and other service organizations and, most importantly, caring for her young son. These commitments sometimes kept her occupied from 4 a.m. to as late as two a.m. the next day.

To Deborah's delight, the hard work paid off. When she received her MBA, she had the added confidence of knowledge and speaking with conviction, and was better prepared to deliver more sophisticated, value-added services to a high net-worth clientele that she would later pursue. She was also armed with a solid business plan and a mission. Her high-net-worth and corporate business has exploded since entering Columbia's executive program.

To compensate for the smaller accounts she was helping in the early part of her career, Deborah prospected business owners and corporate clients, who would later become a major component of her business. Typical services she offered these clients included lines-of-credit, debt restructuring and commercial mortgage programs.

When establishing objectives for individuals, Deborah carefully fine-tuned her planning-based business. Each relationship begins with a formal, written financial plan. She specializes in providing estate planning and comprehensive wealth management strategies, and as a result, Deborah has developed a wide spectrum of clients—professionals, corporate executives, small business owners, celebrities and professional athletes.

When New Jersey Nets forward Jayson Williams was forced to retire in 1999 due to a knee injury, he sought advice from his panel of advisors about establishing an effective investment program. Shortly before his injury, Jayson had received a guaranteed $100 million contract and was actively searching for a financial advisor to help him manage his assets.

When the six-foot, ten-inch athlete asked his panel to recommend a financial advisor, two of his trusted advisors almost simultaneously spoke up; coincidentally, they were both Deborah's clients. Both remarked, "Deborah Frazier is highly trusted in the securities industry and in the African-American community in particular. She has proven her ability to effectively manage investment portfolios and does a fantastic job of helping individual plan their financial futures." They also commented on Deborah's extensive experience working with trusts, establishing family foundations, estate planning and philanthropic services.

"Deborah immediately understood my financial needs," Jayson says. "She took the time to understand my life's plans—another career, college planning for my children. She addressed my early retirement issues and, importantly, understood my family's strong desire to contribute time and finances to the community. Once she understood our needs, she meticulously mapped out a plan of action. Few people I have worked with exhibit the high level of integrity and professionalism Deborah consistently demonstrates. I'm glad she's on my team!"

Another wealthy client segment in which Deborah caters are those with concentrated stock positions. "These clients—whether founders, high-level executives or early employees of the company—have typically spent their career at one firm, have large employee stock option plans and often have also accumulated large concentrated positions of company stock in their retirement accounts," she says. "They usually have modest incomes and live moderate lifestyles but their total net worth is substantial. These clients are often reluctant to sell their company stock."

Deborah provides extensive consultation to these clients. "For example, if one of these clients wishes to purchase a home, he or she may not have the cash they need for a meaningful down payment. Their first instinct is to take a distribution from their retirement account to address their cash flow needs. I may advise that they pledge securities instead. With a Pledged Securities Account, a client could be eligible for a 100% mortgage financing program."

To encourage diversification, Deborah may introduce strategies using the highly appreciated stock they own. Working with Merrill Lynch estate-planning specialists and attorneys for the client, Deborah helps clients analyze the benefits of establishing Charitable Remainder Trusts or utilizing a Net Unrealized Appreciation, special tax rules to plan tax-advantaged strategies for their highly appreciated stock positions.

For Deborah, everything has come full circle: the more successful she becomes, the more she is able to contribute to the community. In fact, her rise to the top was aided in part to community-related business. She now manages investment portfolios for a significant number of religious and not-for-profit organizations. In conjunction with specialists from Merrill Lynch's philanthropic and gifting services, Deborah provides consultation to non-profit organizations on structuring and managing endowment accounts and other gifting strategies.

But the service that brings her the most riches, only not in dollar terms, is the work she does for individuals with modest means or minimum experience in financial matters. "Working with families who really need my help the most is the most important work I do," she says. "It makes me very happy when I can influence the planning, savings and investment habits of individuals in a way that may substantially enhance their financial future.

"My natural avocation has always been teaching, so it's easy to understand why I enjoy sharing knowledge about finance and securities with people who otherwise would rarely have the opportunity to gain such insights. Whether it's helping clients structure savings plans to fund their children's college education, plan for retirement, or create a lasting legacy for their families, the fact that I can make such a difference has had a profound effect on me. And it has allowed me to actively pursue one of the most important objectives in my own life—a sincere desire to give back to the community."

Deborah continues to open many of her lower-income family accounts, and she receives large numbers of referrals from these clients. At one point, a client referred close to 20 friends to her. Most were small, individual accounts. One of these smaller accounts referred many more clients, including a prospect named Bishop Donald G. K. Ming, of the African Methodist Episcopal Church.

The Bishop had been in the market for over 20 years, but complained that poor advice led to poor performance. Not knowing where to place his money, he sought the safety of Treasury-backed zero-coupon bonds, which had appreciated in value. After carefully reviewing the bishops' goals and objectives, Deborah recommended he realize the substantial gains in his zero-coupon investments and diversify his holdings into alternative tax-deferred growth vehicles. A few months later, when interest rates shot up and the value of the bonds plummeted, Bishop Ming truly understood the value of Deborah's advice.

"I have never met anyone who has taken as much personal interest as Deborah," the Bishop says. "She has taught me a great deal about investing. With her, I was able to raise my level of investing to a very sophisticated level." The Bishop has built his net worth substantially due to Deborah's leadership: "Never in my life would I have imagined that I would have this much money!" At his request, Deborah has spoken to many of his referrals, and she is managing investments for a number of his district's Episcopal churches.

"Having the opportunity to develop professional and personal relationships with clients like Bishop Ming has been one of the most rewarding aspects of my job," Deborah says.

In the late 1990s, Deborah was referred to a couple in their early fifties who had hoped to retire in another decade. She noticed that the family's only investment was a $100,000 retirement account, which "was sitting in cash," she says, shaking her head in disappointment. Deborah spent several weeks convincing the couple to invest their money. "This couple was similar to many other clients I have worked with. They did not feel they had the knowledge or expertise to make the investment decisions they knew they should make. They were so afraid of making the wrong decision that they made no decision at all. They also felt that because their assets weren't significant, they wouldn't be able to seek proper advice." After many conversations, they followed Deborah's advice and completed a formal, written financial evaluation. She broke the news gently. "I had to tell them that if they continued with their current plan, it was unlikely they would ever be able to maintain their current lifestyle in retirement."

The couple eventually acquiesced and followed her advice to diversify their money in the equities market. The retirement portfolio is now worth several hundred thousand dollars, and the couple calls Deborah frequently to tell her how the quality of their lives has changed forever. "It's just an incredible feeling," Deborah says. "This means they are going to be able to retire early, travel, and send their sons to the colleges of their choice! It's been wonderful building this relationship with them."The couple later opened accounts for their college-age sons so they could get an early start on investing. One of the sons arranged for Deborah to speak at his school, where one student was so inspired he plans to become a financial advisor. "The sooner individuals start planning for their financial future, the easier it will be for them in the future," she says.

One of the non-profit organizations Deborah works with is a foundation that provides fellowships for minority students to enter medical programs. The client that referred her says, "I referred Deborah to them, and they instantly took a liking to her. She spent a lot of time educating them and guided them through the investing process. They've told me how grateful they are that Deborah has encouraged them to invest in a way that has enabled the assets to grow significantly."

The foundation entrusted a significant portion of the current grant to Deborah, to personally invest for them—around $5 million. Due to cutbacks in corporate contributions a few years later, the organization determined that it would have to lay off a number of employees. "They were very concerned because, in addition to four people losing their jobs, the foundation's marketing and fundraising campaigns were going to suffer," she says. Based on the growth in the investment portfolio Deborah managed, the foundation was able to supplement their operating cash flow and avoid four employee cutbacks. The foundation has since doubled the amount of assets they hold with Deborah."It's amazing to me what kind of impact a financial advisor can have on people's lives," Deborah says thoughtfully. Meanwhile, the four employees whose jobs were saved by her investment expertise gush when they speak of Deborah."She saved my job!" one of them cheered.

Deborah's involvement in the community has also helped her to earn business with religious organizations. One client referred his church's board to Deborah. The board requested that she make a presentation. She impressed the board members and immediately won them over. Additionally, she earned a second account, which is dedicated to a major capital improvement for the church. The account holds the church's collections, which are then invested for growth."The account has grown substantially," the client says."We're looking at major interior improvements in the church sanctuary. What we're looking at is a major project that includes redoing the stencil in the ceiling of the sanctuary. It's nice to know that the growth in the portfolio is going to go a long way. We actually have much more funds for improvement than we initially projected."

Deborah also credits her involvement with the Brooklyn Chamber of Commerce for helping her gain credibility in the community during the early development of her career. Acquaintances in the Chamber were instrumental in connecting her with the New York City Transit Authority. The NYCTA was interested in providing financial-planning seminars to small business owners. The three-day series dealt with assisting these business owners with obtaining the proper licenses and certification to work with the city in obtaining government contracts. The program added a business financial services department, and Deborah was invited to speak. This lead to a large number of new accounts with business owners. "I enjoy working with business owners because they're decision makers," she explains. "They're informed and know their business better than anyone, and they're extremely straightforward. I appreciate that."

Deborah's role in the community has created countless opportunities for her to continue helping people with her professional insights. Deborah spends a great deal of time as a board member for the New York Chapters of the National Urban League, Easter Seals of New York and the African-American Advisory Board of Spence-Chapin Children and Adoption services. Deborah has also served for a number of years as a Sunday school teacher.

The financial insights that Deborah lends to these organizations has led to many more clients, as well as seminars for different groups, primarily within the African-American community. Deborah seldom asks to give a seminar, and she almost never asks for anyone's business through community-oriented channels. If someone is interested, they approach Deborah. Because she has earned credibility in the securities world, "People know that's my expertise, so they ask me to speak at their church groups, alumni groups, business groups, and the like."

Deborah believes so strongly in providing financial advice, she often lectures at groups—frequently traveling out of state—to spread her word. At the invitation of Mr. Carl McCall, Comptroller for the State of New York, Deborah went to Buffalo and Syracuse where she was the keynote speaker at the 1999 Savings Awareness and Investment Opportunities Conference for African-Americans and Latinos. These conferences attracted around 800 attendees.

"The purpose of the conferences was to raise awareness of the huge business gap the African American and Latino communities are facing," she says. "Because the savings and investment rate is so low for these communities, many will face extreme financial hardships in future retirement years."

During the seminars, Deborah urged individuals to invest, no matter how small their savings. "You don't have to wait until you get a huge lump sum. You can build it over time," she implores. "I talk to them about starting up a mutual fund for $500 or $1,000, and give them a list of companies that they can call to handle these transactions. It's important to me that they realize they can make a difference by investing a small amount of money, and continue to invest more sums over a long period of time." She also gives an overview of the economy and how it affects the markets. "I give Merrill Lynch forecasts to show them where the economy is going," she continues. She concludes the seminar by providing sobering retirement statistics that show many people in this community will not be able to support the retirement lifestyles they desire.

No matter the size of the event, whether it's a handful of attendees or 800, Deborah often receives letters, e-mails and telephone calls thanking her for her time, concern and dedication to helping others. At the time of the conference in Syracuse, Deborah was featured on the cover of *Black Enterprise Magazine*.

To her surprise, the audience in Syracuse gave her a standing ovation as she approached the podium. "Honestly, I was very surprised by the ovation. It was spontaneous and such a beautiful gesture. But it just goes to show the work I'm doing—and many others like me—is meaningful. There is a real need and people appreciate our effort. I believe in my heart, if you do well and help others, God will always take care of you."

Deborah's success on Wall Street, as well as Main Street, has snagged a great deal of media attention. *Worth Magazine* has twice named her one of the "Top 250 Financial Advisors" in the country, in September 1999 and August 2001. NBC featured Deborah as one of their annual "African American Profiles in History" for the month of February 2000. Since 1996, she has been a regular "Investment Roundtable" panelist for *Black Enterprise Magazine*, and was featured on the cover of that international business publication in April 1999.

She has also become a media spokesperson for Merrill Lynch, appearing often on television programs such as CBS Financial News and Black Entertainment Network News where she speaks on topics such as estate planning tools and strategies, establishing trusts and comprehensive wealth management for high-net-worth individuals.

One might think that with Deborah's success she might slow down a bit and maybe even sleep in on a Saturday morning. Wrong. She has determined that she is going to devote more time to her family with the adoption of another child.

"I'm always amazed how I can really change someone's life by offering my experience in investing," she says, completely unperturbed by the tremendous success she has displayed at Merrill. "My job is also my way of working with the community. Somehow it all seems to be part of my mission in life to use the talents God has given me to help others. The difference I've made in people's lives is the real payoff for me.

"I think my mother would be proud of me," she says.

Barbara Jaffe
The Financial Philanthropist

Prudential Securities Incorporated
Jacksonville, FL

As a successful woman in the securities business, Barbara Jaffe's financial opinions are highly valued. So what is her number one investing recommendation? "The community," Barbara says in all seriousness.

She speaks from experience. Remarkably, she is able to spend around a quarter of her working hours doing community work. She devotes the rest of her time to the 3,000 clients and $500 million in assets that the Jaffe Group, a team of Prudential Securities financial advisors, manages. She has discovered that both endeavors tend to feed off one another.

It's obvious this Jacksonville-born leader loves both jobs. She's been with Prudential Securities since 1979. Shortly thereafter, when she felt she could afford to leave the office, she began her involvement with the community. She entered the securities business with no experience other than one selling exercise: as a child, she won an award for selling the most Girl Scout cookies. And the only time she ever prospected was at the beginning of her career as a financial advisor, under pressure as a single mother of two boys. "I was selling money-market funds," she says. "And it was only to prospects I knew."

She began her working career as a journalist for Jacksonville's biggest newspapers. From writing obituaries she graduated to the political beat. Eventually she participated in the gubernatorial campaign for the state of Florida and acted as regional campaign chairperson for the gubernatorial candidate. When the party lost the election, she lost her hopes of moving to Tallahassee to run the governor's public relations. But, because of her devotion to journalism and campaigning, she amassed nearly 1,000 names in her Rolodex.

With her political aspirations grounded, Barbara had to regroup. One day she happened to notice an article in a local paper featuring Bache, a predecessor to Prudential Securities, and thought it might lead to a challenging career. The next day she contacted the firm. Later, she applied for a position, and within a few weeks she was training to be a financial advisor.

Rather than taking a shotgun approach, making 100-plus cold calls a day, Barbara sought 25 solid conversations with people she had come across professionally. She began with her Rolodex. "There was no way I was going to call anyone I didn't know," she says emphatically.

From the beginning, Barbara made a point of seeing each prospect in person, whether in her office or at their location. The first meeting typically consisted of establishing a relationship, with Barbara eventually turning the conversation to the prospect's financial situation. This is when she would listen and learn. In this friendly way she was able to gather relevant information, then modestly prove her financial know-how when the prospect asked questions or provided inaccurate information about the markets.

A follow-up meeting was set up. "It takes more than a couple of meetings to fully understand a person's financial situation," she says. "Many people in the business feel they can have one conversation, look at financial statements, and then know what needs to be done and make recommendations. I disagree with this approach."

A typical recommendation that Barbara might offer was money-market funds. This accomplished two tasks: First, she was able to provide 10% returns for a safe, liquid investment. Second, Barbara was perceived as being very non-threatening. "After all, these people are entrusting me with their money; I needed to prove myself, and take more time to understand their needs," she says. "If they wanted risk, I would recommend that a small portion—risky money—be apportioned to these investments."

During Barbara's first few years, her business grew briskly. And as her investing experience deepened and her sons grew up, she decided to devote time to her community interests. It was almost an afterthought that she would lend her most valuable skill: financial know-how. And the fact that people would determinedly seek her for financial advice never entered her mind.

As Barbara soon recognized, financial competency was to be her greatest contribution to the community. She act as chairperson for several committees, including being a trustee of the board of Jacksonville's Police and Fireman's pension fund and the Jacksonville Jewish Community Foundation's investment committee. She has also been involved—whether as an active member, board member, or chairperson—in a number of other organizations, including the Jewish Community Alliance, the Ronald McDonald House, and the Hebrew Home. Interestingly, she turns down the organization's board requests to use her services professionally as financial advisor. "I would lose objectivity," she says. "It's better for the organizations if I spend my own time on it."

Barbara's knowledge and experience don't go unnoticed among other board members and volunteers; they frequently ask her if she can perform the same type of services for their personal accounts. And whether she is building a home for the needy, or organizing a charitable golf tournament, her financial advice is eagerly sought.

Even though her team uses extensive technology in managing a large client base, Barbara considers her business low tech. "Unlike most in the business, we have no cookie-cutter approach," she says. "Our real differentiator is thoroughness. Each recommendation, each piece of advice, is customized for each client. We have a very manual, hands-on practice. If we're preparing an extensive strategy for a client, he or she can't expect it overnight—unless it's urgent. We take our time to prepare it right the first time, and then go through it again just to make sure everything is perfect. We have close relationships with clients, and we create a history with each one. Additionally, we provide a degree of fulfillment and services they can't get elsewhere."

The Jaffe eight-person team is comprised of Barbara, Senior Vice President of Investments, four associates, and three administrative team members. Among the associates is Racquel Zisman, an Investment Evaluator who specializes in equity products and investments, manages equity portfolios, and evaluates outside portfolio managers. Diane McDonald, First Vice President-of Investments, specializes in fixed-income products and investments. Barbara's two sons, Brad Zimmerman and Sandy Zimmerman, manage client relationships as First Vice Presidents of Investments.

Barbara's gift for giving is contagious. Her team members share her vision, and most people she comes in contact with are inspired by her example. Frequently, during speeches she gives to financial advisors, organizations, or other community leaders, she promotes the benefits of giving time to community activities.

Once, Barbara decided to build a home as part of a Habitat for Humanity project. Typically, a family in need pays an affordable, no-interest mortgage to Habitat for Humanity, which in turn subsidizes the home from contributions. Typically, corporate sponsors finance these homes; however, Barbara chose to pay for the home herself.

During the weeklong build, more than 100 of Barbara's clients showed up to join her team. All wore T-shirts that read "Build for the Future with Barbara and Larry Jaffe" on the front, and "Habitat for Humanity" on the back.

Toward the end of the project, Barbara treated a group of volunteers to a drink at a nearby convenience store. A woman behind the counter asked what they were doing, and Barbara shared their plans of building a home through Habitat for Humanity. As the woman listened, tears welled up in her eyes, and in a cracked voice she said, "You don't know how much that means to me." As it turned out, the woman's sister was living in a Habitat house.

Once Barbara's crew finished building the house they visited a site where volunteers had failed to show up, and they completed that job as well. "It was such a successful week, and so much fun, we've decided to do this every year," she explains. She helped build her third house in 2001.

Barbara highly recommends community work to rookies in the business "if, however, they sincerely believe in what they are doing. If their purpose is to generate business, it's not for them." she says. "There's no single better way to build a rapport than to work side by side with community leaders, business leaders, and others, to build lasting relationships based on mutual interests. In this case, those interests involve the improvement of our society.

"I've always been told that if you pursue what you truly love," Barbara says with a warm smile, "it'll come back to you in spades."

In her case, it turned out to be all hearts.

CHAPTER 4:
DIFFERENTIATION

Marvin "The Wizard" McIntyre
There's Something Funny About the Wizard

High Net Worth Group
Legg Mason Wood Walker, Inc.
Washington, D.C.

See related sections:
Building a Brand: The Wizard of Washington
Managing a Billion-Dollar Book: They're off to see the Wizard…
Prospecting and Marketing: Who you gonna call? The Wizard

Someone once said, "Laughter is the shortest distance between two people."

If this is true, then it's no wonder Marvin "the Wizard" McIntyre has been so successful at building a large book of solid relationships. His finance philosophy is such a serious undertaking, that "if you soften the process with levity it yields comfort and trust," he says. In fact, many in the business say his constant kidding and "loving" abuse make him the most recognizable name in the Washington, D.C. investment community.

The Wizard is one of those remarkable individuals who warms you with humor, charms you with witticisms, and impresses you with his vast knowledge and professionalism. And it seems to be contagious. His 11-person team of professionals shares this trait. "Whether it's due to coincidence or capitulation, I don't know," he adds. After spending the better portion of a day interviewing the Wizard and team, I paid the price: a four-hour drive back to New York City with my sides aching from laughter. His extraordinary sense of humor definitely makes him stand out from the rest.

Friends of the Wizard always thought he would land a career as an entertainer. As a young boy, his mother believed he'd become a preacher. Marvin gives a smile and says, "Sometimes I do feel like I'm in a pulpit, preaching about financial discipline. I kind of like the fire and brimstone part, if they misbehave!" From high school through his tour of duty in Vietnam, he wrote songs and sang with rock and roll bands. Other than entertaining, he adds, "I was doing a lot of ducking," referring to the constant helicopter missions he made with the artillery battalion. "My specialty was hiding, so I had some time to write my songs."

After a tour of service, he sought his own tours with his band. He cut a demo album in Nashville and talked his way onto national TV shows. He spent a week trying to get in to see producers. "Those were the only cold calls I've ever made," he says, knocking on a wooden table. "One day while I was pitching my song, it struck me that the public, and the person standing in front of me at the time, wasn't exactly clamoring to hear my music, so I sought an alternative career." Friends told him that his sparkling personality and personal skills might be practical in the securities industry.

The first brokerage firm with which he interviewed was Mason & Co., a predecessor to Legg, Mason. "A young, single guy with a Corvette convertible was not exactly the image this conservative brokerage firm was seeking," he says. Nevertheless, when interviewing, Marvin quipped to the director of sales, "I see no one here with the potential I have–with the obvious exception of you, sir." He was hired on the spot.

The Wizard immediately put his entertainment talent to work. Knowing that he never wanted to make another cold call, he wasted no time setting up seminars. He scheduled appointments at retirement communities and gave free seminars on "Maximizing Income with Minimum Risk." This topic was a very conservative approach to investing, tailored to his audience. Now that he had his audience, he educated them while keeping them in stitches. "I kept the seminar very open and encouraged audience participation," he says. "When they interjected, that's when I could really play off the audience and make them laugh." The participants enjoyed the seminars, and attendance jumped.

"Getting people to feel comfortable enough to warm up to you is the way to instill trust," he says. This approach "gives me the opportunity to get them to open up. Then I just listen and learn. This is the best way to begin the relationship-building process. It's what our business is all about." Recently, the wife of a long-time client, the CEO of a publicly traded biotech company, told a team member: "I always know when my husband is talking to Marvin; it's the only time he laughs!"

The Wizard and his team, the High Net Worth Group, cite referrals from "centers of influence" as sources for nearly 100 new accounts per month. "Often when I'm profiling a new client I'll ask, 'Who is your accountant?' Then he or she will tell me the name. I'll say, 'From time to time I may have ideas or suggestions that might affect you, tax-wise. Would you mind if I called your accountant and discussed our relationship?' Later, I'll call the accountant and say, 'Mrs. Jones has spoken very highly of you, and I'd really like the opportunity to meet you. Can I talk you into coming to my office and buying you lunch?'"

When discussing business, Marvin is never the first to mention his interest. He feels that if people are interested enough, they will bring up the topic them-selves and he will be positioned appropriately as objective, and even more desirable to work with. For example, when he takes an accountant to lunch, knowing that the CPA may be anticipating a sales pitch for the rest of his clients, he never brings up the subject. Finally, towards the end of lunch, if the CPA brings up referrals, Marvin asks, "How can we help you grow your business?" Marvin has found that not appearing predatory invariably leads the other party to become much more accommodating; it is only then that Marvin will consider making an offer to help.

In fact, the Wizard only approaches a prospective client for business under rare circumstances. If he does, however, it is subtle. Marvin once attended a party where he spotted an acquaintance, a doctor who ran a business with a large profit-sharing plan. Marvin approached the doctor and whispered in his ear:"Hey, Doc. People are talking about you, but don't worry, I've taken care of it." Then Marvin walked away.

The doctor rushed up to him and said, "What do you mean, people are talking about me?"

The Wiz replied, "Well, I don't like to talk, but people have been questioning your intelligence." The doctor was astounded. Marvin continued, "They've wondered, if you're really that smart, then why aren't you already doing business with me? I told them you were very bright, just a little slow."

The doctor laughed, and Marvin let the subject go. The doctor then said, "You know what? I really should pay you a visit." Marvin called him on the following Monday.

The High Net Worth Group is very particular about referring business. Only after thoroughly assessing a third party will the group do so. "We're very protective about to whom we send business," the Wiz says. "Hopefully, our referral sources feel the same way. You can never send a client to somebody who might embarrass you. And we would never send business to someone simply to repay him or her for the business."

At the beginning of his career, the Wizard earned the business of an accountant who prepares an extraordinarily large volume of tax returns every year. Marvin helped him plan his future and they became friends. Consequently, the CPA started referring every client to Marvin. If the following year the accountant notices their accounts haven't been transferred to Marvin, he'll say, "Didn't I tell you to call the Wizard?" Marvin has received over 200 clients from this referral. "I believe that everyone who refers business to me is completely satisfied. In fact, I give them a guarantee that I would never embarrass them, and that I would give them extra love because they referred them to me," he says slyly.

When the Wiz receives a referral from an accountant, he'll tell the client, "Your accountant does not benefit financially from directing you to me. And quite frankly, if I did something wrong, you might leave him because he sent you to me. So, the fact that he cared enough about you to send you to me means you may want to go back and thank him." Then, says the Wiz, "the accountant would get an appreciative 'thank you' and think, 'All these people that I sent to the Wiz are thanking me.' That always encourages them to send more referrals."

When a potential client visits the Wizard and his team at his office, they take the time necessary to get to know him. Marvin always loosens clients up with laughter. "Money is the last taboo," he says. "People will sooner tell you about their sex lives than they will about their money. The first time somebody visits, our objective is to discover everything possible about him or her, first on a personal basis, and then financially." The Wizard sits and listens, using his humor to create a conversation steeped in candor. "It's like going to the doctor, except they're getting financially undressed," he says meaningfully, then jokes, "but it's okay if some want to get undressed also."

"Asking the right questions is imperative," he says on a serious note. "Many brokers will begin the conversation by asking 'How much money do you make?' or 'How much are you worth?' That is just too offensive. This is a probing situation—don't pick up a pad or paper or punch data into the computer; get to know prospects as human beings. Get them to open them up." The Wizard suggests finding a common ground, such as golf or tennis. "In my case, maybe they've seen me on television or heard me on the radio, so it's easier for me because they sort of know me alreadyæand my good looks help," he adds with a wry smile.

"Supplementary to his or her entire financial situation," the Wiz continues, "I make a point of learning the person's fears, hopes, and desires. Then I focus on making resolute decisions that will alleviate those fears and fulfill those hopes. If decisions can't be achieved in the first meeting, then an advisor isn't listening. Listening is a crucial skill in our business. Both clients' time and our time are too precious to waste in three or four meetings to make a decision. We're the experts, and as soon as we have our information, we act.

"Most of the time, people just want answers in simple terms. Many clients have accounts all over the place; they have no direction, no focus. Advisors need to make this process less complicated. They need to solve a problem." And the Wiz makes the process less wearisome by keeping clients laughing.

ANDY GELLER
SHOOTING FOR THE STARS

UBS PaineWebber
Century City, California

It's obvious that Andy Geller is a family man. His office is decorated with pictures that tell the story of his family's life, and his eyes gleam as he discusses his daughter, Cari's, wedding. He's thrilled that his son Greg will be partnering up with him in the business, and he laughs when telling the story of how his wife picked him up at a beach, finding his body irresistible. (Unable to tell a lie, he later confessed that this story is only partially accurate.) Andy offered an apprehensive smile when asked about his childhood, and replied: "My childhood is the reason for my success."

Growing up in the 1940s in a Jewish West Los Angeles suburb, Andy learned the meaning of starting from nothing. When he was ten years old delivering newspapers—helping to support his family—he promised himself that he would one day be financially successful. He was well aware of the difference between the haves and the have-nots. It was obvious to him, and to others, that his family's one-bedroom duplex and all of his possessions didn't match those of his peers. He felt ashamed and embarrassed in school when the kids would speak of their new toys or vacations, and then ask him what he received for his birthday.

His only feeling of wealth during childhood occurred to him when he returned home from school; that's when he was with his family, and they all felt rich in love. His father would return from his job in a women's clothing sweatshop, and the family would be once again united. Andy shared a bedroom with his sister, while his parents slept on the lanai. "My parents gave us all they could," he says with a heartfelt smile. "That's all we had, and we cherished it immensely.

"My parents were a great inspiration," he continues. "I learned the value of earning a dollar and frugally managing finances. We appreciated everything we had." This is a virtue that he would eventually bestow upon his clients.

When he was in the sixth grade, he wrote a New Year's resolution for the Cub Scouts and won an award. The prize: a $30 watch. "My whole family was so proud of me, owning something with that kind of price tag was a true luxury."

Then one day at the beginning of a piano lesson, his teacher realized that Andy hadn't practiced that week. "He grabbed a ruler, lifted it up, and aimed for my hands," he says, excitedly. "He missed, and the ruler landed with a piercing crack on my new watch. Andy was horrified. "I thought that I could never replace it," he says, saddened. "It really affected me."

Andy became more determined than ever to escape poverty and to make something of his life. After graduating high school, he repaired vacuum cleaners to pay his way through California State University, where he earned a bachelor's degree in education and a master's degree in the arts. He found that the quickest escape from poverty, and to ensure his own survival, was teaching. After being accepted by the board of education, Andy was assigned to teach elementary school in an underprivileged area. "I couldn't help but feel a special closeness with these children," he says meaningfully. "I understood how they were being raised—I felt like I was able to give back, even though I still had little," he says, then proudly shows off a class picture which he keeps on a credenza behind his chair, and points his younger self standing high above the students. The caption reads: "1967 6th Grade."

Still in need of money, and determined to break out of the low-income cycle, he took an additional job teaching English as a second language for adults. He decided to invest his entire savings, around $800, in a company that he was fond of called Data Products. The stock subsequently appreciated in price, and he saw his investment balloon up to $2,000. He continued to research companies that he liked, and invested his money accordingly. This is when he realized he had found his niche. "I loved teaching, and I loved investing," he says. "It made complete sense to give it a try."

As a true conservative with his money, Andy landed a part-time job with a mutual fund company. He worked this job in addition to teaching and tutoring. He earned his securities license and sold mutual funds at night. After six months, he became the firm's top salesman. A year later, he joined a small municipal bond company. He was so ecstatic about his potential for success that he quit his daytime jobs so he could focus on his new job. "I called my wife and told her the good news," he recalls. "She was so excited." And nervous, he says, because he was still supporting his wife and two kids.

Andy wasted no time building a book. When he first started, his boss told him to let his "fingers do the walking" and find clients. "This is my secret to success," he jokes, "the telephone book." The telephone book helped Andy to become the top-performing salesperson—out of 75—within a year.

In 1973, Andy's success inspired him to start his own municipal-bond business. "We became a very large firm in California, employing well over 200 people," he says with satisfaction. Andy was easily the top-performing municipal bond broker at his firm, which he structured around the customer. " My clients were asking for municipal bonds, so I built them the best product possible," he says.

The difference between Andy and the rest of the salesmen was simple: He didn't start with just one telephone book. "I called the telephone company and ordered every single phone book in the state of California, and had them delivered to my house," he explains with a short laugh. "This included every single city and county phone book. At the time, even though my wife was supportive, I'm sure she wasn't thrilled about the mountain of phone books which occupied nearly half of our tiny home."

He hired high school students to address envelopes to every single doctor, lawyer and accountant in each telephone book. Each student earned a penny per envelope. "I prospected every doctor in Beverly Hills, every accountant, every lawyer and anyone else that I thought had any money," he says of his experience in the early 1970s.

As the list of names grew, so did the number of high school students who stuffed the envelopes. The group of teens working for Andy ultimately numbered 12. For three straight years, Andy's team accumulated all the names, around 10,000 altogether, and frequently sent them flyers. At the bottom of the flyer he provided his name and toll-free number. Flyers were usually sent on a monthly basis to each individual until they started responding and eventually became a client. All told over the three-year period, he sent out in upwards of 500,000 flyers.

Once he started opening accounts and building relationships, he leveraged his clients to arrange seminars throughout California. "I've always provided such terrific service that clients are happy to help me organize seminars," he says."I would tell them that I'd like to give a seminar in their area, and ask them to help me fill the room."This strategy succeeded in generating over 100 attendees, and often 200 or more.

One satisfied client referred a farmer to Andy. "This was during a socio-economic downturn, when farmers were having a tough time," he says. The client, located in a farming community in Modesto, California, helped Andy organize a seminar for the benefit of the farmers. Nearly 200 people attended the seminar, and the majority of attendees became clients. When the economy turned, the farmers became prosperous, and relied on Andy to help them manage their money.

As Andy's mostly tax-free business started to flourish with his mailing and seminar techniques, in the mid-1970s he decided to target another niche: high-net-worth individuals."A great deal of wealth was being created in real estate," Andy explains."Then, in the middle of the 1980s, a lot of people got out of real estate. When they did, they sought alternative investments for their real estate proceeds; preferably something that was safe. Tax-free bonds were an appropriate alternative—especially considering interest rates were still high. He targeted local businessmen and households in affluent neighborhoods."

In 1988, with his business in full throttle, Andy sought more ways to improve his service. He considered moving to a full-service firm. PaineWebber, predecessor to UBS PaineWebber, branch manager Barry Harberson contacted Andy and offered a tempting proposition. "They told me I could provide a high-net-worth municipal-bond business, and have access to PaineWebber's tremendous resources," he says. As one of UBS PaineWebber's consistently top-performing financial advisors, Andy works with nearly $700 million in client assets and currently ranks as the firm's top municipal bond salesperson. Importantly, Andy had access to UBS PaineWebber's vast resources, which enabled him to expand his product offerings, and thus client base.

"I could also expand my business to provide the firm's extensive array of financial services for my clients. It was the right thing to do for my clients. Barry still manages the office and continues to provide tremendous support."

Since a majority of his clientele consisted of accountants and lawyers, Andy's high level of service led to a tremendous referral network among these professionals. Clients that have been referred include other accountants and lawyers, high-net-worth individuals and a host of celebrities. "This was a direct result of the honesty I've always exhibited, the best possible service—in an unselfish manner—and the giving of my time anytime and anywhere a client needs me. That's what I'm there for."

Depending on the situation, Andy typically works closely with the client, or the lawyers, accountants or agents that are responsible for his or her money. In the last several years, he's noticed that more and more of clients are taking an active role in the decision-making process with Andy, instead of relying on outsiders. "Once they get involved, these clients are finding that they very much enjoy taking an active role in their investment program," Andy explains. "And because we handle virtually every aspect of a financial relationship—retirement planning, education funding, loans, and more, they are expressing a greater and greater interest in becoming involved. The referrals from these clients and the encouraging responses they are expressing to their business managers are testament their satisfaction and trust with my team. This in turn reflects very favorably on the managers, who continue to refer new business to me."

Andy has noticed that the more time he offers a client, the more active they become in the decision-making process. For example, Andy generally tries to establish meetings with both spouses at the same time. If the client has a business manager, Andy invites him or her as well. "If the client's schedule doesn't permit the couple to meet with me together, then we'll meet each spouse one at a time," he explains. He guesses that previous financial advisors to these individuals didn't provide sufficient time and attention. "After all, they're human beings—they need to be treated like anyone else, and certainly deserve the same close personal attention we provide any other client."

One long-time client, an award-winning actor, attributes his relationship with Andy and business manager to his proper financial planning: "No one could ask for a better financial planning arrangement—sound financial guidance from my sole financial advisor Andy," he says. "I trust him implicitly."

"Andy provides a high level of financial expertise that I rely on," says a top actress. "I feel very comfortable knowing that Andy is helping me managing my investments."

"My policy has always been to provide the same level of high-quality service to every client, regardless of status or size of account," he explains. "They get the same quality of service." He points out that different clients demand different kinds of service. "For instance, the smaller accounts typically need more service than the bigger accounts, who tend to be more sophisticated with their money." He explains that certain types of clients have their own preferences for service. "The services we provide our clients don't end with their financial needs." For example, Andy and his team utilize UBS PaineWebber's sophisticated information services to provide information relating to clients' businesses. "This could include economic data for businessmen, news stories for lawyers, or the opening box office receipts for a movie that one of our clients starred in."

Andy's love for the business also keeps him in the office up to 12 hours a day, five to six days a week. It's extremely rare that he doesn't return a call by the time he leaves the office (in fact, one evening he returned my call at 9:30 Pacific time). "I accept calls from clients at the office, home, and even the far corners of the earth. If my team can't help a client—which is rare—or the client only wants to talk to me—which is also rare—I will return their call as soon as humanly possible. No matter the size of the account.

"I'm very sensitive to the needs of my clients," he continues. "I hate to think that a client may require immediate assistance, and have to wait to have the situation resolved. Right now the market is down 120 points and the long bond is down $10, and my clients know that if there's a problem, I will call them." He points to a message from a client that his assistant Julia hands him. It reads: "Call me. Need some fatherly advice." "Please excuse me while I call her back," he tells me.

During an initial meeting, Andy spends considerable time with his clients to determine their investment needs and objectives. He likes to have a complete understanding of their entire financial situation, and he focuses on asking a lot of questions about their personal finances, financial objectives and dreams for the future. With this information, he is able to propose an asset-allocation model, and recommends specific securities for bonds, stocks and cash. As Andy monitors the plan over the course of the year, he keeps each client—and each business manager, if necessary—informed on any material data related to the account. Depending on the client's preference, he may provide routine account updates anywhere from monthly to yearly. If Andy has allocated a portion of the portfolio to an outside money manager, he provides quarterly updates and performance figures to the client and the business manager.

Andy credits his team, Julia Yokoyama, who has been with him since 1989, and Michelle Shoot, for their exceptional support and service. "Our clients appreciate the time we put into servicing them," he says. "Accountants, lawyers and business managers, in particular, enjoy our hard work—when it comes to investing, we make their jobs as easy as possible. We are cognizant that there are competitors that would love to earn my clients' business; we keep our clients extremely satisfied so they won't consider leaving." He continues: "My team is so reliable that I have no fears when I leave the office—whether it's for lunch, vacation or a sick day."

While Andy maintains the privacy of his client's names—only mentioning their names with permission—it is widely known among clients and prospects that he manages a very high-profile clientele. One client, just days prior to this interview, recently asked him, "Can you take the time and speak to a friend who needs help with his finances? I know you time is very, very busy with major clients, but my attorney and I both agree that you could be of great help." The prospect, a real-estate mogul with tens of millions of invested assets, was unhappy with her current financial advisor and was impressed with Andy's reputation. The two met for an in-depth consultation with her lawyer, and she transferred her account shortly thereafter.

Last June, he was aboard a cruise in the Mediterranean Sea and received a message from a prospect that had heard of him over 20 years ago. Her neighbor spoke highly of him prior to passing away, and the prospect continued to hear favorable comments about his business conduct. Although the two had never met, he sensed some urgency in the message that was read to him by his office. He called her from the ship—at $20 per minute. "Anyone who would return a call so promptly from the other side of the world is someone I want to do business with," she said. Now a client, she has referred dozens of people to Andy.

Now that Andy has accomplished his boyhood dreams of success, has he forgotten about his past? Hardly. His emergence from impoverishment to the ranks of *The Winner's Circle* has left him with one important lesson. "Never forget where you came from," he says.

He still gives back to the world of education, though not via teaching. He is an active board member of ORT, which provides assistance to children's education worldwide. He provides generous financial contributions, as well as over 300 hours a year. His pet project with the organization is a golf tournament, in which he has recruited major sponsors, including UBS PaineWebber. He's more proud of his Humanitarian Award than any other award, including many of UBS PaineWebber's highest recognition awards. He is also very active with the City of Hope and Young President's Organization (YPO). Andy believes that these words explain his philosophy best: "Give a man a fish and he will have a meal. Teach a man to fish, and he will feed himself for a lifetime."

William F. Nicklin
The Financial Entrepreneur

UBS PaineWebber
Fishkill, New York

Bill Nicklin has always been an innovator and entrepreneur. That soon became clear in our interview. In the course of the evening I learned how his early life on a fruit farm fostered an entrepreneurial spirit that led to an understanding of business and the financial markets. This has served him well in differentiating himself from his competition. And as we pondered new ideas and concepts, I witnessed firsthand the inventiveness and ingenuity that eventually helped him reach the upper echelons of financial advisors in the securities industry.

Bill grew up in a home his family shared with his uncle's family, and both fathers earned their living off the land, as did other members of the Nicklin clan. The Marlboro, New York farming community provided Bill with an early understanding of the risk and reward associated with business ownership and investments. "You learn the basics very quickly on a farm," Bill says. "There's a lot of risk specific to a region or a single farm, like the weather, over which there is little control. Sometimes you just get whacked. Farmers know this, and the good ones are prepared to survive. There is also macro risk, which includes future demand over both the short term and long term, for which you can plan. With due diligence and good instincts you can find profits, occasionally significant profits. Running a farm is a lot like managing a portfolio. My father and his brothers did both, and were very entrepreneurial and inquisitive deep down. They were devoted to the farm and had little time to apply their business smarts on other entrepreneurial opportunities. But this was not all bad, because what they did was find a way to make a living on the farm and at the same time build wealth through fairly astute investing in the financial markets."

Bill, however, did find the time to explore. Whether he was trapping game, making maple syrup, or raising poultry, he was constantly pursuing ventures that might be rewarded by innovative production and markets for those new products. "Because I was in the trenches, I had hands-on experience with producing and selling. These were experiences that would remain with me throughout life." And where did he put his savings? In the stock market.

His formal training in the stock market began as he was earning an economics degree from Lafayette College. His economics professor, Dr. Harold Tarbell, asked him to write a paper on the economic theory of risk, and the paper won Bill an award sponsored by *The Wall Street Journal*. In 1962, while still in school, he assisted in the management of a fund endowed with unspent money collected from American troops in Europe during the Second World War. "By the time I got involved with this money, earmarked for investment, no one was quite sure who the funds actually belonged to, so the goal was to make it grow, and gift it to educational institutions." The portfolio's annual returns were nearly double the overall market and earned him respect at the school. These events led him to consider a career in the securities industry.

Before that venture, Bill headed off for the rigors of General Electric's Financial Management Program. Bill claims that, although he was armed with a formal education in economics, accounting, finance, and a smattering of engineering courses, "I learned more about how financial numbers are put together, and what they mean, at GE than any place before or since. But gathering financial data and generating reports was not my calling."

In 1969, Bill entered the securities industry with a small brokerage firm with a branch office in Poughkeepsie, New York. "I knew there was a way for me to realize my entrepreneurial desire to build a business," he says. "But first I needed to figure out what that business would be."

Bill found that what he enjoyed most was getting a look at business operations. People liked to tell him stories describing their businesses. "These conversations yielded a lot of insight into an individual's financial situation, their interests, and how they conducted business. All that discussion got me the attention of the owners and managers. These people were the foundation of a customer relationship."

During his early years, he wore out shoe leather knocking on doors. "The only products back then were stocks and bonds," he explains. He would prospect by finding an industry whose growth and profit prospects appealed to him, and then narrow down the opportunities to his favorite stock within the group. Before he hit the pavement, he would learn everything he could about the stock. He would create a story around the stock's prospects that would relate to the prospective client's business. "That way they could relate to the stock," he explains. If the prospective client was a banker, accountant, or CFO he would highlight the solid fundamentals and strong cash flow. If it was a small business owner or CEO, he would bring the management into the conversation. "Either way, I would relate the investment story to their personal business or professional situation." After telling the story, he explained how the growth of the company would benefit them as shareholders.

Additionally, at the end of the day he would call his municipal bond trader and take down $50,000 of coupon bearer bonds—book entry had not been conceived yet—and refused to end the day until he sold them. "Back then, $50,000 in bonds seemed like all the money in the world," he says. "Someone at the time said to me: 'The $50,000 I'm giving you to invest now may seem like a lot, but to an ambitious guy like yourself, it's going to seem very small as your business grows.' It seemed hard to believe at the time. However, as time passed, many of the people who bought my stock ideas created great wealth and are today very substantial clients."

One of Bill's early customers, a relationship that began with a knock on the client's door, recently passed away. "When we took a look at his gifting to his children and grandchildren in recent years, we realized that an investment of $3,900 in 300 shares in one company that I recommended in the 1970s, became 13,500 shares worth over $600,000. His entire estate became very substantial." Bill's clientele now includes a great deal of high-net-worth individuals like this client.

Bill prized himself on acting as a gateway to information, collecting as much knowledge and understanding about a company and its investment potential as possible, and disseminating that information to his clients. Though many financial advisors stand clear of this approach given the advent of the Internet, this remains a major thrust of his business. "I provide access and insight into ideas that investors generally don't get until it's too late," he says.

"My entire business model revolves around becoming intimately familiar with a particular industry, or a subset of an industry, and utilizing that information to benefit my clients," Bill explains. "I go to where the wealth is being created and obtain first-hand information."

With this strategy, Bill accomplishes three things. First, his existing clients benefit from valuable information and receive investment insight. Next, the people that he's meeting typically become his clients. "People generally say, 'He's taking all this time to get to know me and he understands my industry—that's the type of person I want to handle my money.' They can benefit from my combination of knowledge of their industry and the financial markets, because they can bounce around their observations with me, and I can help them find investment opportunities and plan their finances." And last, he develops credibility. He explains this technique by saying, "I try to simultaneously develop credibility that attracts new business and improves investment judgment. I immerse myself in an industry or industry segment where wealth is being created by the catalyst of change."

Bill also stresses the importance of becoming extremely knowledgeable in the industry for a particular company. After learning all he can, he will contact that company's CEO. "Because these are typically small- to medium-sized companies, the CEOs are fairly easy to approach, especially if they sense that you understand their business," he says.

"When meeting with a CEO, I find that it pays to be very passionate about the industry and the company," he says. "People who sense this generally want to help you, and give you information. I ask a lot of questions beginning with personal questions, such as 'How did you get into this?' Then I transition into questions about the industry. I ask, 'What is there about this particular industry that makes it attractive?' Then I talk about his competitors: 'Tell me why you're better than your competitors.'"

Bill may spend an entire day at the company: half a day or less with the CEO or other high-level executives, and half a day touring the plant or operations. He will also spend ample time talking with employees at all levels. "They are great sources of grass roots knowledge and understanding."

After his visit, Bill maintains phone contact with his new acquaintances and periodically meets the companies' executives for dinner, at a conference, or an annual meeting. These are functions where he often finds a firm's financial backers and board members as well. He also keeps in touch with the firm's public relations department. This way, if the company is holding a dinner or meeting, he can expect to be invited. Bill typically doesn't solicit a high-level executive for business, but subtly offers insight on restricted stock sales and taxes. "If the executive sells the business or joins a new company, I'll be the first to discuss their 'money in motion': stock options, IRA rollovers, whatever the need is."

Bill can't stress enough the importance of positioning himself as someone trying to become an industry expert. "My goal is to impress my prospects and customers with my understanding of their business." Bill adds that the company feels comfortable recommending him due to the relationship he has built with the company. "And the credibility I have when that potential source of new business does call me is critical. Sooner or later these people send me business because of what I know about their company and the industry."

The first industries in which he became involved, in the early 1970s, were oil and gas. "I was intrigued by the fixed prices of natural gas," he explains. "I realized early on that the price of natural gas compared to the energy equivalent of oil was extremely low, and based on a host of factors I believed that at some point this would revert back to a rational state."

Bill also became intimately engaged in this industry, particularly with the service and distribution segments, by taking regular trips to Houston to call on related companies. "Every month I'd hop on a plane, camp out in a hotel, and build my business," he says. "I got to know the manager of every single company in the valve business that serviced the natural gas industry.

"I figured that the companies were going to grow and eventually consolidate," he continues. "One after another, these companies merged or became acquired. Often the merged companies merged again into larger and larger companies. Each time my customers made money on their investments in these companies and I picked more assets from the relationships that I built."

Later, Bill identified a company that was heavily affected by growth in the demand for aircraft engines as well as the sharp rise in gas prices. This company specialized in a major component of the aircraft engine. "I spoke to company management about their marketing efforts," he says. "They told me they didn't need a plan because they were one of the only providers and that customers called them when they wanted product. While this attitude did not please me, the timing was right because the price of oil went through the roof, and transportation related stock prices were depressed. The offset in this case was that the company had a natural gas field in their backyard with a lot more gas than they could use. That provided value and a potential kicker for the company." Bill bought the stock in the teens. According to Bill, the company was acquired north of $100 per share.

"I saw a lot of people benefit financially from the upswing in the oil and gas industry," he says. "I was side by side with them the whole time, and when it came to finding an advisor they could relate to, they talked to me. I made a lot of clients and great friends."

The experience in the oil and gas industry he gleaned during the 1970s still serves him well. "After coming up dry for over a decade, I believe the oil service industry is again hitting pay dirt."

Bill recommends several tactics in which a financial advisor can pursue industry immersion: "You can get this information from prospectuses filed as these companies re-capitalize in the public markets and as principals of the companies diversify their wealth. Read a few trade journals to be able to 'talk the talk.' Go to an industry conference. Read financial research. Make some calls."

Bill's next stop in the early 1980s was agriculture. His interest was initially piqued as new technologies were enhancing productivity levels. After traveling across the Midwest and meeting key executives in the industry, he found a company that controlled a business that makes weighing systems used mainly in agricultural markets that had all the markings of a great spin-off. "The firm's revenues were growing at a 50% clip with healthy 18% net profit margins. The outlook for the company was excellent." Bill established a large position for his new agriculture clients and his existing clients. In fact, the position was so high that it attracted the attention of Charles "Charlie" Allen, the renowned founder of Wall Street banking firm Allen & Co.

Bill was aware that this high-profile investor owned 40% of the firm through the parent company, but was surprised when he received a call from Charlie's office requesting a meeting for early the next morning. That morning, Charlie asked him about his interest in the firm. Impressed with his answer, he then asked him what else he was buying. Bill described another company where he was establishing a position for his clients. Charlie responded, "Yes, I'm familiar with that company. That's very interesting. What else do you have?" Bill rattled off seven more stocks, along with a brief explanation of their investment appeal. Suddenly, Charlie stood up and left the room. At first he felt a twinge of rejection, but Bill Harder, Charlie's partner who was in the room, assured him that it was not what he had to say that sent Charlie out of the room, but a recurring migraine. After chatting a few minutes more with Mr. Harder, Bill headed down to the street where he made a call from a pay phone back to the brokerage office he was managing.

"My assistant told me I needed to talk to our wire operator right away because something odd had occurred. The wire operator told me that she just received a call from the trading desk at Allen & Co. The head trader company placed eight separate orders for 20,000 shares each. They were for the eight stocks I had mentioned." Bill continued to do business with Charlie Allen, a man who obviously made his mark and his fortune by doing business on gut instinct with people he liked.

In the early 1990s, when the Federal Communications Commission began allocating wireless telephony licenses through a lottery process, Bill saw opportunity. "Billions of dollars of wealth are being transferred to thousands of individuals through government spectrum lotteries to promote the growth of wireless communications," he says. How did Bill identify where this wealth was being created and develop new business from it?

First, it goes without saying that he learned everything he could about the industry. In fact, he was so excited about what he learned that he entered the lottery with a cousin he grew up with on the Marlboro farm, and a few other partners. This led to ownership in a cellular phone business in Kentucky and Michigan. The last of the two companies was sold to Dobson Cellular in the spring of 2000.

While acquiring experience in the wireless industry, Bill aimed his interests toward prospecting for new customers, gathering assets from the wealth being created, and seeking opportunistic investing ideas for his clients.

"Under the Freedom of Information Act, you can access information about the ownership and transfer of electromagnetic spectrum used for cellular, PCS, and other methods of communication," he explains. "The enterprises built on rural cellular spectrum, known as RSAs, are particularly attractive business development opportunities because half the spectrum awarded by the FCC went mainly to smaller companies and individuals through the lottery. The FCC requires rigorous and detailed filings identifying these principals and their affiliations. FCC filings not only point out who owns spectrum and their percent ownership, they reveal when they sell it and to whom. Because spectrum for a given frequency in each geographical area is comparable in value on a relative basis, you can get a good idea of the wealth build-up for each individual. The nature of the investment in both money and time to secure this spectrum assures you that the investors you find are active risk-takers and entrepreneurial."

He encourages other financial advisors to immerse themselves in emerging and re-emerging industries where wealth will be created. "Look for 'money in motion' and 'people in motion.' Read the industry press for changes of ownership. Attend conferences where these industry participants and enthusiasts congregate."

Bill believes so strongly in this asset and relationship gathering technique that he once built a database of over 800,000 unique individuals and their "money in motion" and "people in motion" profiles that he then provided to brokers in the firm where he was working at the time. "I found that matching the right brokers with the right investors, based on their interests and knowledge, provided the best results for all involved."

One of Bill's top stock picks resulting from his "industry immersion" provided profits of over $100 million for his clients. "It occurred to me back in the early to mid 1990s that satellites were going to be an integral part of global communication as well as research and military assets. I found a company of passionate entrepreneurs bent on changing the price and utility of software for the satellite industry. It took a while for them to get traction in the marketplace, but once they got going and investors noticed, their shares soared from a split-adjusted price of $1.50, to a price of over $55. My clients' average cost basis was around $3.

"By applying energy, technique, and ingenuity, a financial advisor can become knowledgeable enough to establish credibility within any industry. The visibility attained by attending industry events highlights your common interest with the community that surrounds an industry," he points out. "It shows that you are interested in their success. It shows that you do your homework.

"Through industry immersion you will establish a sense of credibility that transfers to your activities as a broker. Your industry connections will assume that you will be professionally knowledgeable and go the extra mile for them, their companies and their employees. This show of knowledge, judgment, and interest will not only open doors to new clients, it will connect you to both credible sources of investment information and sounding boards for investment ideas. The knowledge and judgment that determine the credibility you establish, the connections you make, the clients you establish, and the assets you gather will endure far beyond the periods of surging wealth creation."

This is Bill's recipe for becoming an industry expert: "Learn about parts of the economy where wealth is being created. Think about industries that are benefiting from technological, political, social or economic change. Think about what interests you. Pull together thoughts about the economy, changes you see happening, and your personal interests. This is where you should focus your energy. Immerse yourself in the books, magazines, Web sites, and conversations where 'knowledgeable considered opinions' and the dynamics of a wealth-creating opportunity are presented for the taking.

"Learn the buzzwords. Learn which trends and technologies are driving the industry. Rub elbows with industry participants at events. Be visible. Listen. Give you thoughts. Gather resources—trade journals, specifics on trade associations, financial research, Internet communities, a calendar of industry events, industry 'bibles' published by experts, names of industry gurus, information on venture capitalists with industry focus, names of universities with industry-specific departmental focus, names of college friends in the industry of your focus, profiles of clients who have been involved in your focus industry, and industry leaders' newsletters. Start with a few of these resources. Continually examine the opportunity in a cost/benefit analysis of the time, energy, and attention required to build your stature with prospects in this industry. Make a few low-level calls to test your knowledge and effectiveness. Build profiles of people that are creating wealth or are gateways to both corporate and personal wealth. Provide these people a window to Wall Street. Meet and have conversations. Enjoy the experience."

He continues: "You will meet people at all levels of business that need your services. Their professional activities put 'money in motion.' They buy and sell securities associated with their areas of knowledge and expertise. They need your advice on these transactions. They exercise options. They become 'people in motion.' They change employers opening the opportunity for IRA rollovers. They lead you to corporate opportunities: stock repurchase, financing, retirement plans, etc."

When seeking customers at growing companies, Bill relies on several sources. He regularly checks proxy statements filed with the Securities and Exchange Commission. "These can be found by checking the Edgar database for detailed salaries, bonuses, stock grants, employee stock options, and any other form of compensation received by a company's management and directors. These proxies also list the number of shares of stock held by top management, directors, and other significant shareholders. Not every employee owning stock and receiving options is listed, but being known by the people who are listed can help assure that you are remembered and referred to their associates. Financial officers can be particularly helpful. Contacting human resource personnel about company benefit plans is another useful approach."

Whether or not Bill decides a certain company that he is prospecting is also a suitable investment for his clients, he always remains in close contact with the business representatives. "This is one reason why I decided to bring on a partner," he says.

"I was seeking a partner with a consultative demeanor. I was lucky to find Nat Prentice, who also has a research and banking experience as well as solid retail and institutional experience sales experience."

"Nat brings a whole new depth to my business," Bill says. "As the nature of our business changes and my client base ages, there are requirements for more attention to financial planning and other complex services, such as estate planning, that I haven't had the time in which to focus. His broad experience is also particularly helpful in driving the business that's coming from my corporate contacts. This includes 401(k)s, stock purchase plans, and corporate cash management. Additionally, as my client base grows, Nat is helping to develop the business."

So, after such incredible development, where is Bill currently immersing himself? The answer may come as no surprise: the Internet. "I'm reinventing myself in the information age," he says with a smile. While he's involved in many aspects of technology, he is particularly interested in broadband, as well as Internet opportunities that will help him guide other financial advisors.

He has spent considerable time in mentoring programs and trainings throughout his tenure as a branch manager and financial advisor. He and his son Bill created a service called Horsesmouth, LLC., which is accessible at www.horsesmouth.com. This Web-based learning service is devoted to helping financial advisors identify, serve, and retain clients via customized approaches to developing business, building knowledge, and continuing professional skills.

"Telephone is one to one," the Bill explains. "Television is one to many. The Web is many to many. There are very few mentors left in the business, so we created a state-of-the-art Internet resource that acts as a real-time mentoring faculty to support the many business models of financial advisors. We believe that true learning takes place in a blended environment of face-to-face contact, live Web-based events, and a continuous flow of content that both teaches and reminds financial advisors about best practices."

When he's pursuing an industry immersion, how does Bill keep on top of the myriad of industries he covers? "I skim through over forty magazines a month, looking for things that might change my perspective," he says. These range from satellite industry-related magazines to oil and gas, Internet, engineering, construction, computer software, hardware, environmental, demographics, agriculture, defense and aviation publications. The list goes on. Additionally, he spends time in industry-related conferences, annual meetings and, in particular, talking to people through the network of contacts he continually builds.

He recommends that other financial advisors start pragmatically. "Start by asking yourself, 'Where is the world headed? If the world is headed there, where will wealth be created? And of those areas, where do I have a personal interest in learning that will hold my attention? Is it going to be computer software, education, peer-to-peer computing, pipelines or power lines? Am I really interested in peer-to-peer computing and is the opportunity big enough?' I find that you can only sustain a high quality of knowledge in an area in which you have an interest. In the past, I would have to jump on a plane and travel three hours to find information. Now much of the early exploratory work can be done over the Internet. It does not get you in front of prospects, but it is a good place to start."

Besides his extensive business and mentoring interests, Bill with his wife Adah remain committed to community involvement. "Being involved is an excellent way to meet people and support your communities of interest," he says. They have has served on the boards of the Hudson Valley Philharmonic, the Duchess County United Way, the Cedar Hill Cemetery Association, Meals on Wheels and the Amos and Sarah Holden Home. Adah is also actively involved with Mount Saint Mary's College in Newburgh, New York, the town where they raised their sons: Bill, a graduate of University of Pennsylvania's Management and Technology program, and Jonathan, a computer engineer graduate of the University of Michigan. Bill, Sr. is a former trustee of Marist College in Poughkeepsie and sat on the Lafayette College Leadership Council.

CHAPTER 5:
BUILDING A BILLION DOLLAR BOOK

Alan Jusko
A Generational Business

The Jusko Group
Prudential Securities Incorporated
New York, New York

On a sunny afternoon in June 1999, Kevin Jusko and his team completed a week's worth of work building a home in Houston for a deserving family as part of a Habitat for Humanity initiative. The proud new owner gave an acceptance speech on behalf of himself and his family of five. He had never dreamed of owning his own home, and his minimum wage job was barely enough to support his family. Wiping tears from his eyes, the new owner managed a smile as he took the keys from Kevin. He hugged Kevin, and then let his family and himself into their new home.

"This is what it's all about, to have your hard work truly valued," Kevin says, reflecting on that summer day. "It's one of the basic principles I've learned with my father and the Jusko Group, a team of financial advisors at Prudential Securities. It's our true motivation."

Indeed, the Jusko record speaks for itself.

A financial advisor's business doesn't get much cleaner than the Jusko Group's. With 3,000 clients (at last count and excluding thousands of retirement plan participants) entrusting the Jusko Group with a billion dollars in assets, Prudential Securities has never received one formal complaint during Alan's tenure since 1969. And based on *Winner's Circle* studies, the Juskos' client-loss record, as a percentage of total clients, is one of the smallest in the entire industry.

Alan Jusko joined Bache & Co. in 1969 and credits success in the business to his relentless hard work. This is due mostly to cold calling and mailings. While building his business, he drove six hours every Saturday to host seminars at hotels in the Catskills mountains.

Alan still works hard, but he gave up his weekly jaunts to the Catskills years ago. Also gone are the cold calls and the mailings. "Our business continues to grow from referrals. Happy clients are spreading the word," he says. "We're also doing very well with my clients' second and third generations.

"For 30 years now I've been providing advice and guidance, servicing my clients on a very conservative basis," Alan says. "I've grown up with many of my clients, and now we're seeing the families grow. Their children are getting older and coming of age. We felt that it would be very important, from a continuity point of view, for my son, Kevin, to get to know the children of my current client base. As a result of that decision, we've built a client base with not only second generations, but third and even fourth generations. I developed relationships with the great-grandparents and grandparents, and Kevin has done the same with the parents, grandchildren, and great-grandchildren. Kevin has truly followed my footsteps—both in terms of getting into my business and developing my clientele."

In 1988, Kevin graduated from George Washington University. He joined Prudential Securities' training program, then built his own book of business. Nearly two years later, he and his father decided that it was more important to service existing clients and earn referrals than to actively seek new business.

The wisdom of their decision is in the numbers. Before Kevin joined his father's group, Alan had around 1,400 clients. Today the duo has a number more than twice that, in terms of both clients and assets.

"It's given us continuity," Alan says, "and it's given our clients a comfortable feeling knowing that at some point in the future their children will have the same type of guidance and opportunity." He pauses thoughtfully. "This turned out to be a win-win situation for our clients, and a win-win situation for us. It has worked very, very successfully."

Kevin points out that they actually service all clients together, but they simply have more common experiences with the generations that are their contemporaries. Both Juskos service the corporate plans—such as 401(k) plans and pension plans—and they always back each other in the event one is out of the office.

"We've basically built our business by recommendations and referrals from our existing clients," Alan says. "We don't cold call, but if we're told by a client to call someone, we'll make the call."

Before Kevin joined the group, two client service assistants—Julia Romano and Patricia Chamoun—assisted Alan. Once Kevin came on board, and the business began to escalate, the group expanded to seven people: an additional client service representative, Maria DeSimone, was added, plus two licensed financial advisors—David Abrahams and Derek Albanese. The client service representatives are responsible for all administrative assignments, and the registered associates talk to the clients about investment-related activities. Telephone calls are typically answered by the client service assistants, then forwarded to the appropriate individual for expedited service. As a rule, whomever picks up the call owns the call. That person is designated to handle the request, unless there is a person specifically suited for the task. Another rule: all calls are returned on the same business day. "Just about all issues are handled same-day," Kevin says. "It's unimaginable that any financial advisor in this business would place a client in a position of feeling that an issue was unresolved. This is in the best interest of the client."

Alan is a firm believer in prompt response. "Clients have learned that if they want to reach us, they can," Alan says. "With seven people in the group, we have ample resources to respond to client requests, and I'm usually here from 6:30 a.m. until 6:30 p.m. Additionally, we eat lunch at our desks, and we don't use voice mail during the day. Our client reps rarely tell clients we'll call them back, because we can generally pick up the call, get right to the point, and find a solution. If a message is taken, and we return the call sometime later, we may be interrupting the client without focusing on the reason they called in the first place."

As the Jusko Group's business continues to grow, so will the team. "Most of the additional resources I plan to add to the team will work with our growing number of high-net-worth individuals, as well as support our asset-allocation and estate-planning initiatives. These are constantly reviewed." Alan explains. "Our business is growing both in terms of the number of accounts and the increasing asset levels of our clients."

Long ago, Alan introduced his wealth preservation strategy. For example, by constructing laddered bond portfolios, and investing the income in conservative growth stocks or mutual funds, he can help investors manage the risk of their original investment, while providing potential for upside stock appreciation. "Clients are comfortable knowing their basic portfolios are diversified to manage risk," he says. "Plus, it enables me to handle more assets."

Alan's strategy has further implications for the times. "The baby boomers are an interesting group because they're at a career point where their earning capacity is close to its peak; they do spend, and they're very interested in investing. My feeling is that this is when we're needed most. Those baby boomers that are arriving, and are making money, don't want to deal with an online broker, and they don't want to spend the time trying to do my job. What they want is the advice and guidance of a financial advisor who's been around for a long time. Someone in whom they have faith and trust. That's where the Jusko Group shines.

"In the managed money area, I'm very selective with the managers I use," Alan continues. "I do quite a bit of the Prudential Target® program, which allows me to allocate clients' funds to managers outside of Prudential Securities. But, most important, it's an asset-allocation business, which enables us to be in the right investment style, during the right period of time."

Alan leans forward in his chair to emphasize a point: "Discipline is the most important factor when executing an investment strategy. We have our own disciplined program for investing in the market. Most people know when to buy. However, most people don't know when to sell. We've put together a strategy that utilizes the Prudential Securities Select List. When you combine this strategy with asset allocation and diversification, it is a winning combination."

The Jusko team doesn't handle speculative accounts, or those that seek to trade actively on a daily basis. "We handle the serious money," Alan says. "Our feeling is that the markets should be used as a marketplace for creating wealth through well-thought-out investing strategies, not gambling. This perception is well known among our clients, and, together with our high-quality service, it's been a prime reason why we receive such large numbers of referrals." If a client desires to trade actively online, the Juskos will open a Prudential

Securities account which enables clients to trade through the company's online trading service.

"This gives them the ability to place a small percentage of their assets in a trading account," Kevin says. "Our clients benefit because they have full access to our team; we monitor their activity, and they can consolidate their assets with us."

As the Jusko Group's business continues to grow and evolve, so does team member expertise. "We familiarize ourselves very, very well with our clients. We ask ourselves: 'What are their needs? What are their responsibilities? What are their aspirations?' Our goal is to fulfill these individual needs and expectations with carefully produced financial strategies. In doing so, we bring in experts. These experts are Prudential Securities' resources; they're not selling anything; they're here to strictly give advice and suggestions. If a client decides to draw up a new will, trust, or whatever, we'll bring in their own lawyer or accountant and work with them. We don't solicit legal work or accounting work; our role is to advise clients as to what their options are. Then it's their decision to proceed. We're with them through the entire process."

Have the Juskos ever been concerned about the competitive threat from online brokers? "On the contrary," Alan replies. "What we're finding is that the discounters cater to a certain category of people, typically the twenty-year-old fresh out of college who's got time on his or her hands, and perhaps a small amount of money to invest. But we've found that those who were using the discounters, such as the baby boomers, realize they don't have time to go online. Nor do they have time to do their own research. They don't want to log on at 2 a.m. to review their account; spend two hours of valuable sleep time trying to determine what they should be doing tomorrow, or to review what they did the day before.

"When we meet with these people, we explain to them that there is a cost for doing business," Alan continues. "And there is a cost for professional advice. We'll handle their account, and we'll take away some of the burden that they're imposing on themselves, and we'll do it in the most professional way possible. We seek to preserve their principal, which is very important to us, as it is to them. When they realize that a small percentage of that amount could be used to retain us or pay for our services, they know they're better off with a professional than doing it alone."

This is Alan's rationale: For the best outcome, you would hesitate to put yourself in the hands of a discount doctor or discount attorney. You truly get what you pay for. "If people want professional advice," he says, "and if they want our decades' worth of experience, and knowing where to go, what to do, and how to do it, the small cost that they will pay in fees is well worth the virtually unlimited amount of time that they can spend seeking our guidance." On a regular basis, the Juskos receive several accounts that are transferred from the discount brokerage firms.

"It all comes back to working hard and providing value for your clients," Alan says. "For every client you do well by, it will come back many times over. And you have to love what you do."

That's the lesson Kevin has learned at the office, and from his involvement with Habitat for Humanity NYC.

In 1996, Kevin was inspired by a television documentary on Habitat for Humanity International, a non-profit enterprise that seeks to eliminate a global lack of affordable housing. The show featured former President Carter as an active member participating in the development of a home in South Dakota. At the end of the show, information was provided for volunteers. "Building and construction has always been a hobby of mine," says Kevin, "so I called the next morning."

Kevin went to work immediately, and since then he's been contributing his building skills one day every other week. The highlight for him is the once-a-year "Blitz Build," which is directed by the former president. "For one week, we'll build anywhere from ten to 100 homes, depending on the location," he says with pride. That's when he helped build a home in Houston.

"It's been a tremendous experience," Kevin says. "I have met the greatest people, people I never would have normally encountered—whether they're the people we're building the homes for, community leaders who are pounding the nails next to me, or CEOs who sit on the board with me. And like me, they're deeply involved."

Kevin has since become a member of the board of Habitat for Humanity NYC and spends several hours each week working on their behalf, mostly on the phones and attending meetings. "It's great making new contacts and friends, and some of them become clients. What's important to me is building homes for families and having fun doing it."

This past summer, Alan and Kevin helped raise enough funds through Prudential Securities to build a home in New York City simultaneous to the construction of the one hundred thousandth Habitat House.

Kevin pauses thoughtfully, then says: "It's one thing to build the house, but the real pleasure is seeing the family open the front door for the first time."

IRA WALKER
THE INNER CIRCLE

Morgan Stanley
New York, NY

Ira Walker is one of Morgan Stanley's most venerated financial advisors. He has built a highly successful practice by following a very basic, though highly effective, business model. He communicates with clients regularly, provides outstanding service, and relies on a strong team-oriented work ethic to serve clients' varied investment needs.

And while other financial advisors claim to provide exceptional service, rarely do they offer services as unique or exceptional as Ira's. In fact, Ira's integrity and belief in personal relationships are so impassioned that he eschews the popular partner approach pursued by so many in the securities business. He avoids partners for the simple reason that he wants to maintain a certain closeness with his clients. "The buck stops here," he says, pointing to himself. The superior level of service he offers his clients is so exclusive that they are almost unheard of in the business.

It's no wonder Morgan Stanley has never received a complaint about Ira. It's also not surprising that his clients entrust him with a billion dollars in assets.

With experience dating back to the mid-1980s, Walker admits that the roaring bull market has played an important part in his success. But he also points out that he has spent nearly a lifetime honing what he calls his "open-architecture relationship building," a level of service designed to surpass every client's expectations.

As a young boy growing up in Brooklyn, New York, Ira spent many after school hours working in his father's antique shop. He easily developed a rapport with his father's clientele, a colorful array of personalities passionate about collecting and craftsmanship. To this day, he believes that early initiation into the business world gave him a competitive edge in his investment career. "When you're exposed to a lot of negotiating, buying, and selling at a young age, you earn the ability to communicate effectively in business, which is essential."

Of course, it was years later that Ira would test his skills in the securities arena. But due to his days in his father's shop, he'd developed an instinct for value and salesmanship, as well as a pleasant demeanor that remains with him today.

Ira's success is a product of both formal and self-education, combined with insatiable curiosity and ambition. After graduating from Brooklyn College in 1978, he put his communications skills to work in the real estate industry. For someone comfortable with people and schooled from an early age on how to close a deal, it seemed a natural fit.

The turning point in Ira's career took place one evening at a friend's party, where nearly the entire room was huddled around a stockbroker who was fielding questions about the market. "I was so impressed that one person could command the interest of a party of 50 people," he says, "that I decided to pursue a career in investing."

Ira was so taken by the potential of the investment industry that he immediately set up interviews with virtually every major brokerage firm in Manhattan. Eventually, this led to an offer from a major New York-based securities firm. That was in 1985, when the market was soaring. For two years, Ira worked the phones, cold calling prospects every morning, and convincing them that he understood market psychology and financial planning better than most traditional brokers.

"A lot of investing isn't complicated. It's simply understanding the concepts of value, diversification and asset allocation," explains Ira. But he's quick to point out that it's equally important to make sure his clients understand the same concepts that he does. "If they don't," he says emphatically, "you run the risk that they will bolt as soon as the market tanks."

After prospecting in the morning, Ira would meet with potential clients every afternoon, patiently explaining the world of investing. He was sure that if he could educate these individuals as he had educated himself, they would, over time, give him the opportunity to help them meet their financial needs. His strategy worked.

For the next two years, Ira systematically accumulated his clients' assets, and quickly built a thriving practice. In 1987, he transferred to Dean Witter for its broad array of products and services. There he turned his attention to a market that he has become proficient in corporate services and retirement investing.

This is when Ira decided to differentiate himself from other financial advisors. He wanted to become knowledgeable in pension rules and regulations, steer clear of the stereotypical "stock jockey" role, and become, in effect, more of a financial advisor. "At the time, many other advisors were positioning themselves as great stock pickers or as specialists in some unique research process," Ira says. "I simply preferred to analyze a person's full financial situation. That opened me up to providing a full range of services, from asset allocation modeling, to estate and business planning."

By becoming a Corporate Services Specialist and Retirement Planning Specialist at Dean Witter, Ira has indeed set himself apart from the everyday "stock jockey" that many investors still associate with brokerage firms. But he's done more than build an image for himself. He's built a solid reputation. And it's easy to see why. He's a voracious reader in the field of investing. He attends seminars, takes classes, and builds relationships with legal experts in the field.

Ira decided early on that corporate and retirement money was the path of least resistance. "Most people understand that pension money is long term," he reasons. "They are much more inclined to invest assets that they can't touch until the age of 59?, rather than invest their personal dollars that might include liquidity needs."

He also found that prospecting for pension money had a kind of sweet simplicity. "First of all, you get an annual contribution without calling the client," he explains. "Second, trustees of corporate pension plans have to invest—it's not like they can keep the money idle and get a low rate of return."

In addition, as an unexpected perk, pursuing the trustees of pension plans ultimately landed him some very high quality referrals, including CEOs from some of the biggest companies in the U.S.; Ira had found his niche.

As Ira took on more and more clients, he began to bump up against the limits of his ability to properly service them. "In the first couple of years, I quickly understood the need for leverage. A doctor doesn't take his schedule out and set up an appointment for you. I felt that I shouldn't, either. In this business, your time is all you have. I figured if I budgeted my time correctly, I could grow the business properly."

So, in a visionary but somewhat brash move, Ira set out to hire his own support staff, and financed it himself. "Most people in the brokerage industry felt that the firm had to support them. I decided to invest in myself."

Remember, this was 1988, just after the bull market had experienced some unprecedented slaughter. Nevertheless, Ira bought a state-of-the-art workstation and hired a part-time technical support engineer, which was almost unheard of among financial advisors in 1988. He also brought in a full-time administrative assistant to help organize seminars to increase Ira's exposure in the marketplace.

The seminars—educational events that covered generic investment and stock market topics—put Ira in front of 100-plus people a night, and have proven to be one of the best prospecting tools he uses. At the conclusion of each event, Ira and his assistant distributed questionnaires that concluded with an inquiry about additional one-on-one investment help. This simple device allowed him to quickly identify those who would be receptive to follow-up calls. He also reserved space at the bottom of the response sheet for one more question: "Would you like us to speak at any of your local organizations?" This simple query was very beneficial to his business.

"It's been great for my business because we've been asked to speak to important groups, like those made up of major firms' retired employees," he says. "I've also spoken to local organizations for senior citizens, unions, hospitals, and more. I didn't think I was going to get any business out of this gesture. It was intended purely for goodwill."

Ira's only dilemma was that the seminars generated too much interest. He was again faced with a time-management issue; there weren't enough hours in the day for him to contact every prospect. His solution? He hired two more people to focus on calling potential clients. They put calls through to him all morning, and he would gear the phone conversations toward setting up face-to-face appointments in the afternoon. These afternoon appointments allowed him to meet with prospects, solidify relationships, gather assets, and produce a full, customized financial plan.

In the early 1990s, Ira was bringing in enough business to justify a team, currently numbered at nine. Dinah McCoy, Senior Registered Sales Assistant, ensures that trades are executed smoothly, offers prompt service, and oversees the team. She has two individuals reporting to her. Andrea Dagnelli is a Senior Registered Sales Assistant and, like Ira, is a designated retirement planning specialist. She is in charge of marketing, and generates sufficient leads for all seminars, mailings, special events, and appointments. Andrea follows up on all seminars, calls prospects in the database, and establishes appointments. Three individuals assist her with marketing and client contact management, and keep her organized so she can regularly speak to prospects.

"We frequently joke that we are all parts of one body," says Ira. "One person's an arm, one person's a leg, one person's the head—everyone has a different function, but we fit together into a whole, and that's what makes us go. It's a very healthy environment to work in. We focus solely on making the clients happy."

Ira is constantly raising his own bar on customer service with innovative services he offers to clients. As he puts it: "The key to satisfying a client is to provide service well beyond their expectations—they can have anything within reason, within our rules and regulations," he says emphatically. "If there's a problem, we'll do whatever is in our power to remedy the situation. And our staff goes out of its way to ensure everyone has what they want and are very happy."

His clientele can best be described as an "inner circle." In addition to Ira's exceptional service, his clout on Wall Street makes things happen for his clients. For example, his clients enjoy access to some of the hottest IPOs—not to mention access to some of the smartest minds in the business, including top analysts, money managers, and strategists. "It's my way of showing that there's no such thing as going out of the way for a client," Ira says.

Ira is so intent on maintaining a high level of service for each client that he limits the number of new clients he will accept. In fact, it's now rare for him to accept an account worth less than $1 million. Moreover, to be considered, a prospect must be a sophisticated investor who understands the financial markets, who will abide by investing strategies that are long-term in nature; that is, not be inclined to pull out of the market just because the market is in a short-term rout.

"If you have your client's money invested properly, if you're using a truly diversified asset allocation model, and if your clients have a full understanding of their strategy, then client questions become minimal," Ira says, explaining one of his keys to client satisfaction. It would be very difficult, he points out, for a broker to properly manage and service a book of clients if they were predominantly trading on an active basis.

Perhaps Ira's most unique service is his annual client dinner, which is off limits to prospects. The dinner's highlight is a seminar from a high-profile individual. "Although we never intended it to work this way, a lot of prospects become clients prior to the seminars so they'll receive an invitation," he says.

"Additionally, our clients discuss these high-profile, invitation-only, seminars with their friends and family, which further boosts our exceptional service and helps us to differentiate ourselves further. This is an excellent way to receive high-quality referrals."

The real core of Ira's business consists of his deep knowledge in asset allocation and the research behind his selection of money managers."And this is in addition to other services such as estate planning, insurance planning, and all corporate services,"he says."Now we round this off with Morgan Stanley's initial public offerings, and our clients can receive some real full-service treatment."

Ira is quick to admit that without a solid team working together, leveraging his experience, they wouldn't be able to provide this high level of service, including client communication and money management, to around 100 active clients. His clientele primarily consists of high net worth individuals and institutional-type clients.

To prove the effectiveness of his strategy, Ira gestured toward the phone and asked me to guess how many times the phone rang that morning. He provided the answer:"Just a handful of times over the last two hours, and this is our primary telephone number!"

It is critical, says Ira, to get to know a client from the start by asking the right questions. The process begins before an individual or organization is accepted as a client. His assistant gathers such information as goals, current financial situation, and current investment holdings, and then passes it on to Ira, who determines if the prospect is the right fit.

The next step involves a meeting with the prospect, whether over the telephone or in person. At that time, Ira begins with a series of fact-finding questions:"'What rate of return are you getting on your money?'I'll ask. If the client is getting 26% a year on his money and he's unhappy, that's a major red flag to me. It means that nothing is good enough. But I'm also curious because maybe he's really not getting that kind of return. He just thinks he is. If the client says he's getting 5 or 6%, and he's 50% vested in equities, that usually tells me he's not invested properly. And unfortunately in our industry, not everybody receives solid advice. In my estimation, the client who is not dealing with a full-service broker does himself or herself a tremendous disservice; for the kind of service we provide, our fees are quite reasonable."

Dozens of the questions Ira asks help him gauge a prospect's risk tolerance. He'll ask:"When do you plan to retire? How much money do you spend annually? How much will you want to spend when you retire?"With the prospect's answers, he can turn to Morgan Stanley's analytic models to help estimate risk tolerance.

When the information-gathering portion of the meeting ends, Ira explains his business, providing an in-depth description of his investment styles and the money managers he works with. He then presents an actual model that he may recommend, which will determine how their money will be invested, and gives them information about the particular money managers he has in mind for them, including their track records and investment philosophies. At this point, he is able to sum up how these managers will complement the client's investing needs and may provide a potentially greater risk-adjusted return than the one they receive at the present.

Ira feels he is ideally suited for prospects who are not currently comfortable with the diversification of their assets and want to work with someone who understands the markets and can provide guidance. "I think our clients understand that there's not going to be a lot of buying and selling; there's just going to be good core investing in public companies with long-term, solid track records," he says.

Because Ira entrusts his clients to money managers, he takes every precaution to make the right decisions. Unlike many financial advisors who leave background research to their firms, he spends hours combing through the qualifications of money managers to find those who fit well with his clients' investment styles. To Ira, such attention up front—matching a client's needs and risk tolerance to complementary investments—ensures a happy customer down the road. And that leads to a low-maintenance enterprise. "My business has never been transactional," he explains. "I don't have to sit in front of a screen and worry about a stock going up or down. I have my money managed by people who have great track records and a consistent philosophy that makes me, not to mention my clients, feel very comfortable.

"During our selection of money managers, we do tremendous research, including interviewing, to make sure that there's a right fit for each client's individual needs. The research we do is in addition to the terrific approach Morgan Stanley takes, a service that we fully use to our benefit." He notes that it is critical to rely on the firm's expertise in the money management area to provide the optimum assessments. If Ira finds a money manager that he thinks might be a good fit, but isn't on the Morgan Stanley's recommended list, he will swiftly turn to Morgan Stanley for another opinion.

In addition to discussing typical issues like investment philosophy, Ira asks money managers in-depth questions such as, "What percentage of your rate of return has been attributed to IPOs? Who actually manages an individual's money: a person, or an electronic program?"

Ira's close-knit universe of money managers has evolved to nearly 100 professionals. He maintains a close relationship with each manager he recommends to a client, and wants to be the first to know if there is any change that might be material to the management of the assets. This might include an alteration in the investment process, or turnover at the money manager's office.

"We want to ensure that a small-cap manager isn't straying off from his focus and buying a large cap," Ira says. "I once interviewed a mid-cap manager and noticed that some of his top holdings were clearly large caps."

Ira takes extraordinary pride in the selection of managers, not only because they serve his clients, but also because he develops his own proprietary asset diversification models. "For that reason, the money manager has to be very complementary," he says.

"Recently a prospect transferred over a multi-million-dollar account to us," Ira continues. "The prospect was with money managers who bought all large-cap growth stocks." He points out that the lack of diversification has led to wild swings in the portfolio, and required more small-cap, mid-cap, and international exposure. "He was wondering how he ended up with negative returns during periods when the overall market was up. After we reviewed his investments, he became very unsettled that he hadn't been properly diversified.

"Another benefit of establishing relationships with money managers," Ira says, "is that clients may attend the managers' quarterly meetings. Additionally, clients are able to get better quarterly reporting." That, along with Ira's diligence and exceptional communication means fewer questions from clients in regard to their overall strategy.

Ira tells the story of an early customer whose charitable-gift portfolio originally comprised low-interest bearing money-market accounts. She ran a successful company in New Jersey and had an excellent head for business but little knowledge of financial planning. Ira realized that her portfolio would quickly run dry unless he could move her into higher-growth investments. After several visits with her in which he carefully explained market movements and various risk-return relationships, he was able to convince her that stock funds held the best potential for her money. The account—worth approximately half-a-million dollars when Ira first met her in 1989—grew to a $5 million foundation in ten years. "We've been gifting money ever since," says Ira.

That, to no small extent, is one of Ira's greatest goals: to give back. With his head clear of day-to-day market jitters, and his customers settled in for the long haul, Ira now spends his time bringing in new business and honing strong customer relationships. No fuss, no worry. And that leaves time for the good stuff in life. Ira Walker no longer needs to make cold calls to get noticed. Whether standing on the sidelines cheering for his sons at a soccer game or counseling one of the 16 charitable foundations whose portfolios he manages, Ira Walker's visibility both in the business and in his community are enviable products of team spirit. He is also constantly improving his base of knowledge. For example, in 1993, he received an Executive Education certification through Morgan Stanley's exclusive alliance with the Wharton School, University of Pennsylvania. But for all his success, he is oddly—and perhaps unduly—modest. "If you get involved with the right people and do the right thing for your clients," he says with a shrug, "money management is easy."

To Ira, the greatest gratification his work provides is simply this: "I have hundreds of clients who have been building their net worth their whole lives, and now they're entrusting me with their life savings. And to top it off, they thank me for a job well done. It's really quite satisfying."

Marvin "The Wizard" McIntyre
They're Off to See the Wizard

High Net Worth Group
Legg Mason Wood Walker, Inc.
Washington, D.C.

See related sections:
Differentiation: There's Something Funny About The Wizard
Building a Brand: The Wizard of Washington
Prospecting and Marketing: Who you gonna call? The Wizard

High praise for "The Wizard" comes from Legg Mason Chairman and CEO Raymond A. "Chip" Mason: "Legg Mason has, for the past 30 years, been blessed to have someone of Marvin McIntyre's talent and ability. In addition to having a great sense of humor, Marvin works hard, has a very high energy level, and is devoted to his clients. He has been very successful in retaining clients, receiving referrals from clients and professionals, and, most importantly, enhancing client values without undue risk."

Successfully managing almost $3 billion and over 2,000 client relationships has come naturally to the Wizard, who says the exceptional results are due to his capable team, the High Net Worth Group. "I have carefully selected each team member with an eye toward enhancing our business and adding value for the clients," says the Wizard. "I look for team members who are competitive, care about people, and are oozing with integrity."

Marvin, a senior partner, is joined by: Bob Parr, a certified financial planner™ and tax-free, fixed-income specialist; A.J. Fechter, a chartered financial analyst and equity portfolio researcher and strategist; Don Metzger, a corporate-benefits expert and former head of Legg Mason's Retirement Plan Division; and David Gray, a former investment banker with extensive public and private equity experience. Colleen Bradley, a registered associate who directs all administration and funnels issues to either the appropriate individuals in the group or to Legg Mason, supports them. She is also involved in complex and demanding situations. Registered associates Alyson Chrzan, Annmarie Bilger, and Natascha Blake, who handle client trades, inquiries, and requests along with Stephanie Weir and insurance specialist Patti Wandres, further enhance client support.

Most referrals meet with A.J. or Bob for an initial consultation. During this meeting, they assess the client's current situation, obtain all pertinent details, and determine the client's future goals. Marvin will typically join the meeting, review the data, determine the strategy, and outline the final recommendations. "We take the complexity out of the equation and give our clients focus and direction,"

A.J. says. "We will show them their overall asset allocation and discuss what it means for them."

Even if the team is managing the portfolio of securities, individual stocks aren't discussed at the initial meeting. "Are they properly positioned?" Bob asks. "This is the real key. Are we taking the appropriate path we designed?"

After beating performance expectations for the past 15 years, the system seems to be flowing properly. "We have clients who are actually receiving over four times the projections because we were fortunate to have them well positioned at the right time," the Wiz says. "It's very rewarding."

The team has discretion over virtually all money. "If we're going to control a client's money, we give him or her different options," the Wiz explains. "They could be in a portfolio of mutual funds, with outside money managers, or we'll manage the money in-house, tailored to their investment objectives."

"We establish a direction for our clients for the long term, and we constantly monitor their investments to ensure we're on target," says A.J. "Because of this long-term horizon, our clients only feel compelled to call us when something changes in their financial situation. If appropriate and required, we'll work in concert with another expert—such as a tax attorney or CPA—whomever we need. We keep it simple for our clients by customizing and managing their portfolios in-house, and hence, simplify their lives."

"Because we make a substantial up-front investment of time as part of our process, our clients contact us fairly infrequently," Bob says. "On a rare occasion, such as if we need to discuss altering their financial strategy or if we have an administrative question, we'll call them—and then we have their full attention." An almost non-existent attrition rate, a constant flow of referrals, and client thank-you notes and compliments suggest the team's strategy is working.

The High Net Worth Group meets biweekly to maintain communications. The office is designed in an open trading-type environment, which encourages free flowing communication and the generation of ideas. Informal meetings spontaneously "break out" among team members to discuss a client situation, investment merits or strategy. As a result of the open environment, teammates who have something to contribute are expected to join in the fray. These sessions are encouraged, and Marvin is usually the focal point.

What keeps the Financial Wizard motivated? "First, I have a responsibility to my clients," he says. "Second, I have a responsibility to my team. And finally, I love what I do. I'm not going to stop until they make me."

CHAPTER 6:
GETTING TO THE NEXT LEVEL

MARK POLLARD
A HERO IN LIFE

Merrill Lynch
Princeton, New Jersey

How many people have left a lifelong impression on you? For many, Mark Pollard is one such person. Getting to know Mark for the first time is like getting to know your father all over again. He takes such a sincere interest in everything you say, you feel as though you can trust him with anything. His clients rely on him for his financial acumen as well as for his advice and leadership. It's no wonder that nearly 500 clients entrust him with $1.2 billion of their money.

Mark is an inspiration to nearly everyone he meets. His athletic six-foot-two-inch frame has been confined to a wheelchair since 1981, when a freak accident left him paralyzed from the waist down. Yet calling Mark's condition a handicap would be misguided; he dismisses it as a mere bump in the road as one travels through life. He has competed in ten marathons, including the New York Marathon, has toured the Great Wall of China, skis the Colorado Rockies, hikes, and more. Indeed, what he now considers fun makes other people feel they're missing out. This attitude is how he lives his life, how he has always lived his life: facing its great challenges, proving that nothing can stop him. His desire to move up to a next level didn't begin with his accident; it only seems to have made it more interesting for him.

It's obvious that what's most important to him is his family. The first half hour of our interview consisted of a tour of his great display of family pictures in his office—ranging from travels to the far corners of the planet to intimate moments with son Stephen or daughters Miriam and Deborah. His face lights up when he tells stories of his family and jokes, "My wife, Carol, frustrates me when she puts the M&Ms on the top shelf, out of my reach."

The day after he received an American University MBA in 1967, Mark started working for Johnson & Johnson in Princeton, New Jersey. With no time to waste, he was determined to begin his life—he even got married a month later. After six months, and ranking as one of the top supervisors, he decided to seek a new challenge in the securities industry.

He joined a now-defunct brokerage firm as the office's supervisor. "But it didn't go under because of me," Mark says in his usual sly manner. "Only kind of." The firm was a parent company for many smaller brokerages that were involved in unscrupulous business practices. When Mark first learned of the potential harm to investors, he quickly picked up the phone and dialed the

NASD. The brokerage firm was quickly shut down, and Mark received his last paycheck. He had no regrets. "From there, getting to the next level could have only been up for me," he says with a broad smile.

It's a good thing, however, that he received his last paycheck, because he and his wife were expecting a child. For six weeks he drove a truck to make ends meet, all the while trying to convince Merrill Lynch to hire him. Earning $5 an hour, and twice that amount for overtime, he was working many 16-hour days. Finally, in July of 1970, Merrill hired Mark.

In seeking ways to build a business, Mark came up with an idea. Since Merrill was recommending the stock of Goodyear Tire, he decided to call all Goodyear tire dealers and car dealers in his area and sell them stock. "I didn't know what I was doing," he says, smiling. "I didn't even know how to talk to investors."

Mark wasn't able to sell any Goodyear stock. But he did learn something valuable. Even if he didn't make a sale or strike a deal during his first contact with a prospect, there was much to be gained in the meeting. He found that discussing Goodyear stock with the tire and car dealers opened the door to conversations in which they had a genuine interest, and in these discussions he was able to prove his investing acumen. Perhaps more importantly, he learned to listen, even if contacts weren't interested in what he was offering. "When the dealers told me they weren't interested in the stock, I asked them what interested them. Then, I just listened, and they told me what their needs were.

"That one skill, listening, played a large part in my success." he says.

Hard work was also a major factor in building Mark's business. Back then, he was typically in his office by 7 or 7:30 a.m. (he still is) and he didn't leave until nighttime.

Once he had built a solid business, he decided to take it higher by prospecting high net worth individuals. "At first I had to get used to talking to people worth millions of dollars. I was young, I didn't come from a lot of money, and I only had ten bucks in my pocket," he says. "But I figured I knew my business better than they did, and that gave me confidence.

"Interestingly, I realized that there are many people with money who don't have a lot of people they can talk to," he continues. "Most successful people get lonely at the top, and as they climb the upper echelons of the corporate world, they really talk only to the people above them—the president or the CEO—or to no one if they're that high up. Even so, people at the top generally don't want to talk about their personal finances with each other, nor do they have simple conversations, such as, 'You won't believe how tough a day I had.' The only people they talk to about their financial success is their spouse, their accountant, or a financial advisor they can trust. I found that I can fill that void for a lot of people."

In the early 1990s, Mark earned the business of several executives at a publicly traded company. When he learned that the president had been dismissed from his position, Mark thought to himself: "'Gee, this guy probably needs some help.' So I called him up, introduced myself, and said, 'Can I talk to you?' He replied, 'I'm busy, I don't have time for this.' I shot back, 'You just got thrown out of your job. You have nothing but time.'"

As it happened, Mark did get to talk with him; in mid-town New York City, he ran into him as he was headed toward a cab. "I'll never forget this—I jumped into the cab with him!" Mark exclaims. "He was headed toward Grand Central Terminal. He told me he was very upset at being thrown out of his position, and he didn't know what to do. He was really talking to himself, trying to sort things out. I simply listened and helped him think things through. As we were nearing the station, I told him, 'If I can be of help, or if Merrill Lynch can help, please give me a call.' That day, I dropped him a note again offering my assistance."

The executive eventually joined a major corporation and earned a great deal of stock. "I called him to see how he was doing," Mark says, "and he told me he had received a large bonus check, and he was sending it to me. We developed the relationship from there." The new client eventually transferred all his financial matters to Merrill, including his retirement account and checking account. One day he called Mark for account-related information and told him that the company was issuing a large equity offering. Mark asked if Merrill could participate.

The client said, "It's pretty much a done deal with another firm, but for you, I'll give Merrill 25% of the transaction."

"It's very satisfying living through the tribulations of a client, and seeing him land on top," Mark says. "He thanks me for my candid advice and tells me that I'm the only person who ever tells him he's wrong."

Just as Mark's success raised him to the highest ranks of Merrill financial advisors, the unthinkable happened. Mark was making his usual drive to work on a beautiful January morning in 1981 when a rabbit jumped onto the road. Mark, no stranger to the risks living in a rural area, simply swerved around the path of the rabbit, easily avoiding a collision. To this day it is still unclear why the car rolled; both the road and the car were thoroughly examined. Mark awoke in a Princeton hospital to learn that he was paralyzed from the waist down. "I'm actually fortunate I didn't die from my internal injuries," he says.

Incredibly, Mark took the incident in stride. "The most depressing part," he says, "was when I entered the Kessler Institute for physical therapy. So many people there were depressed, and many were just waiting for me to get depressed, too. I was definitely upset and somewhat angry, but never deeply depressed."

True to the caring, sincere individual that he is, Mark takes a moment to talk about the wonderful nurses, doctors, orderlies, and physical therapists he met at the hospitals where he was treated. By the time he left a hospital, he knew every person on staff by name. Doctors would stop by during their breaks or after work to relax and talk with Mark. Nurses regularly went out of their way to pop their heads in the door to make sure he was okay.

He's most proud of the time he spent with his physical therapist, Sue Anne Sisto. "The first day I met her she said, 'This is going to be the most intense relationship you've ever had with anyone. But it's going to be as short as I can make it.'"What she didn't know was that this was no ordinary individual. Mark says, "My real challenge was to make her work hard, because I was going to work harder than anyone."

Shortly after Mark and his family learned of his paralysis, he wrote his wife, Carol, a note. It said, "We will walk. We will run. We will ski. All my love, Mark."To this day she carries the note with her wherever she goes. Since his accident, their quality time together includes journeys around the world, marathons, and skiing vacations. In fact, he taught his two youngest children how to ski.

When asked if he had made a reassessment of his life he replied pragmatically,"Well, I knew we were going to have to make some major changes in the house—ramps and so forth." He then points to a picture on his desk of his daughter reaching up to kiss him while he's on the phone."What else could I ask for?" he says."I have the most loving family ever. I also value the warm friendships I have with my clients."

After finishing physical therapy, Mark decided to pass on occupational therapy because he was anxious to catch up on his work."I was calling clients from my hospital room," he says."Not to discuss business, but just to keep in touch. I didn't want them ever to feel awkward about talking to me about my accident."

Mark's frankness has always been one reason why people tend to open up to him. Now, because he doesn't want anyone to feel uneasy about seeing him, he always tells people over the telephone that he is in a wheelchair. If he meets someone for the first time, he'll mention that he had a car accident that left him paralyzed."It just seems like the right thing to do," he explains."It's easier than watching someone shuffle their feet, and not look me in the eyes. If I tell them upfront, they tend to relax, and feel free to talk about themselves. I share something that many are afraid to share. I think people appreciate that."

Mark's openness and sincerity are probably why he virtually never loses an account to the competition."My clients trust me implicitly," he says."We're way beyond the usual client-financial advisor relationship."

A few years ago, a neighbor who was familiar with Mark's reputation in the business, but didn't know him personally, referred an individual who had just sold his business for $50 million."The man was looking for financial advice and needed someone he could trust," Mark explains.

Mark had the opportunity to get to know the businessman on a personal basis. Then, during a conference call with the man and his lawyer, he impressed them with his advice. When asked how the $50 million would be allocated, Mark replied: "$15 million in asset management, $5 million with an outside money manager, and I will invest $5 million. So I'm going to take $25 million."

There was a brief silence on the phone, interrupted by the lawyer:"What about the other $25 million?"

"You're going to leave it in the bank," Mark told him.

"What do you mean?" the businessman asked incredulously.

"You don't want all your money in one place with me," Mark said.

"But your reputation at Merrill is spectacular."

"Let's give it six months just to make sure you're comfortable with what you're doing."

The man followed Mark's advice. "It was obvious to me that he felt more comfortable with this arrangement," Mark says. "I knew that if he was happy with my service, I could always earn that business."

Mark takes a moment to reflect on his career. "There are a lot of good financial advisors out there," he says. "I'm sure many of them are outperforming me in terms of market performance or are more skilled in certain areas. The bottom line is that I have such a unique relationship with every one of my clients that they wouldn't consider going elsewhere."

What keeps Mark going in business today? "I deeply believe I can help people and organizations meet their needs and achieve financial independence. It's my objective to help them attain greater fulfillment in their lives. I enjoy what I'm doing so much that I don't want to do anything else."

It goes without saying that Mark is actively involved in the community. He is Chairman of the Henry H. Kessler Foundation, and the recipient of the Triumph of the Human Spirit Award from the Kessler Institute, where he spent time in physical rehabilitation. He was also a campaign chairman of the Princeton-area United Jewish Appeal Federation. In 1986, he gave the commencement address at Greensboro College, his alma mater, discussing "The Difference Between Winning and Losing."

A few years ago Mark received the Philip Forman Human Relations Award, and concluded his acceptance speech with these words, which he repeated to me in very deliberate tones: "If I can leave you with one message it's this: Look a little deeper. See the whole person. Offer respect, and demand some for yourself. To me that's the essence of human relations, the essence of that great and golden rule. Individually and collectively, let's work a little harder to continue to make this country and this world a better place. And let's start doing it one person—one human relationship—at a time."

NICK BAPIS
THE NEXT LEVEL...AND BEYOND

Morgan Stanley
Salt Lake City, Utah

Nick Bapis, Senior Vice President, is too modest to view his rise from the tough reality of a mining town to the upper echelons of the brokerage world as a heroic achievement. As he sees it, his success is simply "a consequence of hard work and treating people with respect."

In fact, hard work has been the hallmark of Nick's life since childhood, which began in the small town of Midvale, Utah, in the 1940s. While his father worked from 5 a.m. to 5 p.m. in the Kennecott Copper Mine, Nick, his brother George, and his sister Geanie were left to tend the small family farm, rising early to feed the animals before starting off to school. By age 11, Nick landed his first paying job, harvesting crops in a local orchard. "I was the best fruit-picker in the orchard, the one who picked the most," he says with pride. After that, he worked as stock boy at Sprouts Reitz, a local variety store.

The extra money Nick and his brother made through odd jobs went to buy clothes and school supplies for themselves and their younger sister. "But the pressure to work didn't feel like hardship," he says. "We never thought in terms of what we couldn't afford. We just wanted what the other kids had," he explains.

However, stocking shelves was not what Nick's father had in mind for his sons. A Greek immigrant with a third-grade education, he was determined to see his children better their lot. So with a stellar work ethic, a high school transcript that displayed good grades, and his relentless involvement in student government, Nick headed off to the University of Utah in the mid-1960s. There, he studied finance and joined the ROTC at a time when the country was pouring troops into Vietnam. But a tour in Southeast Asia was not to be his fate. Soon after graduation in 1968, he was sent to Panama as a first lieutenant in the U.S. Army infantry, serving there for over two years before returning to his hometown at his father's urging.

Nick's father felt strong ties to Kennecott, where he had toiled for 50 years before retiring from his post as powden foreman in 1916. Motivated by loyalty to the company, he convinced Nick to take a job in Kennecott's accounting department. One job was not enough for the tireless younger Bapis, however. Nick took on a night job at a sporting-goods store to supplement his salary. That second job was fateful: The owner, who saw a special spark in his part-time salesperson, encouraged Nick to consider becoming a stockbroker.

Bapis liked the idea of combining his financial background with his sales acumen, and applied to every major firm in the Salt Lake City area. But, he says, "This was the 1960s, with a roaring bull market, and the brokerages wanted people who came from money." After many rejections, Nick eventually found his way to a new firm open to hiring hungry young beginners, and thus began his career.

Nick was initially stuck with back office jobs, but in 1969 he found his way to a sales position with a local brokerage firm. Unfortunately, the market turned against him just as he was learning the trade. By 1972, a bear market set in, and the brokerage business was in turmoil. It was then that Nick began to hone the client-building methods that have become permanent parts of his personal approach.

"When I was training in New York in 1969, a partner from my firm had a formula for success: 40 plus 18 plus 2 equals 200,000. In other words, if you contact 40 people a day, send 18 qualified mailers a day and make 2 personal visits a day, you'd be a $200,000 producer at the end of the third or fourth year in the business." Not afraid of hard work, Nick changed the formula to 50 contacts and 4 personal visits. "To this day, I still do it," he says proudly.

That might seem like the basic hard-sell approach, but this unassuming Utahan is actually as tactical as he is driven. "I didn't just build my book by cold calling. I built it by being quiet and clean in my dealings. So as brokers left the firm, the manager would give me some of their accounts. I loved to get the accounts that really didn't have a lot of trading on the ledger sheet because I knew the client had an interest, but the broker hadn't burned them out by over-trading them. Those are the accounts I'd really work on."

After a few years in the business, Nick began to organize seminars, sending out personal invitations and making phone calls to remind prospects to attend. Nick soon discovered that such face-to-face communication with a larger audience was the bridge that could bring him to a wider market. "I began to concentrate on the seminars because it was easier to get in front of 20 or 30 people at one time than it was to meet with them individually," he says. He considers this a major thrust of his business.

"From then on," he continues, "I just kept growing every year. I was determined to keep cold calling. It's hard to contact 40 people each day, but if you start doing it at 8 a.m., you can have most of it done by 10:30 or 11 a.m. And I knew that the lifeblood of the business is making contacts and proving that you can provide a high level of service."

For Nick, making contacts consists of a complete review of portfolios, for both existing and prospective clients, determining if their asset mix is on track with their goals, and recommending changes if necessary. Nick emphasizes that he never pressures clients into decisions that don't serve their goals or respect their risk tolerance. In fact, one client took nine months to decide to follow Nick's recommendations, with no in-between prodding. To Nick, trust and respect, not sales pressure, are critical to any thriving business relationship.

"I've always done what I told the client I would do," he says, "and that includes backing off when the client needs time to think."

At first, Nick conducted portfolio reviews himself. When the concept of hiring money managers arose in the late 1980s, Nick began directing his clients to this new benefit. It was around this time that he moved to Dean Witter, now part of Morgan Stanley. "The resources at Morgan Stanley have always been top-notch," says Nick. "In particular, the money management program has always been terrific.

"This program allowed me to place a strong emphasis on the fee-based business. The money managers had more information and more expertise than I had, so I said to my clients, 'Let's try it for a couple of years and see how it works. They have solid track records, and we've done our best to diligently screen for the best ones.' I monitored what the managers did and reported to the client every quarter."

Over the next few years, Nick found that his firm's money-management expertise was an effective tool for building client confidence as well as assets. Perhaps more important, though, passing buy-and-sell decisions on to the money managers gave Nick more time to pursue new clients and continue to give good service. Instead of hovering over a monitor for hours tracking stocks, Nick was doing what he did best: making phone calls and developing personal relationships. As he points out, "I had to meet with the people if I was going to get the big money."

To meet high-net-worth individuals, he attended major social events and benefits, where he networked with Salt Lake's high society. "I just kept my ear to the ground," he notes. Another tactic was to comb through local newspapers and financial publications for leads. That approach led him as far away as Sheridan, Wyoming—a connecting flight with a four-hour drive—to court a rancher featured in the *Wall Street Journal*. "I wrote the rancher a letter complimenting him on the article," he says. "Then I followed up with a phone call. We had a nice conversation, and I offered to fly to Sheridan to talk to him about his financial situation." Nick earned the rancher's account, and many more leads as well.

As hard as Nick works, he has always found time for family life. He and wife, Elaine, have two grown children: Alethia, who is a Training and Recruiting Associate in Morgan Stanley's Investment Consulting Services department in San Francisco, and Michael, a Financial Advisor, who joined Nick at Morgan Stanley in 1998.

The community, too, is important to him. "To be involved in the community in an honest and sincere way," he says, "is a great way to contribute something of value and at the same time to make some important contacts." Nick has worked with the board of directors of the Art Council of Utah, and after serving as a board member at his church for nearly 10 years, he is now completing his fourth year as president. Additionally, he's been involved with his children's activities, and beyond this, he's in his twenty-fifth year coaching Little League, and he coached the high school varsity basketball team at the Catholic school his daughter attended.

All this involvement and activity, along with his work, adds up to a great deal of pressure—pressure that Nick has never minded, to be sure. "I like to be at the top of the pack," he says. "When I was growing up, I was always in the middle of the pack in athletics: good, but not good enough to be the star. Here, I'm a star for my clients, my family, and my firm."

Who could refute him on that point? And Nick became a star through nothing more or less than relentless diligence and treating his clients well. "I learned early on that this is a numbers game," he says. "The more contacts you make, the more clients you have. Also, the better you treat your clients, the more referrals you receive."

What drives Nick today? "I love the business," he explains. "I like to help people with their finances. I know I can give them an honest shot at meeting their objectives—and I'm not sure that they'll get an honest shot everywhere they go."

CHAPTER 7:
BUILDING A BRAND

Marvin "The Wizard" McIntyre
The Wizard of Washington

High Net Worth Group
Legg Mason Wood Walker, Inc.
Washington, D.C.

See related sections:
Differentiation: There's Something Funny About The Wizard
Building a Billion Dollar Book: They're Off to See The Wizard
Prospecting and Marketing: Who you gonna call? The Wizard

What does it take to become the financial advisor for over 50 professional athletes? It takes more than a name. It takes a brand.

Early in his career, Marvin recommended a stock to a client and it quickly appreciated in value. "At that stage, it was probably an accident," he admits. After they sold the position, the client called him a "financial wizard." He instantly quipped, "How did you know my nickname?" One week later, the client presented Marvin with new business cards sporting the moniker. Ever since, he has encouraged people to address him as The Wizard.

That's when the buzz began. Marvin lightheartedly asked friends, clients, and prospects to mention "the Financial Wizard" to anyone who wanted to consult with the best in the business. "That seemed much more believable than simply speaking highly of myself," he says. Then the referrals started coming in. What clinched his "brand name" identity was the publicity he developed along with it through seminars, financial articles, and radio and television interviews. (See *Prospecting and Marketing: Who you gonna call? The Wizard.*) For instance, at the beginning of each radio show, after he was introduced, the station played the *Wizard of Oz* song, "We're off to see the Wizard."

Marvin has developed such a high-profile business that prospects ask him if amounts such as $15 million are enough to open an account with him. "The means by which I've positioned my business has given me an edge over the competition," he says. "The competitive advantage in this business occurs when a financial advisor differentiates himself or herself from the others. In my case, I've developed a business that exudes a certain distinction. After all, it's human natureæpeople want what they think they can't have." He adds that the major difference between his business now versus 20 years ago is the publicity. "I wasn't on television or the radioæI didn't have a brand. But I was cuter back then and had a full head of hair," he adds with his trademark humor.

His brand gained more notoriety several years ago when he received a telephone call from Donald Dell, who was referred to the Wiz. Dell is legendary in the sports agency and marketing industry as founder of Proserv, which catered to countless professional athletes. After the first meeting, Dell told the Wiz that he really liked him and wanted to give him some of his own money to manage. The Wiz replied, "Well, I appreciate your confidence, but that's not really the way I do business."

"What do you mean?" Dell asked.

"I always sit down with a prospective client and get to know him first," the Wiz answered. "I need to learn about his or her current financial situation and his needs and objectives. Then I'll work with him." Dell thought this sounded like too much work, and he was dumbfounded that Marvin wouldn't just take some money and manage it.

Over the course of the next two years, even though they became good friends, Marvin never asked Dell for his business. Then, Dell called the Wiz and said, "Hey, I want you to manage some money for me."

"Your memory is about as short as your drives from the tee," the Wiz answered, waiting for a reaction. "We've had this discussion. I'd love to work with you, but this is what you've got to do first."

Marvin and Dell had a long conversation about his financial goals. Shortly thereafter, Dell asked Marvin to work with his agency's athletes and began sending the business to the Wizard. The Wizard's picture and an endorsement were added to the agency's brochure. The Wiz and his team then earned the company's 401(k) and other executives' business. "I'm a sports fanatic," he admits, "so it's a great deal of fun for me to work in this arena."

Once the Wizard earned this business, he established himself as an expert in this niche. With permission from certain athletes, Marvin subtly "name drops," but only when he's meeting with other sports agents. "Once you start a niche, it's easy to approach others in the field," he says. "Those in the industry tend to hear about your practice. It's a kind of 'follow-the-leader' mentality."

Marvin and team treat all clients equally, whether they're professional athletes or retired individuals. "We work with them to set up an investment plan, then implement it," the Wiz explains. Often, as he would with any other client, he and his team develop close friendships with them. Another difference between working with professional athletes and other clients is that athletes' financial goals are slightly different. For example, a typical client may plan for retirement in his or her fifties or sixties, while a professional athlete may have an objective of half that number. In addition, athletes' spending patterns can be unusual.

The Wizard's tremendous referral system does not exclude professional athletes. Almost half of these athletes are referrals from other athletes. And, as he would with any other client, he "trains" his athlete clients in how to give him a referral. "Instead of asking a client to call a referral, I simply ask them to tell the prospective client that I will be calling. This ensures that a call will be made and that the potential client will be comfortable when I call."

A referral recently spoke of being "hustled" by a financial advisor at another brokerage firm. "I told him I was referred to Marvin McIntyre," the prospect said. "The broker replied, 'Marvin is the best.'"

All of his joking about it aside, Marvin takes his brand name seriously. "Building a name for yourself in this business is everything. When they finally carry me out of here, I hope to leave a legacy of integrity."

STEVE BLOCH
A BUSINESS BUILT ON QUALITY

Morgan Stanley Dean Witter
Miami, Florida

"I'm more concerned about the return <u>of</u> my money than with the return <u>on</u> my money," Steve Bloch, Senior Vice President, says, borrowing a witticism from humorist Will Rogers.

"When it comes to other people's money, I don't want to have to apologize," Steve says firmly. "For an extra sixty cents a day on a $100,000 investment, it doesn't make sense to sacrifice, say, an insured bond for something of less quality. I don't want a client to have to explain to his wife that he lost a million dollars because he wanted the extra $6 a day."

Whether it's his product, his service, or his image, Steve runs a quality business. No wonder he's only received one written complaint (it turned out to be a mistake and was rescinded by the writer) since he started with Morgan Stanley's predecessor in 1972.

Steve's interest in investing and managing finances began early. He watched closely as his father, a cattle buyer, managed his meager wages, and as his mother made do. They put what little they could into the stock market. His cousins, Erika and Ernest Hockster, were influential: they taught him some profound lessons that he would take with him the rest of his life. "Mostly, they instilled the meaning of family, striving for success, and always doing the right thing for others," he says. Then he perks up and laughs as he tells the story of how his cousin talked him into going to college by promising, "All you do there is party."

As it turned out, Steve realized he had to create his own strategy for success, and studying was the first step. High scores at the University of Oklahoma got him accepted to University of Tennessee's law school, but when his father died, financial problems forced him to drop out. Nevertheless, he was determined to enter the securities industry.

At first, Steve sold life insurance because he couldn't find a job selling securities. Then, after being rejected by seven securities firms in Miami, Reynolds Securities (which eventually became part of Morgan Stanley) took a chance on him in 1972.

"It was a very difficult time in the market," Steve says. "The market had just broken 1000 for the first time in November 1972, and it didn't return for another decade. Brokers were having a tough time making a living. Investors were mad at their brokers. It was a great time to start in the business."

When he began, Steve lacked the luxury of being well connected, for he knew few people who could invest. His plan was to reach investors that might be interested in finding a new broker by cold calling.

He took advantage of syndicate offerings. This gave him the opportunity to offer something few other firms could offer. "I was particularly interested in new bond offerings or secondary offerings of utility stock, which paid a very high, stable dividend," he says. "I would always reserve 100 shares, or a small lot of bonds, and not leave the office until I'd opened an account and sold it." Steve would begin work at 7 a.m. and stay until he knew the West Coast investors were sitting down for dinner, around 8 p.m. Eastern Time.

When seeking prospects to cold call, Steve tried to minimize the cold-call effect as much as possible. For example, when he had an inventory of attractive insured municipal bonds or utility stocks, he would get the telephone numbers of residents in retirement-based buildings.

Only, he didn't want to do it completely cold. "I wanted to at least know something about them," he says. In retirement areas, he called those who would most likely be interested in stability and income. He was emphatic about sticking with quality, and with stability: that meant insured municipal bonds.

When Steve came across investors who were interested, whether they became clients or not, he would ask them for a referral. This, he learned, was the ultimate way to prospect, and to avoid cold calls.

"Our business all comes down to two magic words: *who else*," he says seriously. "If you truly believe in what you're selling, and it's right for the investor you're dealing with, all you have to do is ask them: 'Who else?'" Steve continues to use these two words today.

"'Who else do you know that I should be showing this to?' I'll ask. 'What about your brother-in-law, your neighbor, your cousin? Who else?'" If an individual is reluctant to give Steve a referral, he'll say: "I've just given you the best I have. Why can't you give me a name so I can show them the same thing?"

Steve stresses the importance of his favorite two words when he trains rookies around the country. He recently spoke to a large group of financial advisor trainees. After giving him an astounding ovation, they presented him with a hat that read: "WHO ELSE?"

In Steve's view, quality investments go hand in hand with quality service. "It goes without saying that you're less likely to run into trouble if you avoid investments that are lower than high quality," he says. "It's also a lot simpler to service people if you're meeting their expectations, and not having to explain money problems.

"In the early 1980s, I didn't do any tax shelters because they didn't make economic sense to me, even though many other advisors seemed to be doing them," Steve says. For a similar reason, he didn't get his clients involved in junk bonds during their heyday. "I'm not the smartest guy on the lot, but I know what makes sense, and I'm looking at the long run. I was always afraid of limited partnerships and other related deals." During the limited partnership days,

Steve would tell investors who had an interest in these investment vehicles, "The difference between the general partner and the limited partner is that in the beginning, the limited partner has the money and the general partner has the knowledge. At the end, the general partner has the money and the limited partner has the knowledge."

Like fixed-income securities, Steve's equity business is comprised of "quality" stocks. "I really believe in quality equities," he says. "This includes the large companies of the world, companies with long-term track records of consistent earnings growth and solid businesses." Steve eschews gambling in the market, especially with unproven Internet-related stocks. He borrows another witticism from Will Rogers. "The quickest way to double your money is to fold it and put it back in your pocket," he says with a smile.

When it comes to clients who like to trade short-term, he still only recommends a quality stock. He advises selling the losses and riding the gains, and always minimizing capital-gains taxes by eliminating losses. "I stress stability, even when the Dow is roaring to new records." When things go sour, Steve is on the phone again explaining to his clients what happened and offers a course of action. "When the bad news happens, it happens," he said. "The important thing is to call your clients. I'd much rather call a client than have them call me."

Steve can't stress enough the importance of continually staying in contact with clients, and reminding them that you and your team are there for any questions or concerns relating to their financial situation. "This is part of what they're paying us for," he says. "So why not keep in touch with them and tell them that you care? Prove to them that you're looking out for their best interests."

Steve acknowledges that he only plays a part in the extraordinary service his business provides. "I have the greatest team you could imagine," he says. His partner, Mindy Brown, Financial Advisor, joined Steve in 1983. "We're very close, and our lines of communication are excellent. She and I know everything that is going on with each client, so there's always someone readily available to provide service. Also, we think similarly, both in terms of investment philosophies and creating service."

Bob Axelrod joined Steve's team in 2000. In 1996, the team hired Cynthia Lombardo, Registered Sales Assistant, to provide additional expertise in the fields of customer service and public relations. "She's loyal, smart, interesting, and has the type of personality that everybody loves," says Steve. He has a similar opinion of Nancy Acevedo, Registered Sales Assistant, who was brought on board in 1997 to handle the group's technology needs, to update records, and to help streamline the account opening process. "I'm a great delegator, and thankfully I have a team that I can fully rely on," Steve says. "And there's one thing we all have in common. We really, really care about our clients."

Because Steve benefits from a supportive team, he is able to provide additional types of service. "The more service you can provide, the stronger the client relationship becomes," he says. He will provide advice and introduce clients to the highest-qualified individuals that will help with purchases and negotiations, such as cars, homes, restaurants, tickets, and even doctors, lawyers and accountants. With financing needs, he will help them negotiate for the best deal. Because they know that he's well traveled, his clients often seek his advice for travel tips.

Steve's team is recognized as the backbone of Morgan Stanley's Miami branch office. "My team is very supportive of every financial advisor," he says. "We work with all the rookies, and we help to ensure that not only are our clients covered, but we also make sure there's always someone to cover the other advisors' clients."

Steve also credits Morgan Stanley, the only full-service financial services firm he has ever worked for, as a major factor in his success. "I pride myself on the leadership and quality of my company," he says. "One of the most important things that I did in my career," he says, "was make a conscious decision that I was going to find a high-quality firm, and stay with the company."

Back in 1973, Steve helped an investor buy 100 shares of a four-dollar stock. Seven years later, the investor called and said he had a broker and needed some financial advice. Steve looked up his account and saw that it was his own client. The client appreciated the fact that Steve was still there, and gave him an update on his financial situation: he had just inherited money that he needed to invest. His two sisters had received an inheritance as well. Steve told them that, given their financial situation, the right choice was 11?% triple-A rated bonds. Less than a year later, the bonds were pre-refunded, and called at a premium. Steve then invested the proceeds in more high-quality bonds.

"My clients appreciate the fact that I have longevity, and that I'm established," he says. He feels that this image of success and stability helps clients understand that he's looking out for their best interest. He's not a new broker relying on transactions to pay the bills. "My clients relate to my success, and know that there's no trade that can make a difference to me financially," he explains. "There would be no motive whatsoever for me to hurt anyone. I can focus only on what's good for them and never consider the consequences to my finances."

Steve is emphatic on this point. "It's important for clients to understand that my advice is given because I think it's the best advice possible for their situation," he says. "It's not generated to make a commission. And if I'm ever wrong, I tell people ASAP."

When a client refers a prospect to Steve, it's his image as an established, honest financial advisor that speaks for him; an advisor with a proven track record that—through the high-quality investments that he recommends—consistently works toward meeting the investing expectations of his investors.

His physical image speaks volumes, too. He's rarely seen in the office without a well-cut, expensive suit, and appropriate, not flashy, jewelry. He owns a nice home, drives a nice car, and is a member at the country club. "People want to do business with successful people," he says. "It's a matter of confidence. I wouldn't want a doctor who drives a beaten-up car to do brain surgery on me; I'd have my doubts he was successful."

Steve's office signals success as well. In fact it closely resembles a sports shrine—signed basketballs, baseballs, Olympic tickets, tickets from the major boxing matches. The Chicago Bulls play the most prominence, with jerseys, including Michael Jordan's, and a Dream Team basketball.

He has an open-door policy at the office: "People are accustomed to my presence in the office," he says. "We always welcome visitors." Now that he's more established, however, his operating hours are shorter than they were in his beginning days. But they're not short by any means. He's in the office by 7 a.m., and leaves around 4:30 p.m., unless a client needs him or a situation demands his attention. "I paid the price early on, working long hours and spending time away from my family," he admits. "Now I can leave earlier and enjoy spending time with my wife, Jill, or visit our children—Cara, a photographer in New York, and David, who lives here in Miami."

Steve also commits a great deal of time to the community. "I'm very active in our temple, Beth Moshe, and I'm very close with our rabbi, Jory Lang, and his family," Steve says. He and Jill help the temple in many ways: financially, and becoming involved in as many projects as they can.

"The true joy to life involves lifetime relationships, and caring for those friends or clients," he says. "These are quality relationships."

CHAPTER 8:
PROSPECTING AND MARKETING

THOMAS B. GAU, CPA, CFP™
THE RETIREMENT SPECIALIST

Oregon Pacific Financial Advisors
Ashland, Oregon

> *See related sections:*
> *Going Independent: Building a Franchise*
> *Building a Fee-Based Business: The Fee-Based Conversion*

It's a good thing the franchise Tom Gau has built is fully capable of handling large volumes of new business, because he seems to attract money like a magnet (see *Going Independent: Building a Franchise*). Tom's tremendous success is due in large part to his financial-planning seminars—his ability to fill a room with attendees and convert over 80% of them into clients.

The first thing Tom did when he started his business was to develop an area of expertise. "We branded ourselves 'The Retirement Specialists,'" he says. "With all the layoffs occurring at the time and retirement planning moving to the forefront of people's financial concerns, there was clearly a need for a specialist in this area. Add to this the fact that statistically, this is where the money is, and it's the fastest growing segment. Did you know," Tom asks, "That by the year 2010, 36% of Americans will be at least 65? Right now, they represent 20% of the households, yet 40% of the nation's total personal financial assets. This segment also has a greater proportion of assets invested in individual stocks and bonds, and in mutual funds. Consequently, my typical client is in the 60-plus crowd."

When Tom and his partner, Phil Kavesh, first opened their doors on September 15, 1997, they ran retirement-planning seminar ads in local newspapers and in the *Los Angeles Times*, hoping the right people would come their way. Their target market was broad: anyone interested in planning for his or her retirement distribution. The initial response was lackluster. Tom's own market research told him that he wasn't attracting the individuals with significant assets, those who knew that they should give some serious thought to future planning. "I realized that I needed to create a new breed of seminars relating to retirement planning, one that targeted clients with the assets to work with. I would have to appeal to attendees' emotions and show them how much they could benefit from the advice of a retirement specialist."

More pointedly worded was the partners' next seminar: "Don't Let the IRS Take Up to 79% of Your Retirement Distribution!" Tom's intent was clear. "People would think to themselves, 'Can I really lose *that* much of an IRA to taxes?' That would open the door for us to explain how they can reduce or avoid this circumstance."

With this seminar, a new approach took shape. "Here is one way that we could really differentiate ourselves," he says. "While everyone else was advertising common retirement seminars, we were raising provocative questions about the state of people's assets or portfolios, attracting an audience of potential clients who would say to themselves, 'Oh my gosh, I didn't realize that!' And better yet, these seminars were aimed at individuals with significant IRA assets."

One day Tom read an article about an IRS rule—a rule that has since been phased out—that placed an additional 15% penalty on oversized IRAs when individuals withdrew their money. "So we created a seminar titled, 'Are You Accumulating Too Much in Your IRA?'"

Another attention-getting seminar title read: "Is the Beneficiary of Your IRA the IRS?" Tom received many calls from interested clients, asking the meaning of this. "This gave us the opportunity to give a brief overview, then encourage them to attend the seminar for further details."

Tom later decided to precisely target affluent clients and prospects by advertising this topic: "Is your estate over $3 million? If it is, you will most likely be paying over $1 million in taxes. Consequently, attendees were generally worth at least $3 million," he says.

In his seminars, Tom stresses mistakes that many people are apt to make. "I don't want you to have a problem with the IRS," he tells them. While Tom may present some information that may appear alarming, he is also quick to add humor. "You need to ask humorous questions, and get your audience involved and have them raise their hands as much as possible."

Seminars are advertised in several newspapers, including the local paper at his Torrance, California office called the *Daily Breeze,* and in the South Bay section of the *Los Angeles Times.* Tom explains, "People don't want to travel too far for a seminar."

Seminars are usually held in a hotel conference room "because we want it to be a non-threatening environment," he says. "Many financial advisors claim that they can't get anyone to show up. That's because they're holding the seminar in the conference room of their company."

Because seminars are usually scheduled for the evening, between 7 p.m. and 9 p.m., Tom offers an assortment of desserts, coffee, tea, and water. If they are held during the day, say, mid-morning, a continental breakfast is served. The event lasts two hours, with an additional 15 minutes for questions.

Attendance varies from 40 to 60, and Tom might hold as many as 70 seminars in a single year. While this number may seem high to most in the business, Tom finds that he can consistently generate a large number of new clients, not just for himself, but also for the other financial advisors at his firm, as well.

Tom has also tapped another source for new clients: businesses. He will arrange to have his retirement flyers stacked in high-traffic areas such as business lobbies, posted on bulletin boards, and even under the windshields of cars in the parking lots. He has found that the more strategically you place the flyers in the corporation, such as in the coffee areas, the more impact they have. Flyers in the entrance, or close to a receptionist, can easily get lost among other communications.

Using this strategy, Tom's seminars may see 150 to 200 attendees during peaks of corporate downsizing. "This is a very effective way to fill a room," he says.

While Tom requires that attendees RSVP prior to attending, many simply show up unannounced. "At least 20% of our attendees are walk-ins. Everyone is required to sign a guest list, which asks for name, address, and telephone number. Otherwise, they're not permitted to enter." An astounding 80% of the attendees make a follow-up appointment with Tom before they leave the room. "Most advisors gauge the success of a seminar by how loud the audience is clapping at the end. I measure it by the number of follow-up appointments," he says. "My seminars are terrific learning experiences for the attendees. They feel very compelled to act immediately."

One of the people who acted immediately was a woman who attended a seminar on "Inherited IRAs." "Her husband passed away and left her as the beneficiary," says Tom. "She then rolled over the assets into her IRA and made her two children her beneficiaries. Twenty years later, she passes away; the children have inherited an IRA worth $2.2 million, but taxable, to be shared equally. Understandably, they wanted to know if there was a way to reduce the tax implications. The brokerage firm holding the assets encouraged her children to take the distribution all at once."

Tom recommended an "Eternal IRA," also known as a "Stretch IRA," an election that allows a beneficiary to stretch out the distribution of the money over his or her lifetime, with the remainder being tax deferred.

"This year alone I have uncovered mistakes just like this that exceed $120 million!" he exclaims. "Do you know that a lot of custodians are unaware of this election to continue the IRA indefinitely if the proper choices are made?" he asks me. "I've mailed many IRS rulings to custodians, and the prospects are usually outraged. I will ask them, 'What other areas is your custodian uninformed about?' Then I continue, 'I would be happy to be your financial advisor, but if you want to use that custodian, you're going to have to do some research to make sure it gets done right, because I'm not here to give advice for free.' This approach has generated significant business, especially since many people want you to give them the specific information, but are not willing to transfer the account to you."

Tom has interested many local companies and associations in his retirement-planning seminars. He has held seminars for members of the Elk Lodge and the Moose Lodge, and for employees of companies like Xerox, Northrop, TRW, Aerospace Corporation, Rockwell, and Hughes Aircraft.

Other demographics Tom targets include the retirement of key employees. If he sees a retirement story in the newspaper, Tom will write the individual a letter, extending an invitation to a particular seminar. He will also present retirement seminars for executives or key employees preparing to retire.

Another group he targets are companies that allow retirees to take out their defined benefit pension plan in the form of a lump sum. Tom has found this to be an excellent way to generate large amounts of money to manage per client.

One of Tom's greatest strengths is his ability to think like his clients. "This enables me to act on their behalf, to do as I would for myself," he says. "It's important that clients get what they deserve. That's what I'm here to do."

MARVIN "THE WIZARD" MCINTYRE
WHO YOU GONNA CALL? THE WIZARD.

High Net Worth Group
Legg Mason Wood Walker, Inc.
Washington, D.C.

See related sections:
Differentiation: There's Something Funny About The Wizard
Building a Brand: The Wizard of Washington
Building a Billion Dollar Book: They're Off to See The Wizard...

When the market tanks, who does the city of Washington, D.C., turn to? The Wizard of Washington. "That's because I whimper well," Marvin McIntyre sighs. The Wiz usually appears on several television stations when there's any sign of market turmoil. With a penchant for publicity, he has parlayed his network of acquaintances and his outgoing personality into radio shows, market updates on television, and media appearances. "I am an acknowledged media harlot," he admits.

There are some financial advisors who avoid publicity because of a fear of public speaking. Others enjoy publicity, knowing it might help increase their business. And then there's the Wizard, who was born to perform. His break occurred early in his career when his branch manager, aware of Marvin's knack for entertainment, told him that a radio station was looking for a commentator for a financial show. Although it was an all-sports talk radio station, the hosts were looking for someone to offer financial insight and could interact well with the professional radio personalities. The Wizard's eyes lit up when the manager told him he would have latitude for creativity. The show was an instant hit. The Wiz spoke about the market for one minute and bantering for the remaining nine minutes.

For five years, the Wizard headlined the segment via telephone from his office, car, the beach, a client's office, his home, or wherever he happened to be. "Everything was unrehearsed and spontaneous, so I knew I had to be on my toes," he says with a sly smile. "These clowns would wait all day and plot to try and one-up me." When asked how often he felt bested, Marvin replies, "Not once in this lifetime!" His quick comebacks helped ratings go through the roof. A fan told the Wizard he almost drove off the side of the road because he was laughing so hard.

Along the way, Marvin took careful steps to develop his Wizard identity. For instance, at the beginning of each show he received a brief introduction, then the radio station played the song from the Wizard of Oz "We're off to see the Wizard." Is this self-promotion? "Nah," answers Marvin, "it was their idea, and I felt it would be presumptuous to interfere." He says that his fans felt that his irrepressible, natural sense of humor was better than any musical intro.

After a particularly ugly day in the stock market, the host referenced the Crash of 1929 by asking Marvin, "What would you do if one of your clients jumped?" Without missing a beat, Marvin shot back, "I would catch them!" Subsequently, the radio station used that exchange as a promo for the segment.

The Wizard has clearly established himself as the broker of record in the D.C. area. If the market tumbles, the Wizard is the one they rush to. The Fed raises interest rates? Call the Wizard. Nikkei Index crashes overnight? You get the picture. And the moniker "Financial Wizard" doesn't hurt, either. "What name would come to your mind first as a credible source of market-related information, Financial Wizard or Tom Smith?" he asks. A local station once mentioned simply on a show that they were going to seek the advice of "the Wizard." (See *Building a Brand: The Wizard of Washington*.) The Wizard continues to receive many calls from his radio and television audience.

On one particular occasion, the Wizard received a referral from an accountant. The prospect was interviewing three other financial advisors as well. When the prospect called for a second interview, he said, "By the way, I heard you on the radio."

"Uh-oh. It must be an omen," the Wizard replied.

"An omen?" the prospect asked.

"Yeah," the Wizard said softly. "You've had all these signs. The first sign was somebody telling you to see me. The second was actually seeing me in person. Third, you heard me on the radio! I wouldn't waste any time if I were you."

"I think you're right," the prospect said seriously. "I'm on my way."

"He has become a good client, and a great friend," says the Wizard.

Several years ago, the Wizard asked Legg Mason to sponsor a tennis tournament that his client, Donald Dell, founder of a well-regarded sports agency, was arranging. "Sponsoring a prestigious charitable event like the Legg Mason Classic was an excellent way to expose Legg Mason's name throughout this part of the country," the Wiz explains. "In addition, it was a wonderful opportunity to help inner city kids."

Legg Mason heavily promoted the tournament, including local television interviews featuring Marvin. Between the radio spots, the television commercials, the news channels, the sports channels, and, thanks to tournament advertisements, the Wizard has become a familiar face in his part of the country. Not only has he enhanced his civic reputation through his association with the tennis tournament and the nonprofit organization, he has earned recognition as an expert in the financial marketplace.

When asked how he turns this publicity into new business, his reply is simple: "I don't want to ask for any business," he says. Otherwise, he explains, he would just be just another stockbroker. "When someone refers a prospective client to me, chances are they're not going to need to ask who I am. This publicity is a tremendous differentiator for me," he says.

A case in point: A client once mentioned to an executive who was submitting requests for proposals for his sizable 401(k) plan that he knew of a stockbroker. The executive said, "No way, we already have enough firms fighting for the business and we don't want to look anymore."

The client interrupted, "You'll really like this guy, Marvin McIntyre."

The executive said, "The guy on radio? Yeah, I'd like to talk to him. Just the two of us."

"We have always been uncomfortable with the naked solicitation of business," the Wizard says of his unobtrusive prospecting technique. "It seems that the less I ask, the more business seems to come my way. When prospects find out they can actually do business with you, and they're already familiar with you via the media, there becomes a cache value in becoming your client."

CHAPTER 9:
BUILDING LOYALTY AND RELATIONSHIPS

BERNIE BENSON
GOING THE EXTRA MILE

Benson, Eckerline, Bencini, Boyd Group
Merrill Lynch
Minneapolis, Minnesota

In 1968, during Bernie Benson's first week as a financial advisor, he contacted a veterinarian and asked the doctor if he could earn his business. After some time, Bernie gained the doctor's trust and received an order to buy 50 shares of a $20 stock. "That was a lot of money to them," Bernie says.

Bernie's relationship with the vet and his wife developed over the years, as did their net worth, which is now well into seven figures. At the beginning, Bernie learned all he could about their financial objectives and long-term goals. He then established a disciplined saving and investment plan, which he altered as circumstances changed.

"I've literally been through life with them," he says. "They put children through school, enjoyed the lifestyle they wanted, and built a very comfortable retirement. The vet's wife, now into her seventies, lost her husband in the mid-1980s. When she became a widow, it was more important than ever that I help." He pauses, and then says, "It's my responsibility to go the extra mile for every client, and to exceed their expectations."

When most people say they're entering a business for the money, they're looking to strike it rich. Bernie Benson entered the securities business for money, but not to make a killing. He tributes his immediate success and subsequent rise to the ranks of *The Winner's Circle* coterie, and to the lessons he gleaned from childhood. These lessons are the basis of his mission: to help others enrich their lives through the careful planning and execution of investment plans. Along the way, he has created a team that helps realize these goals for more than 1,000 active clients, clients who entrust him with nearly a billion dollars in assets. His tremendous following in Minneapolis is the direct result of the loyal and intimate financial relationships he and his team have built over the decades.

Interestingly, Bernie has always attracted people whose background resembles his own, and he has grown with his clients through the decades. He feels he can best relate to their needs and provide them with the same type of advice he would offer himself. And as he has entered new life stages, along with many of his clients, he's made sure that his service meets the changing needs of his clients' families and their businesses. Here's how he started.

In the rural community of Cresco, Iowa, still feeling the pain from the Great Depression, Bernie's parents struggled to raise their three children. Both worked multiple jobs for minimum wage; his mother inspected eggs, his father drove a truck and worked in a factory. Their tiny home lacked hot water, a refrigerator, and a telephone. Poverty wasn't unusual in this town; the Benson family just happened to be worse off than others. For them, managing finances was simple. First they paid the rent, then bought food with the leftover cash. They had no bank account, and no luxuries.

At an early age, Bernie helped pay for items like clothes and books with the money he made from his paper route. Serious about contributing to his family coffer, the 11-year-old consistently ranked as one of the top newspaper account openers in the state. Later in childhood, he earned more money setting up pins at the local bowling alley. By learning to be a self-provider, he received a solid lesson in managing finances and acquired a strong work ethic.

After high school, in 1958, Bernie spent four years serving on a naval destroyer. Then, realizing the importance of a solid education, he paid his way through the University of Minnesota with the commissions he received selling mutual funds and insurance. During his senior year, while supporting his wife and baby son, he was struck with mononucleosis. He dropped out of school, but continued to work full time during the day. The next year, he continued working days, and completed his degree in political science at night.

In 1967, he applied for a job with Merrill Lynch. The interviewer liked the work habits he'd acquired, and he was hired. He started building a business immediately.

"I didn't know a single person who had any money," Bernie recalls, "except for my branch manager—but he was off limits!" Bernie's branch manager strongly believed that his protégés shouldn't spend their entire day in the office when trying to build a book of business; they belonged in front of clients and prospective clients. Bernie diligently followed his direction.

One thing was clear to him. "Our biggest competitor in those days was real estate," he explains. "With the terrific tax benefits and soaring real estate values, people wanted to invest in their homes or other real-estate ventures. Many brokers attempted to make quick money for their clients. In the process, they failed to develop long-term relationships or a solid business for themselves. I entered the business to develop long-time relationships with clients. I knew that I would become successful only if my clients became successful, and I could make them successful only if I could develop their trust and confidence."

From 8 a.m. until lunchtime, Bernie knocked on doors and introduced himself, typically asking potential clients if he could have the opportunity to earn their business. He took copious notes, and then followed up the next week with a phone call requesting a meeting to offer investment recommendations.

In the afternoons he made long-distance cold calls. "I owned just about every telephone book in Minnesota, Iowa, South Dakota, North Dakota and eastern Montana," he says, amused by his zealous efforts. "I preferred to make long-distance calls because those contacts were less likely to hang up on me." He specialized in towns where there were no brokerage offices, often calling towns with populations of fewer than 4,000. Additionally, he sent mailings to all the doctors in North Dakota. During his first mailing, he contacted all 650 licensed doctors in the state, and within ten days, received 28 replies. Twenty prospects opened accounts in the weeks that followed. Today, he considers many of them as friends, as well as clients.

While Bernie's success in the business has helped create a comfortable savings cushion, he still places a great deal of value on each dollar he earns, and on each dollar he invests for his clients. "When I was a child, I experienced the after effects of the Great Depression," he explains. "I treat money very seriously. I don't want anyone to ever experience the hardship I endured. I invest my clients' money as if it were my own—very carefully and appropriately," he says. "When I accept someone's money, I treat it with the utmost respect."

He is well aware that the nature of the business includes sometimes losing some money. "That's why it's imperative to know as much as possible about every client, to learn their objectives and risk tolerances."

Bernie feels that the best way to understand clients' needs is to meet with them in person and develop a trusting relationship. "The more complex a client's affairs," he says, "the more important it is to meet with that person to maintain the relationship. And if you really care about the client," he adds, nearly whispering and leaning in to emphasize his point, "then you'll listen very carefully."

When Bernie opens a new account, he is quick to establish a close relationship. "Before I open an account," he says, "I ask a lot of questions. I let the client ask questions about me. Then we discuss our relationship. I explain the type of business I run. I tell them that they are always welcome to contact me or one of my team members with a question, or to set up an appointment to discuss their finances.

"I also let them know that because we're investing for long term, I'm not going to call them every time their stock is up or down a couple of points—we're not concerned about stock movements in the short term because our outlook is very long term in nature."

When a client does receive a stock-related call from Bernie, it's usually because he is recommending additional investments in a current position or initiating a new position. Nevertheless, he also calls clients from time to time just to let them know that he's thinking of them. When he makes these calls, he'll update them on their financial goals and investments as well as acquire new information that may affect their objectives.

To Bernie, every individual's finances are important—whether they're holding ten thousand dollars or tens of millions of dollars. "I love to see a client prosper after starting out fresh in the investing world," he says. "Most of my clients are successful, middle-of-the-road Americans, like me, who probably didn't start out under the best of circumstances themselves."

This illustrates Bernie's affinity with his fellow Midwestern clients. During a difficult stock market in 1974, he found an opportunity to seek investors in small towns. "I read that the price of durum wheat, the type that's used in noodles, was going through the roof," he explains. "I also learned that most of the country's durum wheat is raised in northern North Dakota."

Always eager to befriend a small-town individual, Bernie contacted a farmer in that area and got the scoop. "For a long time, the price of durum was depressed," he says. "So farmers stored tremendous quantities of this commodity. Suddenly, demand was on the upswing and prices soared. A great many of these farmers made a fortune."

Bernie obtained telephone books from several towns in the area. "These were towns with populations of less than 3,000," he says. "I called the local businesspeople, and, as usual, they were very friendly. They gave me the names of the bigger durum producers." In his initial phone calls he introduced himself, talked about their business, and asked them for referrals. When he had amassed a large number of contacts, he flew to northern North Dakota and spent a week visiting them in the small farming towns. He lined up appointments one after another, and left enough time to meet even more farmers.

"They were very pleased that I took the time to make the trip to see them," he continues. "They were flush with cash, and no one was contacting them. I opened 40 accounts that week. It was a windfall for them. Thankfully they invested their money wisely and it grew remarkably over time. They are now enjoying very comfortable retirements." Bernie then speaks of how satisfying it has been to follow the fortunes of these farmers. "We've built our lives together, and strong relationships. I am now helping out many of their families, both children and grandchildren."

As his business flourished over the years, and his clients' families and businesses have entered the picture, Bernie has constructed a team that effectively serves these evolving needs.

His office team now consists of ten individuals: four partners and six support representatives, each with a specific role. The group focuses is on the financial and investment needs of its multigenerational client base, with an added emphasis on high-net-worth individuals and small businesses.

In 1980, Bernie hired Barbara Bencini, a certified financial planner. "When Barbara first started, she helped me to better serve my growing client base, particularly with customer contact and administration. My clients have flocked to her ever since. If I'm not in the office, I know they're in very capable hands," Bernie says. Barbara specializes in financial and estate planning issues, and her expertise has earned her a partnership.

As Bernie and his clients enter their 50s and 60s, their children are now independent, many with families. Who better to meet their needs than Bernie's daughter? Christina Benson Boyd wasted no time getting into her father's business. In 1989, as she entered college, she took a keen interest in the business and worked as many hours as she could, limited only by her father: "I wanted her to have some fun in her college years," he says with a laugh.

Immediately following her graduation from Colorado State University, she went to work for a rival securities firm in Boulder, Colorado. But Bernie persuaded her to join his team in 1995, as a financial advisor, to work primarily with individuals and small businesses, with a specialization in retirement planning. She has since become a partner.

More recently, Bernie gave his team a further shot in the arm by bringing on partner Peter Eckerline. Already a highly successful financial advisor, and a veteran with Merrill since 1983, Peter credits Bernie for much of his success. "Bernie has always been a role model for me," Peter says. "His strong work ethic and customer-focused approach have been a great influence on me." Because the two share strikingly similar approaches to customer service, long-term relationships, and investing philosophies, they feel these synergies create a perfect match. Peter provides investment recommendations and financial planning to individuals and corporate clients.

"The team is very focused," Christina says. "Customer service is our top priority. We're able to act quickly and decisively for our clients, and really spend the time each client needs. This exceptional customer service is how we differentiate ourselves from the competition. This is how we are extending my father's commitment to building lifelong relationships." The relationship-based team approach has proven to be a success. Clients praise each team member for his or her outstanding service referrals, and such referrals are higher than ever.

"Our team is truly full service," Peter adds. "We have the capability to handle virtually all aspects of a client's financial needs."

One client was referred to the team after a tragic accident nearly cost him his life and left him unable to support himself. "In the early 1990s," says Peter, "the man was operating machinery on his family's farm when suddenly he was hoisted into the machine. As a result, the man lost both arms. He ran into his empty house, dialed 911 with a pen in his mouth. Luckily, the doctors were able to reattach his arms, but his movement and coordination are severely restricted. The community responded by making $600,000 in contributions to help with medical payments, and continued support him."

With little investment experience, the client depends on Bernie and team for help in all financial matters: a mortgage for his home, an automobile, a checking account, a credit card, and every other aspect of his financial-planning needs.

Bernie's caring nature, so appreciated by his clients, extends into the community as well. Several years ago when he and his wife were vacationing in Jamaica, they befriended their waitress, a high school senior, while dining out. After spending some time with her and learning of her ambitions, the couple offered to pay her way through college, provided she maintained adequate grade levels. Today, after graduating from West Indies College, she has a thriving career at a major accounting firm.

This is just one of 25 scholarships Bernie has made possible. He also contributes regularly to his favorite community organizations, and he remains involved with several local retirement homes.

Gary Rosenthal
Clients for Life

The Rosenthal Group
Prudential Securities Incorporated
New York, New York

Most people think that customer service means reaching out to a client, whether through a phone call or a letter, and responding quickly when a client has a question or wants to execute a trade. But The Rosenthal Group takes customer service to an entirely new level. They don't merely reach out to clients; they bring something unique to the table.

"We have achieved our success in this industry through our diligent focus on fundamental research, innovative computer technology, and a constant effort to serve our clients' individual objectives," says Gary Rosenthal, senior member of The Rosenthal Group.

"Every time we sell something to a client, we become even more committed to providing exceptional service," notes Brett Rosenthal, Gary's son and partner. "Add to this our unique ability to meet with company insiders, and you'll begin to understand why clients are with us for life."

"We offer institutional-quality service to our retail accounts," Gary explains (*see Investment Philosophies: Performance…and Protection*). "Minutes after a long meeting with the CEO of a company, we're holding conference calls with our clients, providing original, real-time analyses. Our clients get preferential treatment over the institutionals, other retail investors, and even brokerage firms."

Calling the retail clients first contrasts with the way most analysts work, notes Brett. Typically, an analyst visits a company, calls the firm's best fund managers with advance knowledge, and then addresses his own organization. "By the time the average retail broker gets what he or she considers breaking information, it's worthless. Sometimes the client doesn't get the information until the published report is mailed. This is simply unacceptable to us," Brett states.

In addition, The Rosenthal Group goes beyond the standard sales pitch to win new business. Rather than using the archetypal peddler's line, "Hi, I'm Joe Smith with XYZ Company and this is my firm's favorite stock pick," the Group will carefully evaluate a company's balance sheet. They analyze the firm's market opportunities, so that they can speak from first-hand experience with a high level of conviction.

"This approach has been very successful for our clients, and they realize they can't get this type of service anywhere else," partner Dennis O'Hara says.

The Rosenthal Group keeps a client as informed as he or she desires. A client's preferences for frequency of contact become clear after the initial consultation, which consists of fact-finding and determining their financial objectives. In some cases, the Group will call a client twice a day, or a client may call the group several times a day. "Whether a client has $500,000 with us or $20 million, they have equal access to us," says Gary.

"Whether the market's not doing well or something's going wrong, there's never a day that we're not there to pick up the phone," adds Brett. "I think that's something a lot of brokers don't understand. They're afraid to pick up the phone. Or they're off focusing on a new client. The number one thing is that we're always accessible. If you talk to our clients, they'll agree."

Because The Rosenthal Group also maintains close contact with the companies where they hold positions, clients are easily placated when informed of impending negative news or of a sudden stock drop. "It's normal for clients to experience a sense of panic when the market corrects, or when a stock they're holding announces bad news," Dennis says. "This is when our expertise really shines. Because we're so intimate with our holdings, we are able to offer a highly educated perspective. Then, when our clients really take a step back and consider our game plan, it will ultimately make sense."

"And more often than not," Brett adds, "they will ask us to increase their position."

In fact, the Group instills such confidence in its clients that many of its relationships are discretionary accounts. "We've built such trust and a solid track record in regards to strong performance that many of our clients don't even want to be called," Brett says.

"This trust is why we virtually never lose a client," Gary says with satisfaction. "This is the heart and soul of who we are. I've been doing things this way for so long, I know no other way of running a book."

SIGMUND MUNSTER
RELATIONSHIPS, RELATIONSHIPS, RELATIONSHIPS

Morgan Stanley
Columbus, Ohio

See related section:
Corporate Plan Business: The Complete Package

"Relationships are the single most important aspect of our business," Sigmund "Sig" Munster says of his career as a Financial Advisor, which began in 1959. "We try to build relationships with each client and their families in order to help them achieve their financial goals and aspirations. We build life-long relationships."

Sig is well aware that it's not the product that gives a financial advisor a competitive advantage. "All financial advisors sell the same thing," he points out. "Unlike other fields, it's not the inventory that separates one broker from the competition. Any broker can open a new account. That's the easy part. But at the end of the day, keeping them on the books is what's important. You do that by providing great service and building long-term relationships."

Sig's tenure with Morgan Stanley dates back to 1970. As one of Morgan Stanley's top financial advisors, Sig began developing relationships with clients as soon as he graduated from The Ohio State University. That was four decades ago. Today, he continues to build on his base of hundreds of clients. Interestingly, before he finished his first year in the business, he realized that making cold calls to strangers was not the route he wanted to take. Even though he was told "dialing for dollars" would build a clientele, Sig knew that he wanted to create his business one customer at a time.

"The key to being successful in business is doing what you love," Sig says. "I happen to love meeting people and making new friends, and establishing life-long relationships. Even though it's second nature for me, it's something that everyone has to work on every day. It's a great feeling to know that I've nurtured many relationships for generations, and that I now have relationships with clients' relatives, and their friends. That's what's fun for me.

"Our team's philosophy is that one personal call is worth ten phone calls," he explains. "We take every opportunity we have to sit down with the client. We want to see if his or her goals and objectives have changed. With a team of six qualified people, we can usually get someone to a client's home or business that day, if it's necessary." He says this will occur on a daily, monthly, or quarterly basis, depending on the needs of the account. "Some people need more TLC than others."

At the beginning, Sig sought business by visiting investors in person, "eyeball to eyeball," as he puts it. Having lived in Columbus, Ohio all his life, these were people he knew personally; they were friends and acquaintances who served as the foundation for his block of business.

"Sure, I also called on strangers—lots of them—but only when they were referred to me or we had a mutual acquaintance," he reveals. "What I didn't do, however, was take the 'boiler room' approach and make calls to total strangers out of the telephone book, a city directory, or some rented list of preferred prospects. I know some brokers operate this way and they're successful, but that's not my style. It makes me laugh because even *I* get calls from out-of-town brokers who want to sell me. Now, you can imagine how exclusive those lists are when they're on the telephone pitching another financial advisor! For the life of me, I don't understand how they can expect anyone in Columbus, Ohio to give his business to a complete stranger who lives in a faraway place like New York or Dallas."

Throughout his long career, Sig has relied on repeat business and referrals from satisfied clients. From strong, established relationships, new relationships are created. "By doing backbends to serve my clients," he explains, "they not only continue to do business with me, but they refer their friends and relatives to me." It's a similar story you're apt to hear from the top financial advisors in all communities across the country. It's a winning formula that works. Sure, it may be a long, tedious process. Nobody gets rich overnight with this approach. But in the long run, it pays off in spades."

Sig oftentimes receives referrals from individuals who are not clients. "Even if you visit a prospect you've never met before, and for whatever reason they're not interested in doing business with you," he says, "they may be impressed with you, and then they're likely to help you."

Several years ago, Sig and his son Greg, Financial Advisor and partner on the team, took a prospect out for lunch. The Munsters enjoyed getting acquainted with this woman, and had the opportunity to explain their business. Even though she opted not to transfer her account, she held onto their information. Sig had asked her to keep them in mind if she knew anyone who might be interested in their services. Many weeks passed, and then one day she called Sig and gave him the name of some people she thought he might want to contact. Greg and Sig visited the prospects and soon established a relationship. A short time later the prospects transferred their accounts to Morgan Stanley.

Sig Munster's reputation as a professional financial advisor is a credit to the industry. While he's given no indication that he'll retire in the near future, he and his wife, Rita, spend a good deal of time traveling, as well as enjoying their Palm Beach home. "With fax machines, cell phones, and computers, I can be anywhere in the world and remain in touch with my clients," he says.

For many financial advisors, doing work while on vacation may not seem pleasurable. Not for Sig. "It's what I love," he says. "I don't do it for the money. I'd do this for free, I just happen to be making money in the process."

During a short getaway to Florida several years ago, Sig was playing tennis with some friends. In a game of doubles, he was partnered with a man he had never met before. Since then, this tennis partner has become a close friend, and Sig's client. "And now that he has moved to the Cayman Islands," says Sig, "he has introduced me to a lot more people who have become clients."

Sig finds that community involvement is a great way to meet new people and simultaneously perform a great service. "I believe wholeheartedly that you have to be involved in your community," he says firmly, "whether it's pee-wee football, little league baseball, the American Cancer Society, the United Way, or the local hospital." Sig happens to be involved in all these organizations, plus he's a board member of the Columbus Jewish Foundation and active with the Ohio State University and Columbus Academy. "I've met some outstanding people, and many have become great clients. We require that everyone on the team become actively involved in something."

While Sig's clients know he's always on call to serve them, they take comfort in knowing that his talented son, Greg, is dedicated to leading the family business through the twenty-first century.

CHAPTER 10:
BUILDING A FEE-BASED BUSINESS

Bob Jones
A Fee-Based Pioneer

IJL Wachovia Securities
Charlotte, North Carolina

At the age of 14, Bob Jones realized the capitalistic and wealth-creation opportunities available to all Americans."It was a real eye-opener, even at that young age," he says. "I never considered myself a rich American until I lived abroad."

Bob's father, a successful businessman with IBM, had relocated the family from Poughkeepsie, New York, to South America, in order to expand IBM's business. During their travels, Bob made a great number of native friends, "many of whom were impoverished by our standards," he says."I wished there was something I could do for them, but there wasn't. It was obvious that their system just did not offer the opportunities that ours did. They looked at me, a so-called rich American, like I had all the answers."

A decade later, after receiving his MBA from the University of North Carolina at Chapel Hill, Bob found some of those answers. He decided to enter the securities business, first by learning as much as he could about it. In 1981, he joined Interstate Johnson Lane, predecessor to IJL Wachovia Securities, and held several positions in the areas of investment banking, marketing and management. When the market crashed in 1987, he wondered why anyone would abandon stocks."I was thinking like I was 14 again,"he reflects,"knowing that America was the greatest place in the world to invest, a world full of opportunities."

Shortly thereafter, in 1988, Bob left management, opting instead for the life of a rookie financial advisor."This was the opportune time to do it,"he says.

Interestingly, years prior to the formal introduction of fee-based business, Bob knew that he wanted to become an expert on managing clients' finances, and intended to rely on a select group of money managers with proven experience—and track records—to pick the investments. This was a goal that would take effect the first day on the job.

Upon becoming a financial advisor, Bob moved from Charlotte to High Point, NC. He assumed the managerial duties of the small branch office, and immediately began building his business."Looking back," he says,"I felt it was a great advantage to begin my advisory career in a small town."

Every day, Bob walked the streets of High Point, knocking on doors."When I moved to High Point, I didn't know anyone!" he recalls. "I met a number of CPAs and attorneys in town, and tried to meet business owners who might be interested in diversifying some of their assets. I joined clubs like the Rotary Club, the local eating club, which is called the String & Splinter, and the country club. I did all this in an effort to introduce myself, and to get to know them. My goal was to work toward earning a portion of their investment business. 'I would like to meet you,' I'd say. 'I want to earn a portion of your business. Let me tell you a little bit about what I do and how I do it, and why it's different, and earn a chance to prove myself over time.'

"At that time," he continues, "I was realistic enough to know that, at 33 years of age, my stock picking prowess wasn't superior enough to do it myself. On the other hand, using third-party managers made perfect sense to me." When leading prospects to fee-based business, he would say, "I'm smart enough to select experienced people to manage the money for us. And in fact, I invest my own money the same way."

To help him accomplish his goal of building such a fee-based business before it was established within the brokerage world, Bob relied on the firm's fledgling investment consulting department to help him sort through money managers. The leader of the department, Mike Blair, worked full time seeking and interviewing the right money managers for the firm's new managed money program. Once he found a manager that fit his criteria, Mike would negotiate the fee structure. In the beginning, he amassed 15 money managers that offered an array of investing-style options, yet also met his stringent criteria for inclusion in the program.

By the spring of 1989, Bob pioneered the managed money business by opening his first fee-based account. Mike paved the way with one of the first fee-based programs that existed.

Eventually, Mike—with prodding from Bob—introduced new services, such as wrap accounts. Though Mike is now long-gone from managing the department, the firm currently has scores of managers enrolled in the program, and one of the broadest money management programs around. Subsequently, the firm asked Mike to lead the retirement planning and services department. In 1994, Bob convinced Mike to become a financial advisor. Three years later, Bob asked him to become his partner.

The partnership with Mike enables Bob to continue establishing relationships with clients and prospects, as well as leading the third-party managed accounts aspect of the business. Mike runs the retirement plan business, and he manages the Charlotte Myers Park office. The six other team members include four associate financial advisors and two administrative assistants. These individuals ensure that all paperwork and administrative-related activities are fulfilled. One of the associate advisors is a certified financial planner who helps further customize services for our clients.

Bob and Mike seek to meet with every prospect in person. "We begin by explaining our business," says Bob. "This includes giving them a copy of our brochure, introducing each team member, then discussing our investment philosophy. At this point, they are able to ascertain whether our services are right for them. If it is, we discuss their needs and what they're looking for. As we progress, and if we're in the office, we then personally introduce each team member and describe the high quality of service that we provide. It is important for the prospect to physically meet the people that will be doing their best to meet his or her investing needs."

If a prospect is most interested in planning for retirement, Bob and Mike will obtain the information they need by asking pointed questions: "At what age do you want to retire?" Bob begins. "How much money do you think you're going to need in retirement? What do you think the inflation rate is going to be between now then? How much money do you think you can earn in retirement? How much money do you think you can earn prior to retirement on you assets? What type of assets are you comfortable owning and what do you own right now? What have been good investments for you in the past? What aren't you interested in doing? What things do you want to avoid?

"We try to get a complete picture of the client's situation and mentality, and then we try to steer the client towards their strengths and away from their weaknesses. That gives us the framework we need to create the roadmap for the future. And it's not a very complicated process. Most people want the same thing. It's remarkable. They come in all sizes and colors, shapes and forms, but most of them just want to retire with enough money to last."

Bob points out that even basic retirement planning may lead to the team's participation in estate planning, trusts, tax planning, and, Bob adds, "anything else we can do to ensure the client is in command of his or her financial situation."

"After the meeting," he continues, "we promptly send a thank-you letter, which includes a formal proposal." The proposal describes the money-management process, and proposes the next step, which includes an initial investment suggestion. "At that point, we either meet with them in person or over the phone to walk them through the paperwork. After that, we can begin transferring an account or bring assets to our firm.

"Once we know exactly what assets are coming our way, we create an investment policy statement and a long-term financial plan, depending on the client's needs. This is basically a road map for achieving a client's goals. It will include a well-planned asset-allocation and money-management strategy that we implement immediately. This is a very systematic process for us, and the clients are usually impressed with our preparation and ideas."

The team focuses on larger accounts, typically those with a minimum of $250,000. Though Bob considers a large account much higher than $250,000, he is willing to start with that amount if he is convinced that he will earn more of a prospect's assets over time. If a prospect wants his team to prove them-selves with an initial investment, Bob will ask for $500,000 or more so he can obtain the proper diversification.

There are generally two types of prospects the team pursues. One is the case in which an individual's money is considered unsuccessfully or insufficiently invested. Bob explains, "This could be money from the sale of a business or a certificate of deposit or bond that is coming due. The other type of prospect involves a retirement plan. A company may have a retirement plan they're unhappy about, either because the service or the mutual fund performance has been unsatisfactory. The largest part of our business is the management of institutional retirement money. Typically, this is business earned from a competitor. There are different sets of issues with the various services that are required for such plans. These issues include the fiduciary's responsibilities of selecting mutual-fund families, allocating assets among them, and the ongoing education that's required for the various participants in the plan," Bob says.

For the large retirement plans, the team seeks to provide high quality service through information and administrative services. Additionally, the team leverages IJL Wachovia's retirement department and outside mutual fund companies. "It's also important to spend time with groups, or individuals, to explain the plan, and to answer questions so that employees get comfortable with the investing process."

Bob considers his team to be professional wealth managers. "The recently developed technology millionaire tends to be pretty aggressive," he explains, noting that even after the 2000 to 2001 decline in the markets, these individuals still exist and can continue to thrive. "He will have a whole different set of needs than, say, a conservative doctor who is retiring. The technology person will be interested in cashless collars for their volatile technology stock, or they may need loans to bridge the gap between their IPO and their lockup period. And, of course, now that the markets are down from their highs and the IPO business has slowed, there is a whole new set of needs for those who have acquired new wealth.

"Our typical investor is middle-aged, interested in serious investing, and wants the expertise of professionals," Bob continues. "And this often involves a wide spectrum of financial services, such as bringing in an attorney to work with us to create trusts, including charitable remainder trusts and qualified personal retirement trusts. We work with clients to analyze estates and potential estate taxes, create estate plans and build family limited partnerships, create all types of foundations, and form ongoing gifting plans to children, grandchildren, charities, and more." Of course, the team is busy helping clients plan for more traditional needs, such as education planning and tax planning. But retirement planning remains the biggest part of its business.

The team encourages virtually all clients to be invested in equities. "We want investors to be in the stock market as much as they can stomach," Bob says. "Since I began in 1988, I have placed virtually every dollar of my investable assets in the stock market. Over time, it has been very rewarding."

The team provides even greater service during tough times in the markets, "To ensure that our clients don't panic at the wrong times," Bob says. "Whether it was during the Persian Gulf War or in the down markets of 2000 and 2001, we're remaining in equities for the long term."

Empathizing with clients helps keep them at ease during turbulent times. "By telling clients that we eat our own cooking, meaning we invest our own money in the same places they do, our clients seem to feel better about our decisions. And when we remind them that our plan is long term in nature, it's easier for them to hold on."

Bob mentions that his team is extremely diligent with the operations of the managed-money business. For example, they carefully scour the track records of individual third-party managers. "And we have absolutely no bias toward one manager versus another," he says. "We have used managers inside our IJL Wachovia program, and we've used managers outside of the portfolio. We ask that our managers be consistent in the application of their strategies. We ask them to be consistent in their personnel, and we ask that they be consistent amongst the accounts. In other words, we don't want a lot of deviation from one account to the next. We don't want a lot of turnover in the management firm and we don't want a lot of standard deviation of returns over time.

"We have growth managers, value managers, international managers, small cap managers, convertible managers, hedge funds, and venture capital funds. You name it. We try to build the most diversified base for our clients as possible," he continues. "We've been able to deliver a broad range of high quality money managers over time, and it has served us and our clients well over the long run."

Fifty percent of the team's business is directed toward money managers, and around 40% toward mutual funds. Ten percent goes to other investments, such as cash, bonds, or individual stocks.

The types of mutual funds the team uses depends on the client. "For example," Bob explains, "certain retirement plans dictate certain types of funds. Most big plans allow funds from a universe of families, so we can cherry pick the ones we think are most appropriate. We may use a successful large-cap growth manager from one family, and a small-cap value manager from another family. When choosing the right fund, we always avoid front-loaded funds, and we're careful about fund expenses. We also seek a solid consistency of management.

"In a smaller plan, we are careful about expense tolerances," he continues. "In smaller retirement plans, we may have to stay with one family of funds to get solid, consistent administrative support, which is very important. In this case, we may give up a little return for accuracy, timeliness, and a high quality of support services."

When selecting the right mutual funds for individual clients, the team avoids mutual funds with any upfront fees. "It doesn't make sense to me to start off an investment with a significant loss, especially if the client ends up changing his or her decisions. That's unacceptable to us." Bob believes that it's only right to be paid as long as an individual remains a client. "We want clients to be free to leave without penalty if we don't perform for them. Neither the front-loaded funds nor the back-loaded funds can facilitate this. We understand that level loads cost more in the long term, but we just don't want our hands tied. A client's financial situation may change at any given moment and that would be the worst time to penalize someone."

When asked how he's become so successful at attracting assets and growing a business, he responds this way: "I'm always surprised that the first question a potential customer does not ask his or her broker is, 'How do you manage your money?' If prospects asked that question, they would probably avoid 80% of the brokers in the world, because 80% of the brokers don't seem to have any money. So, I'm stunned that the question seldom comes up. We bring it up because we want our clients to know that we have money and we have money in the same places, in the same allocations, in the same price structure as they do and we're all in it together. If we do well, they will do well and vice versa. So, we're very sensitive about the issue of 'eating our own cooking.'"

Bob continues, "We don't recommend anything to clients that we wouldn't buy ourselves or that we don't already own ourselves. We typically invest side-by-side with our clients. In fact, we've even experienced a buying conflict: if we want to buy a particular stock or buy a particular fund, we often have to wait until we get all our clients in an investment before we can buy. It's not a big problem with third-party managers, but it's been a problem at times, such as when certain funds are going to close to new investors."

The team receives many new referrals as a result of their successful approach to managing money and providing high-quality service with a large and growing business. However, they're often challenged to find enough time to meet with prospects without taking too much time away from their clients. Nonetheless, referrals and new accounts are the lifeblood of the business.

"This new business," says Bob, "is a big part of the joy we derive from being financial advisors. Meeting new people is just very enjoyable."

A few years ago, Bob and Mike received a referral from a client. The prospect was a successful businessman in his late fifties who was interested in investing and wanted to profit from the team's financial expertise. Unfortunately, the prospect wasn't in a position to make the several-hundred-mile drive to High Point. Because the duo insists on meeting in person, they set aside a day and made the trip by car.

"It took us half the day to get there," Bob says with a laugh. "It really was a long way from home!" Sometime in the late morning, Bob and Mike arrived at the prospect's office. "We were invited in, introduced ourselves, and then began the presentation."

Bob digresses for a moment to point out how important it is to work closely with a partner during the presentation: to reinforce points, answer challenging questions, and help build credibility. "Additionally, it allows one team member the time to take notes, think, and prepare back-up documentation so that the speaker doesn't have to stumble through papers," Bob says. They followed this procedure here. And after the presentation, they spent considerable time asking questions and learning more about the prospect's needs.

Toward the end of their meeting, Bob remarked, "If you like what you've heard today, we suggest we begin immediately by transferring your assets to our firm."

With that, the prospect said, "Let's go." Bob and Mike looked at each other, then followed the man to his car. They drove to the bank, parked, and walked through the vault gate to his lock box. An associate opened the box, and Mike and Bob stood wide-eyed.

"We saw bundles of stock certificates," Bob says. "We helped him count the certificates, then Mike and I drove back to High Point with $10 million of stock."

The partners immediately deposited the certificates at their firm and put the plan into action. "We planned a charitable remainder trust, another trust for the client's son, changes to his retirement plan, and money placed with three different money managers," Bob says. The team then set up a monthly income system so that the prospect had enough money to support his lifestyle. "Additionally," Bob continues, "we recommended that he sell a large position in a single stock because we wanted to encourage diversification. We didn't sell all of it due to his tax situation, but it turned out to be a wise decision." As it now turns out five years later, the stock has barely budged, while the new stock that was accumulated has nearly tripled in price.

Bob encourages all financial advisors to do their homework so that they can exude a high degree of conviction. He feels that this enables him to ask for the order and close the sale. "At the end of the day, people are looking for advice," he explains. "If they believe you and trust you, you've got to look them in the eyes and tell them what to do.

"We feel that it's also extremely important to make a commitment to 'eat your own cooking,'" he continues, "and prove it to clients. It seems only fair that clients understand that if they make money, then your pay increases. If they lose money, your pay drops. These are very powerful statements. They help clients know that I'm never going to call them to make a change so that I can make money. I may tell clients to stay where they are and I may tell them to change some things. But I am going to make the same money either way, and make recommendations solely on the basis of what I think is best for the client.

"Finally, it helps if you can show some stability," he says, referring to low employee turnover. "Our team has experience, longevity, and maturity. These are some of the secrets to our success."

The team's formula seems to be working. Currently, the team manages over $700 million in client assets, yet Bob and Mike still find time to lend their expertise as financial advisors to the United Way, Charlotte's Mint Museum of Crafts and Design, and others. Bob was also on the ERISA plans committee at Interstate Johnson Lane before the company merged with Wachovia.

"This is the land of opportunity," Bob says, "and it is so satisfying to see our clients and our communities benefit from the investment markets that the U.S. has to offer."

THOMAS B. GAU, CPA, CFP™
THE FEE-BASED CONVERSION

Oregon Pacific Financial Advisors
Torrance, California

See related sections:
Prospecting and Marketing: The Retirement Specialist
Going Independent: Building a Franchise

When Tom Gau decided to convert his business from a commission-based to a fee-based practice, he didn't go about it half-heartedly. Within three months, he converted a significant portion of his total assets under management into fee-based business. Tom's story is unique, considering he was already one of America's most successful financial advisors and business was brisk. But it is also common, as legions of financial advisors across the country see the benefits of seeking professional money management for their clients. Regardless of which fee-based direction a financial advisor chooses to pursue, Tom's story provides an insightful perspective that can serve as a blueprint for financial advisors contemplating the same type of transition.

Tom is probably one of the most efficient financial advisors in the business. Remarkably, he is able to run his practice by working only nine days per month. On those days, he meets with clients non-stop between 8 a.m. and 5 p.m. He is able to catch up on phone calls and eat a brief lunch during his five to ten minute breaks between meetings. Other phone calls are made after meetings, and calls to the East coast begin as early as 5 a.m. Pacific Standard Time.

Some of Tom's secrets to success are his systemized processes. "This way, most of the specific operational duties can be delegated to employees of the firm," he explains. "My practice was built on the basis of strong systems. Therefore, if I were going to specialize in a new product or service, I would need a new system that has every 'i' dotted and every 't' crossed.

"Perhaps the best advice I can give is this: Never offer anything unless you are going to offer a lot of it! This is extremely important. Many advisors try to do everything for everyone and get bogged down in the time, trouble, aggravation, and follow-up required for each product or service that they provide. If you do not have critical mass, then the cost of setting up these systems will often be more than the revenues the product or service will generate. The end result will be an all-around losing proposition: poor customer service and far less business for the advisor."

Most financial advisors agree that fee-based business is here to stay, and more and more are focusing on this market. Many prefer the dependable stream of income that fluctuates less than a commission-based practice. They also prefer lower maintenance requirements, as opposed to traditional commission-based trading. Others appreciate the ability to "outsource" the investment selection to professionals with attractive track records. And when nearing retirement, it's infinitely easier to transition a fee-based business to a new advisor. Unfortunately, many advisors don't know where to start.

Tom had considered transitioning to a fee-based practice for a few years. His financial-planning practice consists of in-depth reviews of his clients' finances. This includes investments, income tax planning, estate planning, retirement distribution planning, and insurance planning. "Unfortunately, my revenue was based primarily on commissions, and I realized I had a dilemma," he explains. "Clients expect top-notch service; many clients come to me because their prior advisor didn't meet with them frequently enough. After building a sizable client base, I was spending significant time meeting with my clients and following up with their investments and financial planning needs. I've always had a close relationship with my clients and felt that it was necessary, from both a business and an ethical standpoint, to meet with my clients on a regular basis, most of them quarterly." This was a trademark of Tom's business, one that he would need to consider carefully when planning the transition to fee-based business.

Because the term "fee-based business" is used fairly loosely, when outlining his business plan for the conversion, he began by thoroughly considering all his options within this realm. "I looked at all the various routes," he says. "My top choices were: keeping my business as is and charging an hourly rate for my time, using third-party money managers, using load funds and class C or M shares, and no-load funds and charging a fee to manage these funds. As part of my systemized process, I was seeking one area within the fee-based business that I would pursue."

In order to keep his business as is, he could assess an hourly rate or flat fee in addition to receiving the commission and trailing commissions he then received. Tom actually tested this scenario several years prior, and found the record keeping and explaining fees to clients to be too time consuming. Tom shakes his head, smiling, and says, "I had clients that either opted against a review because it would cost them money, or questioned our relationship because they had heard they could get the same type of service for free somewhere else."

Tom immediately rejected the idea of hiring outside money managers for his clients. "A significant number of my clients like to track their mutual funds and read various investment magazines," he says. "Some of my clients choose their own mutual funds for their portfolio. Therefore, many of my clients were concerned that third-party money managers would not be as easy to track and compare as mutual funds."

Tom stresses that third-party money managers are a great option for a lot of investors, including his own, and says their service can be impeccable. However, his business systems require all of his clients be managed similarly.

Tom considered Class C or M shares because of his familiarity with the mutual fund families and the fund managers. Using these shares, he would receive a larger trail. "It seemed like an easy transition because my clients were already familiar with these funds," he says.

The downsides were obvious to Tom: There are only a limited number of funds that offer a Class C or Class M share. This would present a problem if a client or prospect wanted to invest in other families. "My biggest concern is the NASD's ruling that C shares should be used on a short-term basis," Tom says. "If an investor is interested in staying in a mutual fund or mutual fund family for a long period of time, the NASD expects that the client will be sold either an A share, or, in some cases, a B share, that's convertible to an A share after a certain number of years."

Charging a fee to manage no-load funds was most appealing to Tom. "I had always managed mutual funds anyway, and thought that I would be able to continue to do research on mutual funds the way I had done in the past," he says. "However, I needed to have a system in place in order to allow my infrastructure to do this, and I wasn't entirely comfortable with my previous broker-dealer firm's systems. If this were a route to be considered, I would have to establish my own systems.

"Once I had the systems in place, I knew this was the route to go," he continues. "And clients seemed very open to paying a relatively small transaction fee for the services they would receive. The next big question was: How do I accomplish this?"

Tom began by compiling a list of clients with mutual funds holdings had that could be repositioned at no cost. He then made a list of questions they would most likely ask when presented with this new service.

Tom describes a typical dialogue with a client he strives to convert to Premier Advisory Service, a program designed by Sun America Securities, Inc. "Hello, Mr. Smith. I have excellent news for you. We now have the ability to invest in no-load mutual funds. The name of this program is called Premier. The great thing about Premier is that there is no cost to get into it or out of it. All of the mutual funds are no-load, with no cost to purchase or sell, and no holding period. There are also no commissions, ticket charges, or other hidden expenses for mutual funds in this program."

The client responds: "Well then, how do you get paid?"

Tom explains: "I do get paid. Unfortunately, like every other business, we have overhead. Mr. Smith, I currently make an average of about 1% per year on your investments. This comes from a combination of the loads, or commissions, that you initially paid when you went into your investments. Plus I also receive part of the management fee that you are assessed directly by the mutual funds, called a 12b(1) fee. Again, the average amount that we earn over a period of time, on an account such as yours, is about 1%. As I have mentioned to you earlier, all of the mutual funds that we recommend in the Premier program are no-load funds. So, instead of receiving a commission, I will charge you a fee. I have decided that a fair amount to charge you would be about 1%, because that is about how much I am getting paid right now for managing your portfolio. Remember, this 1% is not all upfront. We charge by the quarter. Therefore, if it is 1% per year, we will be charging you one quarter of 1% per quarter."

The client asks: "How come we haven't done this before?"

Tom replies: "That's a great question. As you know, the various services that a financial representative can provide are increasing every year. With today's structure and technology, we can do a lot more now than we could in the past. Just think about it: Having a remote control for your TV used to be a luxury and now it is a standard. This is similar to what's happening today in the world of financial planning, with all of the new changes in computers and technology. Now, although you might think the fee is high, it is actually not much more than what you've been paying us in the past. It's important to note that many of the mutual funds that I'm recommending have significantly lower management fees than the ones on your existing mutual funds. For example, the management fees of Vanguard are often more than 1% less than some of the mutual funds that you currently have. By investing in Vanguard, although you will be paying the 1%, your net overall expense may actually be less. However, although I do think low management fees are important, I'm a big believer that the net rate of return in your pocket, after all expenses have been deducted, is more important. That is why one of the things I've done is prepare a comparison of the rates of return of the mutual funds that you currently have to the various mutual funds that I am currently recommending.

"Have you ever heard of a company called MorningStar? MorningStar is an independent company that rates mutual funds. They divide up the mutual funds into the different categories such as large-cap, mid-cap, and small-cap, etc. I've broken down each of your mutual funds into these categories, and have also listed my two top picks of the no-load funds in each of these categories. I have a comparison of their rates of return for the last one, three, and five and ten years—or since inception, if the life of the fund is less than 10 years. As you can see from this report, the rates of return on the no-load funds that I am recommending have out-performed the rates of return of the mutual funds that you currently have. Does this mean that your mutual funds have not performed well? Of course not. Although your current mutual funds have historically done well, the other mutual funds that I am recommending have done better. It is also important to note that historical numbers are no guarantee of future results. However, I had to go by something, and this is the result of my analysis."

If the client seems willing to proceed with the recommendation, Tom will ask whether or not this makes sense to him or her. However, if the client still seems apprehensive, he will make the following statement: "I recommend that we that try the Premier Program for one year and see how we like it. After one year, I'll do a comparison of the rates of return for the no-load funds and compare those returns with the rates of return for your current funds as well. If we discover that it would be better to have stayed with the load funds that you currently have, then we will get out of Premier and go back to the old method."

The client inquires: "Won't I have to pay a load to go back into these existing funds?"

"No, not if we do it in the right sequence,"Tom counters."One of the great things about Premier is that we can buy no-load funds at no-load. However, we can also buy load funds at no-load! This means that if we find an excellent fund, but it is a load fund, we can still invest in this fund at no-load! So if it's one year from now, and we decide that it's best not to continue with Premier, then we will sell the no-load funds, obviously at no-load, and then we will purchase the load funds that you currently have back, also at no-load, and then we will get out of Premier. Remember, there is no cost to go into or to get out of Premier.

"All of this is part of our Gold Medal Service. I would like to explain to you all of the services that we provide for this 1%."Tom notes that it was particularly easy to justify the fees once they see the benefits in writing, which is contained in his Gold Medal Service brochure.

"There are a number of changes that I would like to make in your account, but if we made the changes today, there would be a fee or commission cost to you. Obviously, it would be better to wait until we entered into the Premier contract and make any changes through Premier. By doing it this way, you will avoid any commissions or other ticket charges. Therefore, I recommend that we fill out the paperwork now in order to transfer the account over to Premier. Your account will look identical, with the exception that the account number will start with 05X.Your statement will remain the same.You probably will not see much of a difference, because the actual format will be the same.

"However, it does take my broker-dealer about two weeks to transfer all of your investments into Premier. There is no cost to do this, and there's no income tax consequence. But, you should be reregistered into the Premier account before any changes are made in order to avoid any costs. Once everything is transferred into Premier, then I'd like to meet with you and make specific recommendations. I'd rather hold off from making the recommendations at this time, since the stock market could vary between now and the next meeting.Therefore, I would like to do two things at this point: First, fill out the necessary paperwork to transfer the account over to Premier, and then I'll schedule another appointment with you in approximately two weeks to review the changes in your account."

The average time Tom spent answering each client's questions was less than 20 minutes. He credits Premier for the systems he established to facilitate the transfer of his clients' assets.

Tom stresses that financial advisors refrain from making any investment recommendations at this first client meeting."Your main goal at this meeting is to have the client sign the necessary paperwork in order to convert over to the fee-based account,"he says."After the account is transferred, then you can discuss the various options of which funds to sell and which funds to buy. If you try to discuss too much at the first meeting, the client will most likely say, 'Let me think about it.' My success rate was higher when I had the client sign the paper-work at the first meeting, and then schedule a follow-up meeting a couple of weeks later to discuss the investment alternatives."

Tom also encourages clients to transfer all of the mutual funds that they have directly with the mutual fund companies to a Pershing brokerage account with him. He believes this makes sense whether they have a fee-based account or not. "This enables me to consolidate my clients' investments and reduce paperwork for them," he begins. "I can also help them plan their taxes better, help them better allocate their assets, and make them much more aware of how much they are worth. Additionally, this makes it easier for clients to consider me their primary financial advisor, and think of me first when making a financial decision."

One of Tom's brochures is called "Gold Medal Service." It lists all of the services that he provides his clients for the fee he charges. And, as an under-$50 gift, he sends each client a high-quality three-ring binder, which outlines all the products and services he offers. "It's a small gesture, but it separates us from many other advisors that do not provide such a benefit. Also, as basic as this information sounds, it's a good reminder to clients what I can offer, and not take my services for granted."

CHAPTER 11:
CUSTOMER SERVICE

John D. Cooke
Redefining Full Service

Cooke Financial Group
Indianapolis, Indiana
Prudential Securities Incorporated

John Cooke has seen the past, and he has a pretty good idea of where we're headed in the future. John has always been a visionary in the securities business. When he became a financial advisor in 1968, he was one of the first to have a computer. He was also one of the first to build a team. He later pioneered what would eventually become the largest segment of the brokerage industry: fee-based business. And he isn't stopping there.

Spending the better part of a morning interviewing John, along with his partners and sons Chris and Brian Cooke, left me with the feeling that I'd stepped into history. In addition, they treated me to a virtual tour of the future. But perhaps most impressive is the team's commitment to clients. They continually redefine their business to offer their clients exceptional service, as well as to keep ahead of the competition.

John believes that his real training for the securities industry began in early 1964 when he joined the Air Force. His six-year stint as a pilot included missions during the Cuban Missile Crisis and Vietnam. And how's this for a strong type-A? Incredibly, without wasting any downtime during war, he found time to learn about investments and investing via correspondence classes. But perhaps his greatest lesson was experiencing the professionalism of the pilots with whom he was serving: "You appreciate the tremendous courage and sense of duty of these heroes who were, and still are, serving our country," John reminisces. "It was impressive just to witness their bravery, as they stepped into their aircraft, not knowing if they would return. Everyone had a job to do, and there was no room for any weak links—everything relied on your team effort." John pauses for a moment, then looks up. "Now that I think about it," he says, "my team, and our relationships, are partly the result of my military experience."

In 1969, he joined Thompson McKinnon Securities, one of the many roots that eventually would become Prudential Securities. He had a choice of earning a salary for his first two years or working on commission, the more lucrative option. He chose to work on salary for one important reason: He didn't want commissions to interfere with how he developed and ran his business.

Because he preferred face-to-face meetings over "dialing for dollars," as he calls it, he spent one day out of his six-day work week setting up appointments with local businesspeople, and the remaining five days visiting potential clients. In an effort to minimize travel time, he focused on one office building at a time. His wife, Judy, he said, "ran around town writing down names of prospects from office-building directories." He became an expert in profit-sharing plans: "In those days, brokers weren't selling profit-sharing plans," he explains. "Those plans were mostly the domain of insurance companies and banks."

Five years later, money-market instruments were being developed. John competed head-on with the banks' paltry 1% returns, offering a generous 3% or 4%. His long-term view had no room for the thoughts of commissions, so he opened up as many money-market accounts as possible. In the process, John was inadvertently collecting assets. To this day, the Cookes still do not look at their "commission runs."

Throughout his career, John sought ways to fully leverage his strengths—developing relationships, servicing accounts, and providing financial planning advice. One concern was the amount of time he spent personally managing clients' assets. "I wasn't spending adequate time investing my clients' assets," he says, then leans forward to emphasize his next point: "My clients deserved a better-focused process."

In the mid-1970s, John learned of a small but highly reputable firm called Foxhall Investment Advisors, a division of Thompson McKinnon. The advisory firm managed assets for private accounts from the firm's hometown of Washington, D.C. John's research concluded that he could provide the money manager with some of his clients' assets. The financial advisor arranged for Foxhall to invest the portfolios according to John's parameters. In turn, John would pay them an advisory fee out of the assets. John would continuously monitor the performance of the managers and provide detailed reports for his clients. "I quickly found out that their high performance numbers were far superior to my investing capabilities," he says. "Leaving the stock picking to them gave me the ability to service my accounts and focus on increasing my asset base." With John's new plan fully implemented, and new relationships with other money managers gaining steam, he landed numerous personal accounts and many profit-sharing plans in the $5 million to $6 million range. The executives that John approached were very receptive to this managed-money arrangement.

To this day, John still doesn't understand why this money-manager relationship wasn't fully embraced by the brokerage community. "Maybe brokers feel they can manage money better than the professionals," he says, shrugging his shoulders. "Until they come to the realization that they can't compete with thirty-person research staffs and disciplined investment approaches, they won't understand the benefits of this approach." For this reason, John had only one type of competitor: other professional money managers. During presentations, he had them licked because he was eventually able to give the prospect a choice of money managers, and diversify among them. Toward the late 1970s, due to his familiarity with profit-sharing plans, John naturally progressed into the retirement plans arena: IRAs, 401(k)s, 403(b)s, etc.

Inadvertently, John was defining what would eventually become a true full-service financial advisor, in his words, a "general practitioner." As he explains it, "we work with our clients on virtually all aspects of their financial situations. Money managers leverage our time so we can spend more time managing client relationships, but when it's time for surgery, we bring in the surgeon," he says, referring to the experts who manage the money, help draft estate plans, or review tax situations. Often, the money managers are invited to Indianapolis to meet with clients and prospects. "My clients were thrilled to be speaking to the actual money managers, and my prospects are impressed that I am able to maintain such a close relationship with the managers."

The Cookes believe they have stronger ties to the managers than just about any competitor. "This gives us a distinct advantage service-wise," John says. The team estimates that managed money, including mutual funds, consist of 75% of their business.

Money managers are frequently asked to visit, and Chris insists that they spend enough time to call every client who has money with the manager. "I ask the client if he or she has any questions, such as about performance or objectives, or recent trading patterns," Chris says. "Our clients really appreciate this." The team may also offer a breakfast or lunch with the money manager. They estimate that an average of three to four managers visit the team each week.

Each quarter, the team prepares customized reports for each client, broken down by manager if the client is invested with more than one—many clients have two to three managed accounts. "This gives us the opportunity to spot any potential problems and identify any positive developments," Brian says. "We also include a 'report card' that offers our personal notes and performance reviews." Also included in this package is an investment policy that has been designed for each particular client.

The customized reports evolved from an idea that John implemented in the early 1970s. "Like a doctor who offers x-rays and various other tests, I have always collected as much financial information about my clients as possible," John explains. "These data include insurance programs, disability programs, homeowners and auto insurance, and anything else that's related to their financial situation." The Cookes request that each client provide them with this information. "This information proves useful in spotting financial security blanket holes or possible estate-tax problems," he continues.

In the mid-1970s John determined that to maintain a superior level of service he would need to build a team. He began with one secretary. "I always dug into my pocket to try to stay one person ahead of what was needed in order to really provide my clients terrific service," he says. His team now numbers fourteen members, with six full partners. This includes his sons, Chris and Brian, as well as four other Financial Advisors. "Every father dreams of working with his sons," John says. "But I made a special point not to exact any pressure on them. Both ended up here naturally."

Chris joined Prudential Securities in 1990. He began his career with Ernst & Young, and is a CPA and tax attorney; he recently added a Certified Investment Management Analyst (CIMA) certification to his list of qualifications. He happened to fit smartly into his father's plans of offering additional services such as tax and estate planning. On the first day, Chris reviewed five tax returns and recognized ways in which clients could save significant interest, find deductions, and offered ideas for setting up trusts. Additionally, clients' portfolios could be better positioned to plan for certain obligations.

Two years later, Brian joined the team. Brian earned a business degree from Indiana University in 1989, and was a leading salesman for M&M Mars before joining his father and brother in the securities industry. With a CIMA designation, Brian lends a critical component to the team by providing his expertise in the areas of portfolio analysis and performance measurement. Also, his gift for developing relationships lends an added touch of service.

The team has four additional partners. Nancy Hague, a certified financial planner, is a cash-flow management specialist, and Lisa Grimes is an expert in the areas of annuities and mutual funds. Brian Schuman and Matt Stolle are proficient in the 401(k) arena. Seven others focus on servicing clients and administrative duties. Two of the seven are fully licensed, and well trained to act as financial advisors.

The Cooke team further validated their commitment to maintaining a lead over their competitors while providing exceptional service for their clients with the addition of a technology expert. This expert is responsible for creating high-impact presentations, building and maintaining a client database, and enhancing communications with clients and prospects via the Internet.

Several years ago, sensing a need could be filled, John met with Prudential Securities' former Chairman, Hardwick Simmons, to discuss the formation of a new managed-money program. PruChoice, as it was later named, is a program that provides access to over 40 mutual-fund families, plus extra services like asset allocation modeling and mutual-fund analysis and monitoring for a low annual fee. It is now a highly successful program.

Later, John offered the idea of a high-quality internal money-management division at Prudential Securities, now called PIIMA, Prudential Investments Individually Managed Accounts. "If you look at the assets involved in this program firm-wide, they're in the billions of dollars," John says, referring to the assets currently managed under the program.

More recently, John was a major proponent of Prudential Advisor, the industry's first fee-based program that offers a choice of trading via a financial advisor or through the firm's online trading platform. Many full-service firms followed Prudential's lead with this service. He has also been advocating fees for estate-planning services.

John credits the leadership of Prudential for a visionary outlook, and responsiveness, for moving the company into the future. "In particular, our CEO, John Strangfeld, is the type of visionary and communicator—that not only listens, but executes when he sees opportunity. Virtually every new idea I've ever presented to the leadership of Prudential is immediately considered and often implemented." The Cookes feel that this type of back and forth communication is a significant factor in improving both Prudential Securities, and the Cooke Financial Group.

In 1998 the Cooke Financial Group entered yet another paradigm; one that they feel is far superior to both their full-service counterparts and the online discounters. The Internet has allowed them to become more and more involved in the relationship-building process—offering enhanced communications, online trading, bill paying, e-commerce, and so on. These additional services will complement the team's efforts in the office by allowing them to offer their services at considerable discounts. "By offering our services—money management, transactional business, etc.—and our value-added services—estate planning, tax opinions, etc.—at prices that are less than our full-service competitors, we have a tremendous competitive advantage," John explains, "and the discounted fees are clearly showing up in our clients' performance figures." He also points out that the deep discounters and online trading firms don't offer many of these services.

Chris continues his father's thoughts: "We have attracted a lot of business by being a low-cost operator."

Brian adds, "It's probably the reason that we've seen a surge in the number of referrals we've had over the last few years. At this point, no one is really contemplating this strategy—we're leaps and bounds ahead of anyone"

When discussing the additional services they offer, all three Cookes chuckle, and begin naming some of the out-of-the-ordinary services that they offer: "window replacing, helping clients move, fixing washing machines... we once took a client to a hospital. We've provided pick-up and delivery services, automobile repairs, and job placements." Then Chris adds, "We're pretty much married to our clients, that's how close we try to be." And they all laugh.

John then interrupts, saying on a serious note, "RJ, it's not just about business with these relationships. It's about being alert and kind. I feel just as satisfied fixing a window for a retired widow as I do outperforming the S&P 500."

The Cookes are also serious about lending their expertise to community efforts. John has served as chairman of the board of the Community North Hospital. He has been a director for Community Hospital Systems, is a current Hawthorns Hamilton Proper Golf and Community Club board member, and serves on the board of directors for Butler University. Chris is treasurer of Conner Prairie, a living history museum, and both sons contribute time and resources to the Penrod Society, which raises money for children and the arts.

These non-profit efforts, plus the experiences of working for non-profit clients—have initiated the newest addition to the Cooke Financial Group: A new partner who specializes in non-profits. Together, they have formed Keystone Institutional Consulting. Perhaps with this new venture, the Cooke's pioneering efforts of a low-cost, high-touch model will change non-profit financial consulting for years to come.

"Keystone Institutional Consulting is just one more way we can make a small but significant difference in this business," John states firmly.

The Cookes strike again: Redefining full service.

TOM HILL
HOMETOWN HERO

Legg Mason Wood Walker
Easton, Maryland

"Everyone knows the secret to success in this business," Tom Hill says matter-of-factly. "It's top-notch service." What sets Tom's service apart from that of other financial advisors? "We move heaven and earth to try to give our clients what they need," he says. "You try to meet clients on their level."

Nestled on the winding shores of the Chesapeake Bay, the eighteenth-century town of Easton, Maryland resonates with hometown snugness. Born and raised in Easton, Tom glows as he smiles and chats with fellow residents. He's quick to point out the benefits of life in a beautiful small town, and hospitably invites acquaintances, or clients, to visit his riverfront home.

After I had spent the better part of the day interviewing him, Tom and his wife, Cathy, refused to let me leave on an empty stomach. It wasn't until we skippered his boat to a restaurant that the Hills told me how pleased they were to have me join them for their thirty-first anniversary dinner.

Tom's first exposure to relationship-based sales occurred when he was a teenager selling books and Fuller Brushes door-to-door. Although he didn't intend to pursue a life in sales, he wanted the opportunity to work with people on a personal basis, and, most importantly, to continue to live in the Easton community.

After graduating from the University of Richmond in 1964, Tom joined a small brokerage firm. He moved his business to Legg Mason several years later, and built his business doing what he loves best: "Meeting and helping people," he says.

Walking door-to-door, Tom simply introduced himself and offered to be of service. He was often invited inside for a conversation about the market. In many instances, the conversation led to the prospect's financial goals. One in-person call "resulted in a wonderful 20-year client relationship," he says.

"The woman was widowed and in her seventies," he tells me. She had a broker who was managing her account, but she felt she wasn't receiving the proper guidance or service. After learning more about her as a person, and understanding her financial goals, Tom took the time necessary to educate her about how she should be planning for her financial future. Once the assets were transferred to Legg Mason, he included her in the entire process of managing her account: bonds for income, mixed with equities for growth.

After she passed away, Tom worked closely with the estate attorney and family to help settle her financial affairs."She had a great deal of trust in me," he says."And that was clearly reflected in her family's wish for me to help them with their investments. And it all started with a knock on a door."

One particular cold call resulted in establishing a long-time client relationship with the then-president of Coca Cola. This initial call led to meetings with several members of his family and other leaders of the company.

When Tom opens an account, he gives clients a choice between allowing him to manage the assets himself, or placing them in a managed-money program. The preference essentially depends on his clients' experience and objectives. The money-managed programs he prefers are mutual funds or wrap-fee accounts. His personal style of investing involves a long-term value approach, seeking companies with low price-earnings ratios and minimal debt. For more aggressive investors, he pursues special-situation stocks. His long-term approach to the market is designed to leave his clients unperturbed by short-term market volatility.

Tom maintains a close relationship with Bill Miller, Legg Mason's star fund manager and leader of the firm's flagship Legg Mason Value Trust."Bill is one of the most notable fund managers—he's beaten the S&P 500 ten calendar years in a row,"Tom says. He adds:"The performance he's achieved has certainly made a difference in people's lives.

"One client, the owner of a prominent fast food franchise, experienced limited success selecting stocks for himself,"Tom says."In the mid-1990s, we decided to put his entire equity portfolio into the Bill Miller's Legg Mason Value Trust. The client still boasts about Bill's impressive performance.

"Another client, a corporate vice president at a local trucking company, was getting ready to retire. After several discussions regarding his objectives and risk tolerance, we decided to allocate a majority of his retirement money to Legg Mason equity funds. Since his retirement in 1993, and despite heavy withdrawals his retirement has grown well beyond his expectations. This growth has made a tangible difference in his results."

Customer service is also high on Tom's performance list. He has built his own community in the office, with a team comprised of his son and partner Brad, who is also a CPA, Stephanie Saunders, previously a CFO of a local company, who joined Tom in 1997, and five customer-service representatives: Stephanie's mother, Helga Remington, who has been working with Tom since 1979, and Sharon Lister, Jodi Ohler, Pat Hoxter, and Penny Fontana complete the team. "These are truly some of the most wonderful people you'll ever meet,"he says."To them, nothing is too much trouble for a client."

In fact, the team's exceptional service has a reputation in the area. Recently, an attorney's office called the team to establish an estate account for a prospect with which the team had never had contact. The attorney's office commented that the team's reputation for service was so strong that they were recommending the team to clients. Later, a local accountant sent flowers to the team after tax season saying "Thanks for going the extra mile for us by providing us answers quickly and effectively."

Several years ago, some of Tom's clients asked why cost basis wasn't listed on their statements. The group of professionals responded by manually adding these numbers to the firm's electronic data and incorporating the figures into Legg's statement. The firm later added this feature for every client.

One Friday, late in the day, a client called and said she needed money from her mutual fund in order to close on a house over the weekend. "The client said she wasn't able to do this with her other brokerage account, but was hoping we could pull through for her," Tom says. "We had to jump through a few hoops, and we kept some associates at our Baltimore headquarters working late, but we were able to get the funds. This may seem like a minor event, but for the client it was monumental." The client later transferred over a substantial amount of assets. "It just goes to show you that nothing is too small for a client."

"It's important to us that clients are treated like family," Tom says. "With our group, we just happen to be able to do a great deal for our clients. They can call us any time, day or night, at the office or at home. If they have a problem, it's our problem, and we want to help them solve it."

For Tom, planning a client's financial future involves knowing more than just the client's financial goals. Tom and his team want to know how all their relatives are doing. "We try to get inside our clients' heads so we can view their situation from their point of view," Tom says. "We try to find out how they like to spend their money, so that we can fit those smaller goals into the scenario. Some need a certain sense of security; others like to take trips.

"For example, we had a fellow in today whose wife had just passed on," he explains. "He's at an age where you might be very conservative and live off income. But he said he has adequate income, and that what he'd really like to do is leave money to his kids. In response, we're upping the growth allocation in his account. If he had said, 'I really want income and I want to take trips around the world,' we would have constructed the portfolio accordingly." Tom feels that they may not have garnered that information if it weren't for the confidence and trust they instill.

Tom also feels that educating his clients is imperative. "A number of years ago a client introduced me to a minister's wife, who became a client," Tom begins. "She had little small understanding of what investments she was holding, and wasn't familiar with some of the investing basics such as diversification and asset allocation." Tom and members of the team held meetings with her at both the Legg Mason office and at her home. Many of the meetings involved educating the client, and subsequently, they were able to better understand their client's true needs. "The more a client understands, the more we can help them," he says. "Once this client had a better understanding, she felt more comfortable making certain decisions regarding her financial life, such as which home mortgage is most suitable, how much should she borrow, and how this affects her overall financial situation.

"Perhaps one of her best decisions," Tom says with a chuckle, "was to use a street name account—she had been writing down each dividend received over the previous 30 years. This new format gave her a wonderful sense of freedom. Once we helped her straighten out her finances, she and her husband felt comfortable taking vacations and engaging in activities that they may not have engaged in without an increased sense of comfort.

"When she passed on," Tom says in a softer voice, "her three sons were quite surprised at the amount she had left them." Over time, the portfolio had grown more than 18 times in value.

Tom admits that there have been times when clients haven't opened up. "I always tell my clients, 'advice is important, but you must have a sense of fitting,'" he says. "'If you don't have that sense of fitting, then maybe I'm not the right person. It might be in your best interest to find someone who is better suited for you.'"

Tom's son, Brad, contributes his experience from working with high-net-worth clients at PricewaterhouseCoopers to the Legg Mason team. "Brad has added a new dimension to the business," Tom explains. "We have been able to do some wonderful favors for clients that most financial advisors don't even consider." The younger Hill has helped set up numerous trusts, such as bypass trusts and charitable trusts, which are having a major impact on the clientele. "We're also examining clients' insurance policies, long-term care insurance, and many other gaps in most people's financial situation. And these so-called gaps can result in financial tragedies."

"When we meet with clients to discuss their financial future, we don't stop at their investment portfolio," Brad says. "We ask questions like, 'How is your estate plan set up?' 'How have you planned your estate tax liability?' Most of the people we speak to are unaware that they have exposure to the 'death tax.'" He explains that this punitive tax can eat away up to 55% of the estate, plus any state taxes. "With the proper planning, much of this can be avoided."

Brad works closely with a 91-year-old client who, after much encouragement to organize her finances, walked into the office carrying folders of stock certificates. "She also had diaries of all investment-related activity that she had ever been involved in. The disarray of her finances was just too burdensome for her and her family."

Brad and the team thoroughly examined the investment notes, stock certificate, and her entire financial situation. It was clear to Brad that the estate was going to be heavily taxed the way it was currently set up. "This client relies on a generous monthly income stream from a particular partnership," he says. "The problem was, the way it was set up, it had a very low value. Thus, when she passes away, the asset will be valued at a much higher level." Brad established a plan whereby she gifted the partnership to her heirs at the low value—and free of taxes.

The Hill group often suggests the use of a financial planner when meeting with a client. "The main part of our job is certainly our clients' investments, but it is by no means the only part,"Tom says."We try to look at an overall picture of where someone is and bring in a planner to cover areas outside of invest- ments. For example, to determine the most advantageous way to title their securities or their life insurance program, to determine whether they should consider long-term care insurance, or discussing the possible need for trusts. In many cases, gifting is appropriate and we will certainly provide them appropriate counseling along those lines.

"Financial planning is a growing area of interest with many people, and we feel it is the most complete form of service we offer."

Brad says in his friendly voice:"Whether we're meeting at my office or at a kitchen counter, we'll invite a very experienced financial planner to join us so that we can truly cover all aspects of a client's financial situation. Then clients end up knowing exactly where they stand, assured that their affairs are in as precise order as they possibly can be."

Tom generously offers his financial experience to the community. It is not surprising, given his heavy involvement in the community, that his favorite organization is the local YMCA. As past President of the organization and present member of the advisory board, he has contributed to the YMCA by raising membership to include 25% of the community."Both the adults and the kids are involved in good, healthy, wholesome programs." Tom was also in charge of the major gifts program that raised $2 million for a new building.

The following year, Tom helped raise another $2 million for the local hospice."The community really rallied for that cause," he says. Tom routinely gives 10% of his own income to charity every year.

Tom's sense of community also is evident in his work as a board member of Habitat for Humanity. "We build about four homes a year in Talbot County. Everybody needs a safe, comfortable place to sleep,"he says. Tom also manages to find time for the United Fund and local Rotary Club.

"Everyone has needs—whether they're financial or personal," says Tom. "Business or no business. We all need to give what we can. What matters to me is making a positive difference in someone's life."

CHAPTER 12:
GOING INDEPENDENT

BONNIE WUSZ
AN ADVISER WHO REALLY TEACHES

BW & Associates, Inc.
Torrance, California

It's been said that the future is not something we enter. The future is something we create.

This philosophy aptly pertains Bonnie Wusz's business. Bonnie's interest in managing her clients' wealth involves more than following a successful business model. It's her passion. She has a quest: to constantly exceed her clients' expectations. With her acute business savvy, investing know-how, and client-centric approach, she has remained competitive with the wire houses, and has surpassed them in many respects. But what truly sets her apart is her seeming simplicity. "I teach," she says.

Bonnie's story begins after her graduation from San Diego State University with a degree in mathematics. She knew from an early age that she wanted to teach, and her plans never changed. "I felt a great deal of satisfaction preparing high school students for their future," she says, describing her 11 years in the classroom. "The advanced math I taught enabled many of my students to get started on their way to becoming engineers, architects, and even financial advisors." Some of her students probed her for financial knowledge. "I helped them in any way I could. I loved being a part of their personal growth."

One day in 1983, a friend told Bonnie the writing was on the wall. "'With your desire to guide people to success, coupled with your analytical and communication skills, you'd make a great financial advisor,' he told me. I wondered if it was the next step for me: After all, it seemed perfectly logical," she reflects. Within months, she joined a major brokerage firm and obtained her licenses.

Initially, Bonnie hit the phones, cold-calling for business. "I soon found that the cold-calling method of acquiring clients that is typically taught by the wire houses was inappropriate for the overall financial plan I sought," she says. She intended to enlighten people on how to retire in what they considered to be financial dignity. This entails determining when they wish to retire, how much monthly income they will need in today's dollars, factoring in a projected inflation rate, and identifying their short-term, intermediate-term, and long-term goals. She would then take into consideration other information such as a client's marginal tax bracket, investment temperament, current assets and current rates of return, pension plans, inheritances, insurance and estate-planning needs, and more. According to Bonnie, this information is necessary to devise a financial plan that will enable them to meet their stated financial goals.

It is Bonnie's belief that many people tend to invest backwards. "Many people invest as the consequence of an aggressive sales person telling them why they need a particular product," she says. She prefers to define the financial goals, objectives and investment temperaments, then determine those investment vehicles that are best suited to meet those goals.

Obviously, cold calling was not conducive to Bonnie's financial-planning style.

She decided to revive the satisfaction she once felt as an instructor by teaching a financial planning course at a local college. "Returning to the classroom felt great," she says. "The attendees were very interested in learning how to prepare for their individual financial situations." Much to her surprise, many of the students stayed after class for additional investing information. Several became clients. "This opened up a whole new world for me," Bonnie recalls.

While teaching classes, she was able to assess the full gamut of financial situations her students were encountering: planning for children's college educations, buying homes or new cars, meeting insurance needs, estate planning, managing personal finances, and more. When Bonnie returned to her branch office after class, her manager would often encourage her to sell the firm's products, such as newly formed mutual funds, limited partnerships, and other firm-produced securities. "This wasn't for me," she says, pausing after each word. "I needed an experience that was appropriate to each client's personal objectives. And I felt driven to pursue my clients' individual needs." This was the point at which she considered building her own practice.

Executives of wire houses warned her of the disadvantages of an independent practice, including a lack of staff support, automated computer backup, and name recognition, not to mention limited product. However, Bonnie's research convinced her that they were wrong.

Bonnie performed her due diligence when selecting the right brokerage firm to stand behind her. "I interviewed many independent firms, but the one that really caught my eye was Spelman & Co., Inc. I had dealt with their two principals, Richard P. and Kaye Woltman in the past, and I was impressed with their integrity and professionalism. They made many promises to me at the time, promises that were kept several times over. They are true to their word. This is why their reputation is sterling," Bonnie continues. "Their service is excellent and they're always available if I need anything. Selecting them was the best career decision I ever made."

Spelman & Co., Inc. was purchased by Sun America in 1998; Richard P. Woltman was named chairman of the board and in September of 2000 James Cannon was named president. "Jim maintains the integrity and professionalism of Spelman & Co., Inc," Bonnie says. Through the company, she has found significantly greater product availability. Additionally, she enjoys other benefits. "There is no pressure for marketing quotas on proprietary products," she states firmly, then adds, "We have a much greater selection of mutual funds, variable and fixed annuities, and insurance products. This includes much deeper product selections of disability, long-term care, and life insurance. Neither the wire house nor the regional firm that I worked for in the past had anything close to product selection that was this encompassing."

Bonnie continues enthusiastically: "I have access to wrap accounts, listed and over-the-counter securities, and a prominent bond department. The extensive product availability enables me to recommend investment and estate planning options dictated by each client's particular family needs."

Bonnie is particularly proud of her office's computer capability, which aids in her ability to provide extensive services to her clientele. She believes it far surpasses the capabilities of the wire houses and regional firms. Using her system, she is able to download mutual fund and securities-related information directly from fund companies, as well as detailed information about her clients' Spelman brokerage accounts. She can instantly pull up current account information for any client, including cost basis, initial date of purchase, total purchase price, current value, dollar increase, and how the assets are allocated within equities, bonds, mutual funds, variable annuity sub account, and cash. "This enables me to very quickly and accurately relate to a client the status of his or her entire portfolio and individual holding in question," she says.

She's also proud of the system's additional capabilities. One of these is creating comprehensive yet simplistic portfolio reviews through which clients can easily decipher their portfolio performance. This includes total net (out-of-pocket) investment from the client over the years, total distributions plus the current value, income statements, and Schedule D reports, which calculate the actual long-term and short-term capital gains or losses. "This system is especially useful for systematic withdrawals from mutual funds," she says. She then points out her door to her team, and says proudly, "My team and I built a proprietary client-oriented financial-planning software."

To Bonnie, though she considers the company's computer system among the best in the industry, it's only second to her team. She carefully handpicks each member. "Our team is really top notch," she says. The team handles various tasks, involving operations, estate planning, and office management. They're comprised of registered sales administrators, computer specialists, and financial-plan designers for the best possible implementation of the team's plan.

Bonnie feels her independence from a wire house or regional firm enables her to provide "tremendously greater information, products and service." This independence has enhanced her name recognition as a result. This has led to a client base that has grown exponentially. More importantly, it has enabled her clients to integrate their financial, insurance and estate-planning needs, as well as to implement a strategy to achieve their stated goals.

Once Bonnie achieved her goal of setting up a private practice where she could provide a unique experience to each client and be free from pressure to sell proprietary product, she felt able to freely focus on building her business.

Bonnie initially introduced herself to several local colleges, offering investment seminars. "They requested that the seminar remain generic," she says. "I'm not allowed to discuss any particular product, such as a particular mutual fund or insurance company. When I discuss certain types of investments, it's in a generic fashion, and I make sure all the pros and cons are completely understood.

"In fact, many times students ask me, 'What investment do you recommend?' or 'What's the best way to profit from that?' I tell them, 'This is a generic seminar. During class, I am happy to tell you what to look for and where you can find the information. At the end of the seminar, each of you is entitled to a complimentary one-on-one discussion in my office, during which I can provide you with specific recommendations intended to help you achieve your stated goals.'"

Bonnie soon realized that when prospecting, her lack of affiliation with a major wire house was advantageous. "My seminars, which are typically at local colleges, are unaffiliated with any brokerage firm and free of product-specific information," she says. "The college class description states that I was with a major brokerage firm and now act as president of a firm that bears my name, and that I'm a registered securities principal with Spelman & Co., Inc."

It is with great irony that Bonnie ultimately built a great business through her teaching. She feels rewarded that she's able to offer such a large group of people financial-planning information. The seminar participants certainly value the complimentary financial plan that Bonnie offers. Students are given a data form which asks a series of questions about their financial situation, objectives, retirement aspirations, and risk tolerance. They're expected to return the form by the last session if they wish to take advantage of the financial plan. "I explain to them that the analyses will help them determine whether they're on track for their financial goals," she says. "And if they're not on track I provide them with recommendations consistent with their goals, objectives and temperament. I tell them, 'Don't worry, it's not the end of the world. Our analysis and recommendations will help you get back on track.'"

Bonnie warns her students that the data sheet could take them four to six hours to complete. But they're typically happy to invest the time, given that these plans will help them on their way to achieving their stated goals. "Plus, the plans would cost $750 if they had not attended the class," Bonnie says. "It's a great way to complement what they've learned about investing during the ten and a half hours they've spent in my class. I tell them to make the data form as accurate as possible because it's going to take my staff up to six hours to fully analyze the information and provide solid advice. Many people at this point are so adamant about doing the right thing that they bring in tax returns and other legal documents just to be sure they are filling out the sheet correctly."

After receiving a comprehensive analysis of their financial situation, students can opt to take advantage of the personal consulting Bonnie offers. "If their current strategy doesn't meet their objectives and take into account their risk tolerance," she says, "I'll recommend a reallocation of assets. I always recommend they first invest in their 401(k), if they have one. Early on in the conversation, I hand them an ADV Form Part II, which outlines my registered investment advisory role. I strongly suggest they read it because it discusses my educational background, previous work history, how long I've been in the business, and so on. More importantly, it mentions that I have a high degree of fiduciary responsibilities."

The number of seminar attendees has increased over time. Students frequently ask Bonnie when her next class is scheduled, and they often refer family members and friends. She has also been invited to provide her seminar series to the employees of Fortune 500 companies. Bonnie hesitates to offer more seminars than she currently gives, strictly because processing the financial plans is so time-consuming for her and the team. The comprehensive and quality plans she wants to provide demand significant preparation and presentation time.

Because Bonnie is a registered investment advisor, she discloses all pertinent information to the seminar participants, including the $69 the school charges for the seminar. "The real benefit of charging for the class is that the students really want to be there, and show up for all the classes," she says. "My students apologize profusely if they're late, miss a class, or feel they didn't properly fill out a data form."

Building a business based on a constant stream of new accounts, along with maintaining high-end customer service for existing clients, required Bonnie to build a "practice"-like configuration that could support her business structure. She is quick to note that the key to building an effective organization is, without doubt, hiring the right people. When she opened her doors in 1988, BW & Associates consisted of two people: Bonnie and an assistant. "This is when I really realized that I would have to create my own infrastructure according to how I was going to develop my client experience," she says.

Bonnie vividly remembers how frequently her clients and the clients of other advisors called with questions regarding the current status of their accounts; many brokers didn't have the answers. "I needed to develop a systematic method of tracking clients' reports and activity," she says. It took her a while before she figured out which method would best suit her needs. "I bought one software program because it was very user-friendly, but then discovered it wouldn't provide downloads," she explains. After speaking to many in the industry, she decided on a program that was flexible enough that it could grow with her over time. The program also had to be able to perform certain tasks that Bonnie felt her clients needed, such as asset allocation, and provide instantaneous in-depth information about all investments the client held. She also realized that the majority of the expense wasn't purchasing the software. The true expense was inputting hundreds of clients' previous transaction history. Once it is updated, the annual maintenance is relatively simple due to downloading capability.

"That's where our 'information services representative' fits in—she's a great fit," Bonnie says. "Now all transactional information on securities, whether it's mutual funds, annuities, or any other investment, is downloaded automatically." This makes it easy to format the data on the statement into a clear, concise, easy-to-read statement. She can customize how she wants the data to be viewed on her computer and client statements, for easy comprehensive access.

"My statement is very client-friendly," Bonnie says. "Clients have always asked how the components of their portfolio are performing versus the net. I spell this out in detail, including the date the investment was executed, profit and loss, illustrated asset allocations, and total return. The total return page is unique in that it tells clients how much cash they have contributed to the account, how much they have taken out, and the current value. This is particularly useful for our retired accounts who need to know how much they've taken out in terms of distributions versus the value today. The statement also allows clients to see how their asset classes are performing relative to each other. All data goes back to the first day the clients started doing business with me, or earlier, if they are able to provide us with a history of their accounts.

"We also include year-end Schedule D reports, the IRS form on which all capital gains and/or losses are calculated. Clients' CPAs appreciate this service—it saves the CPAs time, which in turn saves our clients money. Our clients love this type of service, and we get referrals from CPAs because it makes their jobs easier."

In 1992, Bonnie hired Laurel Hackett as receptionist. "She is so adept. Laurel caught on to the business very quickly and has a natural ability to manage and train people," Bonnie says. "She has since been promoted to office manager, and is responsible for hiring the rest of our top-notch team, which now numbers five people."

"Laurel has subsequently passed the NASD securities exams, which enables her to act as our Registered Administrative Assistant. She is instrumental in placing trades, meeting with our client for portfolio reviews and answering investment-oriented questions."

Laurel hired client services representatives who ensure that all activity, whether an account transfer or a direct trade, is processed through to fruition. She also keeps clients current on all activity, and calls them ahead of time when paperwork is being sent. Laurel also established an estate-planning professional to work with attorneys to set up estate plans for clients. She hired an individual to help compute and analyze all financial plans, including the data forms offered at the seminars. This team member also contacts clients for any additional information that is needed.

At Bonnie's request, Laurel devised a bonus system based on the business's year-end profitability. She also helped create a lucrative pension plan, which is funded by Bonnie. "We have formed such a strong team," Bonnie says. "We work very well together and we cover each other to make sure all clients are treated well."

Bonnie and team provide many extra services to clients, some of which are almost unheard of in the industry. "For example, our Schedule D provides our clients and their accountants with the tax gain/loss calculation if they have liquidated, taken systematic withdrawals, or reallocated within their portfolio," Bonnie says. "Simplistically stated, we provide comprehensive reporting depicting the bottom-line dollar amount the client has invested, the total amount withdrawn, and the total year-end value. In addition, we offer updated financial plans whenever life changes occur, such as a new child, retirement, sale of a house, etc."

Clients also appreciate the comprehensive financial planning they are offered, including long-term health care and term insurance. "We do all of the legwork for the client," Laurel says. "During this very administrative process, we take care of all paperwork, guide them with their premiums, and handle their reports."

And of course, there are the intensive portfolio reviews that Bonnie offers in addition to the regular statements. While many in the industry disapprove of the extra expense it requires, Bonnie continues with her costly performance reports. Creating the reports requires the equivalent of at least one full-time employee. "Bonnie feels it's so vitally important that clients remain informed and save time that she would do this at almost any price," Laurel says.

"The most rewarding part of my job is dealing with my clients," Bonnie says. "When I was a teacher, the students would come back every year or two. In my current situation, my students become my clients, so I have them for life. And just like a teacher who gets to teach generation after generation, I am often offered my clients' children's accounts. But best of all, I don't lose my students at the end of the school year. Our relationships continue to grow!"

THOMAS B. GAU, CPA, CFP™
BUILDING A FRANCHISE

Oregon Pacific Financial Advisors
Ashland, Oregon

See related sections:
Prospecting and Marketing: The Retirement Specialist
Building a Fee-Based Business: The Fee-Based Conversion

I magine building a financial advisory business that grows so rapidly that you can't hire people fast enough. As a result, you resort to buying another firm. Or consider a business model so effective that you only work six days a month. Meet Tom Gau. He saw a vision for the future of financial relationships. Now he is seizing the opportunity.

Tom's biggest frustration after earning his CPA was implementation. Fresh out of college and working for an accounting firm, he said, "I felt like a mechanic telling his customers that they needed to fix their own carburetors."

Never one to rest on his laurels, Tom added to his CPA credentials a Pepperdine University MBA, a USC financial-planning designation, and a CFP. In early 1985 he joined an insurance company for sales training. The manager promised trainees $100,000 a year in earnings if they successfully followed his program. The secret to this success, the sales manager told them, was five prospect meetings per week. Tom's instincts as a former CPA told him otherwise: he needed to spend *all his time* in front of clients and prospects. "Five meetings per week?" Tom asks me. "What do you do with the rest of your time?" For a CPA, there is very little if any implementation with financial planning services. In the securities industry there's usually no planning, and he couldn't act as fiduciary to clients. Couldn't there be a situation that offered the best of both worlds?

When earning prospects' business, it was evident to Tom his financial acumen had won them over, and the name of his firm ran a distant second. "At the end of the day, clients don't really care about the name of the firm because they all do the same thing. Clients are buying you," he says emphatically. "You've got to sell yourself, not your company."

Even though he would be giving up what little business he had already built, Tom knew his future depended on building his own firm. "It was very exciting for me," he explains. "As a CPA, I was very reactive, dealing with people's history. I wanted a situation where I could be reactive *and* proactive, helping individuals plan for their future." Tom started his first company, Financial Engineering, which he initially operated out of his house.

His niche was simple. "I'll find the answer to any financial question," he says he used to tell people. "And my account minimum was $1." He believed that once the account was opened and he had the opportunity to boast his financial talents, referrals were sure to follow. He started with family and friends, and always asked for referrals. This was his only form of marketing at the beginning. With a regular stream of referrals, Tom was visiting prospects and clients constantly, accruing over 3,000 miles every month. "I was doing everything for everyone," he exclaims, "but it worked out well for me."

Tax season was particularly fruitful for Tom. After preparing an individual's tax returns, he was sure to earn more business, as well as referrals. "Once I prepared the taxes and offered suggestions on how clients could improve their tax situation, I could take things to the next level and offer investment advice," he says.

As a comprehensive financial planner, Tom required prospective clients to provide a copy of their current tax return and a list of all assets. "If I didn't see the big picture, I wasn't going to help them. How can I give financial advice if I don't know the client's whole story?"

When Tom first met with a prospect, he explained the benefits of his broker-dealer, adding that deposits have SIPC protection since the money would be held in a securities firm. This openness eased many prospects' objections about trusting their money to a small firm.

Tom maintained close contact with many CPAs and attorneys. He found that speaking the same language, they trusted him enough to refer their clients. In 1986 he met an attorney, Phil Kavesh, who specialized in tax and estate planning and was also a tax attorney. Tom began providing financial services for Phil's clients. After nearly ten months of collaboration, their working relationship proved to be a viable one, worthy of a potential partnership. On September 15, 1987, the two opened the doors to a new firm, Kavesh & Gau, Inc. Financial Counselors, which later became Oregon Pacific Financial Advisors.

Tom moved the business to a 500-square-foot office, which he shared with Phil and two administrative assistants. It was then that he fit the last piece into the financial puzzle. "In addition to preparing taxes, assisting with insurance needs, managing investments, and planning for retirement, our firm could now offer estate planning, with Phil preparing trusts and offering legal advice. It's like building a house," he explains, "You need an architect to draw up the plans and a contractor to coordinate all the subcontractors. Otherwise, you would have a lot of people running around building different components of the house, and it would just fall apart. The same goes for financial planning. Everything needs to fit in with your overall plan. This is how we're able to ask our clients questions like: 'How is this affecting your overall taxes? Is this asset properly titled? Have you considered a trust to provide these benefits?'"

On the first day the duo opened their doors for business, Tom and Phil found it nearly unbelievable that they had successfully combined a financial-planning platform with legal expertise. "But why isn't the phone ringing off the hook?" one of them asked.

Business was slow for the first year as they continued to redefine their business model. They identified two necessary components lacking from their plan: a niche, which would be retirement; and credibility, built through advertisements. They tested this by offering a financial-planning seminar designed to appeal to people's emotional issues. They also tested a seminar on estate planning. Both seminars proved to be successful. They continued to rework their seminar by trial and error until they formulated a winning strategy. (See *Prospecting and Marketing: The Retirement Specialist.*) Finally, their business started to take off.

Other sources for seminars were the Elks Lodge, the Moose Lodge, and virtually any organization that would accept speakers. They also offered to provide retirement-planning seminars for both small and large corporations.

Originally, their business model called for charging a fee for the financial-planning service, then charging money-management fees. While there were some takers, "many prospects asked why *we* charged fees for financial planning and the wire houses didn't," Tom says. "Our typical response was, 'When was the last time your broker looked at your tax return? How often does he or she give tax advice?' These are fun questions to ask because most wire houses place disclaimers on everything regarding tax advice. We take full liability—not only do we look at tax returns, we actually prepare them! We know a client's financial situation better than anyone. The wire houses are scared to take the liability— this never made sense to me." Still, the fees that were being levied dismayed many prospects. "We tested these fees for a year, then decided we would provide financial services as part of our compensation for managing the assets," Tom says of the 1989 test year. "We hoped we would make enough through our money-management program to compensate."

The next year was a banner year. "We cut our hourly fees dramatically and our net revenues went through the roof!" Tom says excitedly. "People quickly realized that we were doing ten times the work of our competition. They also realize that our results saved them a lot of money and time and taxes!"

A case in point: A client showed up for his initial meeting prepared with all the tax- and investment-related information Tom had requested. Looking it over, Tom quickly noticed that no distributions had been taken from his $1.2 million IRA. "The man looked at me and said, 'My broker told me that I should let it continue to accumulate tax-free because I have sufficient income from my other assets.' I noticed on his tax return that he had a lot of rental income and a mortgage on his house; he also had a negative taxable income of $80,000. I asked him, 'Don't you think we should at least take $80,000 from your IRA to bring your taxable income up to zero?'" The client later thanked Tom, saying that his accountant prepared his taxes and his broker never looked at the big picture. "Nobody is coordinating these activities," Tom tells me. "That's what we're all about."

In another situation, an individual with a large IRA reached the age of 70—the same year that his wife passed away. He was told he would have to take out a significant distribution that would have cost him $100,000 in taxes. Tom's meeting with this client, fortunately, was in March of 1999. As Tom well knew, the tax law reads that the participant has up to April 1 after the year he reaches 70? to make or change any elections. "My new client told me that he had made his election, and that he took out his minimum distribution last year," Tom recounts. "'I don't care,' I told him, 'you still have a few more days to change that election." The client contacted his broker, who in turn called his tax department, which said that it couldn't be done. Tom then called the tax department and provided a quick lesson on the law. The client saved over $100,000, and decided to transfer all his accounts to Tom. "What else didn't the broker know?" Tom asks skeptically.

Tom believes that the major difference between tax law and investing is one reason there's so much room for error. Tax law is a matter of fact, and investing is a matter of opinion. "I've helped over 9,000 people retire in the last 15 years," he says with satisfaction. "After you've done it a few thousand times, you get the hang of it!" Tom adds, "Most affluent people want a specialist, and retirement is my specialty."

Tom set up his firm with specialists to handle varying client relationships. For example, his company includes CPAs, CFPs, insurance professionals, and attorneys. This local expertise allows him to fully leverage his time. By receiving the prepared tax returns from a CPA, or a newly prepared trust from a lawyer, he can spend as much time as possible with his clients.

In addition to the specialists, Oregon Pacific Financial Advisors has twelve planners including Tom. A vast staff that includes receptionists, administrative assistants, secretaries, file clerks, and a marketing coordinator supports the planners.

The office leverage that Tom constructed allows him to spend six days a month with a succession of face-to-face appointments. "Anytime you're not meeting with clients is wasted time," he says in a serious tone. He is so adamant about meeting with clients that his support staff's compensation is partly tied to maintaining a busy meeting schedule. A busy schedule for Tom means 60 to 65 appointments per week, all back to back. His first appointment begins at 7 a.m. and his last one doesn't begin until 8 p.m. Investment review meetings last half an hour; initial and follow-up meetings last one hour.

After the meetings, Tom's day is far from over. His marketing coordinator arranges several retirement-planning seminars a week. Most seminars are open to prospects and clients, while some are available to major companies around Los Angeles.

The prospect overload Tom experienced from his exceedingly successful seminars has led to a lack of qualified financial advisors to bring in new business. "I'm always looking for individuals with strong retirement-planning experience, preferably with a CFP or equivalent," he says. "Most importantly, qualified applicants need to be good listeners."

To add to his roster, Tom merged Kavesh & Gau with a Phoenix-based financial-planning firm, The Householder Group, Inc., a Registered Investment Advisory firm, which currently has over 30 representatives in Phoenix, and some in Los Angeles. He is also planning an expansion into the San Francisco, Denver, and Las Vegas areas.

The merger represents, in essence, Tom's ability to franchise his successful seminar-marketing strategy and operating model. Upon completion of a merger, he closely trains individuals to deliver the powerful seminars that have proven to be so successful for him. Tom now devotes his time to the Ashland, Oregon branch office, now referred to as Oregon Pacific Financial Advisors.

His success has also spawned another company called "Million Dollar Producer, Inc." which trains other advisors to increase their production while working less. Several times a year, Tom presents two-day "Boot Camps," designed to share his systematic approach to marketing, customer service, and time management to other financial advisors in the U.S. and Canada.

When he isn't in Los Angeles during his six-day office retreat, Tom spends a few days a month meeting with clients in his Oregon office and the rest of his time with his family in Ashland, Oregon. He also finds time to serve on Southern Oregon University's Foundation Board of Trustees.

What keeps him going? "It's simple. I love helping people," he says with a smile.

CHAPTER 13:
INVESTMENT PHILOSOPHIES

MARTIN SHAFIROFF
REDEFINING VALUE

Lehman Brothers
New York, New York

M artin Shafiroff is one of the industry's living legends. Now in his third decade as the nation's top producing financial advisor, he has been featured in several books and countless magazine and newspaper articles. Remarkably, he has used his highly disciplined investment philosophy and approach to gain access to the world's corporate leaders, entrepreneurs, entertainers, and individual investors. His investment philosophy has also helped him access over a trillion dollars in client-related assets.

Although Martin's dream was to become a financial advisor, he initially avoided selling securities because he had no contacts. This was during the mid-1960s, when personal contacts were believed to be the essential ingredient for success in the business. Furthermore, Martin didn't know anyone in the industry he could contact to even set up an interview.

Martin grew up in a middle-class background, working at his father's plumbing supply business during the summer. Wall Street seemed a long way from Brooklyn. Still, it was Martin's dream to enter the securities business. After graduating from Baruch College, where he majored in finance and investments, Martin gained sales experience working for a small industrial company, where he made $8,000 a year. He diligently put every extra dollar into his investment account, and intensively researched his own investment ideas.

Using his finance degree and his investment knowledge, Martin could have become an analyst or money manager. "I decided to go into sales," he explained, "because I enjoyed communicating with people on a personal basis and felt I could apply my knowledge of securities in a more helpful and intimate manner." In time, though, his desire to be a stockbroker became so overwhelming that he decided to pursue his dream, no matter what obstacles he would encounter.

Finally, when Martin was 28 years old, he called five brokerage houses and pleaded for interviews. He was quickly rejected from the personnel departments at four firms, and then got a break at the fifth, Eastman Dillon Union Securities, where the sales manager was willing to interview him. Though impressed with the high level of enthusiasm and knowledge of the candidate, the sales manager pointed out that there were many qualified people but few sales positions. Then, breaking momentarily from the interview, the manager took a telephone call in which he discussed the investment potential of a particular company he personally owned. After the manager hung up, Martin admitted that he couldn't help but overhear the discussion, and revealed that he himself held an investment position in that company. The manager, startled, asked Martin a series of questions about the company, particularly how it was structured and positioned among its competitors in its niche. Martin quickly impressed the manager about his in-depth knowledge of the company and the nuances of the industry itself. By the end of the conversation, the sales manager had determined that Martin wouldn't have to go through an extensive training program. He was ready to move right into the program. Martin would finally become a financial advisor.

After the interview, Martin realized that it had been his first real sales presentation: He was selling himself and the knowledge he possessed. There was no need to oversell or guess; Martin's straightforward reliance on sound analysis was to become an integral part of his long-term approach to selling securities.

In 1966, Martin began his career in the securities industry and in 1969 he joined Lehman Brothers. Early on, he recognized that his success would be the result of high-quality work standards—in short, substance over generalities. His knowledge of investments, acquired by managing his personal portfolio, became his sales tool for approaching prospects. The strategy he had adopted was attuned to seeking out market values and a long-term investment prospective. Martin was determined: His approach to securities would reflect his insights and point of view. "If I were just in the market selling a product that everybody else had, I don't think I would have been very successful," he says. "My investment ideas are unique. They clearly differentiate me from my competitors."

Martin cultivated his approach into a full-fledged business strategy, one that encompassed industry research as well as stock selection and timing. His modus operandi was to work from detailed sources of solid information that included in-depth interviews with competitors and the personal testing of products. His research specialization gave him a leg up toward his goal: long-term investments with long-term accounts interested primarily in unrecognized values with the potential for dramatic results.

"Initially I focused my calls by defining the group I wanted to communicate with, senior people in the corporate world," Martin explains. "I would work with executives of the most highly rated 2,000 companies and call this internationally select group. I have found that many successful executives are exceptional at describing their company's operations and delineating the future of their companies, but they may not be efficient investors. They are completely involved in their jobs and consequently tend to overlook their personal investment affairs, which should be equally important. Sometimes these individuals assign the responsibility for their investment portfolios to others without establishing a sound basis for achieving results.

In particular, Martin's selection of potential clients was geared to mesh well with his approach. The highly placed corporate officers he chose to contact had come to understand the workings of the market, and thus could respect Martin's emphasis on value. More importantly, these were individuals with whom Martin could relate. He spoke their language and he understood their needs. By specializing in this particular affluent market he became increasingly comfortable dealing with people at this level, and they could sense it.

"I work with a client who is interested in preserving and building his or her capital," Martin goes on to say. "In my work, I seek out what can be considered a value area, and I determine where a gap has been created in the marketplace. Since I look for values, I continually review domestic and foreign securities, private partnerships, hedge funds and real estate. I try to find special situations or special timing for investments in these groups. My feeling is that an investment vacuum exists in America today. Institutions are buying into a limited number of companies, and even though individual interest in securities has increased over the past couple of decades, there are magnificent companies with substantial book values that are selling at four to five times their cash flow. These companies have the potential for outstanding returns on capital and on equity, but they lack publicity and sponsorship. In my opinion, this area offers the greatest investment opportunity in the years ahead. I believe that many of these companies could not be duplicated today for two or three times their market values, but one must have patience in these investments until recognition comes. When that time does come, the potential on the upside is quite dramatic. Therefore, I have a strategy and philosophical approach to what I am doing. I find an investment that meets these requirements. I am now prepared to present both my approach and my investment suggestion."

Here is a story that demonstrates how Martin implements his theory. A number of years ago, he called the wealthy owner of a Midwestern coal company from his New York office. He introduced himself and asked the individual a few questions about his investment portfolio. The prospect told Martin that he invested only in bonds. In fact, he had hundreds of millions of dollars in bonds. "I'm very satisfied with my broker," he said. "He's an expert in his field, and we happen to be good friends. Mr. Shafiroff, you are wasting my time and yours by trying to sell me equities."

"I have no desire to work with you in bonds," Martin replied. "Because, at best, I am only mediocre in bonds. This being the case, I would rather not do business with you."

"I appreciate that you're being up front with me," said the prospect. He then told Martin about his successful coal company, which was evidently a source of great pride to him.

"We talked at some length about business in general," Martin recalls. "Then I asked him: 'What other businesses are you interested in?' He seemed to warm up after I asked this question."

The conversation continued like this: "You know, one of my dreams has always been to own a life insurance company," the prospect said.

"Oh, really?"

"Yes, life insurance is what I call a great business."

"Well, who knows?" Martin replied. "We may be able to do business after all. Let me go to my firm and see if the opportunity exists for us to start a life insurance company. If I come up with something that looks interesting, I'll get back to you."

"Now remember," the prospect said very seriously, "I'm not into equities. But owning my own life insurance company—yes, that's intriguing. I'll look forward to hearing from you, Mr. Shafiroff."

After the two ended the telephone conversation, Martin began researching the insurance industry. Before long, he came across a life insurance company that was selling at a very low price after the company rejected a peaceful takeover bid. The stock had taken a big hit and was selling substantially below its book value: in fact, to the tune of nearly 50%. After performing his usual diligent research, Martin realized that he liked everything about the company. And at that discount to book, he thought it was a tremendous value. This company met all the criteria that the prospect had in mind for buying a life insurer. "Everything, that is, except one," Martin points out. "It was a publicly owned company, and he had no interest in buying equities. He specifically said he wanted to invest in a privately held company. This meant I'd have to convert him in order for us to do business."

Martin's first step was to demonstrate to the prospect just what it would take to build a life insurance company from scratch. He worked up a proposal, using a figure of $20 million to represent the initial value. He also illustrated how sales and branch offices would be established, as well as hiring managers and salespeople. Obtaining a top rating from the industries rating company, A.M. Best, would be difficult, he pointed out.

"I took him through all the steps," Martin says. "I estimated that all this would require substantially more than the $20 million. Even with that commitment, I added, we would be only a regional participant until we built up enough capital and experience to become national."

Martin submitted this information to his potential client in a simple and direct package of correspondence. He waited a few days for him to receive it before he called. "Did you have a chance to review the material I sent?" Martin asked.

"Yes," the man answered. "You make it look like quite an undertaking."

"It is," Martin told him, "but I have another possibility. There is a company on the New York Stock Exchange called The Life Insurance Company.* It is selling at nearly one half of book value! If we buy this company on the open market, instead of putting up $20 million for book value, we can accumulate the same dollar amount for $10 million. We won't have to go through all the start-up procedures, hoping to get an A+ rating from A.M. Best. Why, The Life Insurance Company holds the highest rating already! We don't have to recruit a management team or develop a sales force either." Martin paused, then said: "We wouldn't be a regional—we would be a national! The company is about 100 years old and is already well known. So, we don't have to go knock on doors saying, we've been in business for a few months, and we'd like you to have a long-term commitment with us."

* *Fictitious name.*

Martin waited for the prospect to digest the information. Then he asked a question: "Why pay two or three times as much to create something when we can buy a public vehicle—one that we can sell at any time—and receive a substantial cash dividend while we're waiting for the results?"

Suddenly, the man who had opposed owning equities saw the picture: the tremendous discount and value of going right into position with a public company versus the tribulations of creating a private company. "After I showed him that equities could provide exactly what he wanted to accomplish," Martin recalls with satisfaction, "he no longer viewed the transaction as 'playing the market'."

Immediately following that conversation, the client bought a sizable equity position in the company. Over a period of time, the investor accumulated more and more holdings in The Life Insurance Company. "This excellent investment turned out to be the beginning of our long-term friendship," Martin says. "Over the years, I found other discounted bargains in which he took equity positions."

The client later told Martin that his equity portfolio was larger than his bond portfolio. "Believe it or not, I don't view these investments as stocks," he said. "Instead, I review them as values. These are businesses that cannot be duplicated for twice the price."

In this example, Martin clearly demonstrates how a financial advisor must be resourceful and, through an innovative approach, present one's product in a way that fulfills the customer's needs. Martin's fact-finding session turned a quick "Goodbye, I'm not interested" into something meaningful. He understood his prospect's goals, in particular, the dream to own an insurance company. He was able to make the case that owning equity in a public company would fulfill the prospect's dream.

Martin has fine-tuned his investment philosophy into a four-phase design that applies to both new and established accounts. He considers this business plan unique in its dynamic orchestration. The first phase requires a complete understanding of the product. Here, the tools of research and analysis are central, but so are monitoring the changes that can alter basic fundamentals.

"Understanding the operations of a particular corporation and how it fits within its industry niche is the key," Martin explains. "I am interested in situations that show value. I have to gain an understanding of why there may be value in the current price of a company that I'm examining as a potential investment. I also have to know how to find the companies that I believe will give investors the greatest value. Because my clients understand value, they relate to my strategy and investment selection."

In the strategic phase of Martin's business design, he again focuses on the principle of value. "I determine where a gap has been created in the marketplace. Since I look for values, I continually review domestic and foreign securities, real estate, private partnerships and hedge funds. I try to find special situations or special timing for investments within these groups."

When Martin sees an opportunity, such as changing market conditions, he develops a strategy that is in tune with that change. This strategy becomes the basis for a series of individual investment selections. "For example," he says, "if the economy looks weak, and you think interest rates are going down, that becomes the basis for a strategy. I like to buy investments with substantial cash flows and growing cash dividends. If interest rates go down these cash flows and dividends enhance the relative value of these investments. You assume that strategy to guide your research and tune in on a particular investment to recommend for purchase. Thus, you are able to convert a strategy into a practical idea."

Product and strategy are only the first two phases of Martin's successful business design; the remaining sequence emphasizes conviction and urgency. "I want to convert prospects into legitimate accounts, accounts who will have an interest in my approach. I want to build on these accounts with the ultimate goal of tailoring each portfolio to fit the individual's needs and objectives." Martin effectively communicates these ideas to his clients.

"I firmly believe that you must have strong convictions about your approach and your individual ideas," Martin says. "Only then can you effectively communicate with your ongoing accounts and prospects. Essentially, if you want to succeed in investments or sales, the first person you must convince is yourself. When you show enthusiasm based on the kind of information you value personally, the party evaluating your comments is going to react accordingly. For this reason, I believe that an individual in this business must seek out, study, review, and analyze a substantial investment spectrum until he fully comprehends the advantages of both a particular strategy and of a product whose qualities are consistent with that strategy. When I seek accounts, I am convinced that the people I am talking to are missing a great opportunity if they do not choose to participate in the values I am offering. This conviction maximizes the sales potential in any client contact."

The effectiveness of conviction in the sales process, Martin points out, can be measured by elements such as tone of voice or choice of words. "Whether you are in person or on the telephone, an individual can hear conviction in your voice," he says. "Conviction comes across in the way you naturally express yourself. If you don't have conviction, the prospect will sense it and you are not going to be very successful."

To Martin, conviction comes easy. He believes so strongly in his investment ideas that if a prospect's goals and objectives match the expectations of the investment, he sees little reason for them not to enter into the transaction. This is why he places listening skills high on the list of qualities that make a successful financial advisor.

"A good salesperson is also a good listener," he insists. "You have to ask many questions and carefully listen to the answers." Martin will ask a prospect dozens of questions to determine his or her goals, risk tolerance, investing experience, and interests. As Martin carefully—and actively—listens to a prospect, his conviction increases. Why? Because he has a better sense of the client's needs, and the client appreciates the personal interest.

In Martin's business design, conviction and urgency are linked. Because he generates a limited number of investment ideas a year, timing can be crucial. "Once I sense that an investment is a good value, an urgency arises to take immediate action," Martin explains. "Say I am informed of an investment selling near its low. If other people are pessimistic, I become more convinced about my ideas. I look for well-managed companies that are good values and have temporarily lost favor with the investment community. I want to act first with such investments because I believe it's only a matter of time before the investors recognize these good buys."

Through the very nature of this research-focused investing approach, Martin is able to convert prospects into legitimate accounts and tailor each portfolio to fit the individual's needs and objectives.

"You know," Martin says, his serious expression giving way to a look of disbelief, "so many advisors say they're going to stop attempting to develop new business and reduce their research updates so they won't be neglecting their present clients. That is wrong. They'll lose the momentum of their inflow of marketplace information, and that is what I consider the key to success. Of course, one reason I don't have that kind of problem is the way I approach investing. I'm not primarily involved in active trading. I'm essentially looking for long-term investments that enable my clients to build substantial positions in a number of special situations. Because I'm not concentrating on aggressive trading, my clients become accustomed to building up positions over a period of time. On a given account, we make a limited number of investments throughout the year. So, as a long-term buyer, I am not really involved in day-to-day communication with my clients." Martin adds that because his typical client profile is a corporate executive, their mindset tends to think long-term. "They're interested in, and planning for, the long-term."

Martin's approach to focusing on generating investment ideas is very conducive to working with prospects. Along the way, Martin has learned that prospecting and researching his investment ideas go hand in hand. When prospecting corporate-level executives, he is often led to new investment ideas. Over the last several years, his business has grown to include new product lines. Conversely, his approach to discovering new investment ideas is generating substantial new business. This involves extensive meetings and interviews with executives of the companies or partnerships he's evaluating. Many of these individuals become so impressed with Martin's know-how and the value of his research insights that they eventually become clients.

"One of the characteristics of the companies that I look at," Martin says, "is an experienced management team. An experienced team means that the investment characteristics are compelling, and can eventually lead to enhanced valuations. In addition to a strong management team, my strategy involves a return of the client's investment over a period of time. At this point, a client could end up owning an asset, say a master limited partnership, or MLP, worth many millions of dollars when the original investment is taken out in the form of sheltered cash distributions." Depending on the client, Martin may recommend reinvesting the cash distributions back into the MLP to enhance the client's total return. "Over time, the success of the company is likely to result in an increase in distributions and the paydown of company debt. This will mean a substantial increase in the enterprise value."

The MLPs Martin invests in coincide with his wealth-preservation, asset-allocation and growth strategy for clients. Consequently, he is able to utilize MLPs to balance his clients' equity portfolios. He compares MLPs to bond-like instruments without a fixed distribution. "If management performs," he explains, "your cash returns increase. These steady and real cash flow streams are designed to return most of a client's investment in the form of sheltered cash, so, over time, the investor over time has little or no original money in the investment. This way a profit cushion is created. If there is a decline in returns, it will eat into profits, not principal." Additionally, Martin recommends that clients hold a number of MLPs for better diversification within this asset class

Another cornerstone of Martin's business is equity-related partnerships that invest in privately held assets. Martin's proven approach to private-equity investments involves deriving long-term value from fundamental opportunities for growth by selecting proven management teams that have a compelling business strategy. The key to success in this sector, says Martin, is picking the right general partners who appreciate value and stick to their philosophy. "The investments can be very diverse, such as company leveraged buyouts, opportunity real estate and later-stage venture capital. We establish partnerships with very diversified portfolios." In addition, Martin may opportunistically make private investments in operating companies that are already public.

"Each partnership has a management team that is compensated not for simply holding the assets, but for returns that are gained by properly investing," Martin says. Often, the management team will have hurdle rates, where a predetermined rate of return is required before management begins to share in the upside. "This way, the management shares in the upside, but only after they have achieved a reasonable return for their investors."

Martin's primary role in this aspect of his business is making a judgment on the company or partnership and allocating an appropriate amount of funds. When seeking these opportunities, Martin takes a close look at the record of the company, including its management team. He interviews around 200 CEOs and CFOs every year. "I look at the record, and behind the record," he explains. "I'm looking at the disciplines that exist, searching for what's real and what isn't real."

After an investment has been made, Martin arranges "Meet the Management" programs. "As a service to our clients, this gives our investors an opportunity to hear corporate leaders discuss their companies and strategies," he says. "It's a great way for investors to get involved on a deeper level and provides a very tangible element to understanding their investments. For new investments, we continually monitor the management team for consistency and results. We establish very specific goals for these opportunities." He points out that while these investments may not be the next "tech craze," they represent steady and real returns.

Martin's investment philosophy can be illustrated simply. "First," he says, "you have a concept. Then you apply that concept to a real asset or investment and monitor that investment." Martin credits his success in large part to this product focus, which has differentiated him from his competitors. "If you move too far away from your strengths, you become compromised," he says. "I never want to take my eye off the major challenge, which is to protect principle and generate reasonable returns. I am always making a judgment and advising people on how they should invest their money." Martin spends most of his time evaluating investments and determining which ones should be a part of his clients' holdings.

He describes the evolution of his wealth-building investment philosophy as just that: an evolution. "I am always seeking value, whether it's in the private or public marketplace. When I first started my business, cash commitments were much smaller." Today, Martin's clients will each invest anywhere from $250,000 to $75 million in one of his investment ideas.

As Martin's business has grown and become more sophisticated, his operations have been enhanced. The dissemination of reliable and comprehensive information remains a hallmark of his system. He leads a team of people, each person delegated with a particular function to service the client's needs. The team is responsible for reviewing equity research, finding undervalued situations, evaluating partnerships, hedging risk, and servicing clients. Martin's rationale is simple: "Assemble a group of experts who are meticulous in their respective disciplines and work as a team." During meetings with clients, the team of experts is at hand while Martin and the client develop a broad investment strategy. "With this in mind, a client will always be dealing with an experienced party regarding any area of concern that he or she may have."

When Martin first started out in the securities field, he had the courage to cast aside his fears of rejection and develop a discipline for excellence. By doing so, he was able not only to overcome his fear but, in the process, to build a list of clients that today reads like a "Who's Who" in America. The Martin Shafiroff success story is a classic because it sticks to the fundamentals of the security industry. It's a story that proves how knowledge and perseverance are winning tools for success.

RICHARD F. CONNOLLY, JR.
QUALITY IS JOB NUMBER ONE

UBS PaineWebber, Inc.
Boston, Massachusetts

When people speak of high-quality financial advisors in the business, Dick Connolly's name should not be omitted.

"Growing up, I learned from the best," Dick says. Growing up in a tight-knit family of modest means, he acquired a strong work ethic early on. "My father gave all he could—in terms of money, support and hard work. He supported the family, gave to the community, and anyone who asked. He never made more than $10,000 per year, and he was the most giving person you've ever met. Yet I couldn't put on his shoes on the best day I've ever lived," he says. As a teenager, Dick contributed to the family coffer by caddying at local golf clubs. Thanks to his hard work as a caddy, he was able to earn a college scholarship to Holy Cross. As a student, he continued to work part-time, and made sufficient money to support himself, and to send home. "I also learned a great deal about human nature because you see people at their best and at their worst on the golf course." By his sophomore year, he was promoted to head greens keeper. Working on the golf course also helped pay his way through a Babson College MBA. He planned to seek a career in sales, "Because only in sales could I excel at my own pace," he says.

In 1964, after graduation, Dick joined the Ford Motor Company as a field manager on Long Island. "I was in a training program that lasted almost two years. This was a high-powered program where I learned a great deal about customer service and selling. After the training program, I became a field manager, calling on dealers and selling Ford's products. The most important thing I learned from my experience with Ford is how to deal with people."

Faced with the prospect of relocating and ending up in Detroit, Dick decided it was time to find a new direction for his career. Tales of Wall Street told by a friend's father led him to explore opportunities as a stockbroker. He began by lining up several meetings with successful brokers to learn the ins and outs of their careers. Interested in what he learned, he arranged interviews with a number of brokerage firms and soon had his pick among several offers. His choice was a firm with corporate headquarters in the Wall Street district.

When Dick got started in the business, he positioned himself so that he could learn from the best. In his office, during off-hours, he would ask the successful brokers many questions. At one point, he even talked his way into working next to one of the bigger-producing financial advisors. "He was a real trader," Dick says, thinking back to the early 1970s. "When this broker started in the business, the market was strong, and it continued to perform well. This enabled him to trade successfully. He was a very intelligent guy, and he studied his charts, looking for the great trades." The veteran 30-year-old trader was entering as many as five to seven trades per account every day. Most of his accounts were trading accounts.

A year later, the oil embargo changed everything. Interest rates skyrocketed, a major recession ensued, and the market entered a protracted decline. The stock trader lost his entire business, and Dick learned a crucial lesson. "It's obviously pretty difficult to succeed as an active trader in a bear market," he says, "unless you're a great short seller."

He noticed that the brokers who continued to succeed had similar traits. "They didn't have any gimmicks; they just built solid businesses," Dick recalls. "They all worked extremely hard, and their customer service was exceptional. If they sold a customer a stock, it was a high-quality stock. In this business you need a great deal of credibility. Promoting high-quality product and offering superior service is the only way to do it." He also believes that those who build businesses based on trends must be prepared for the day when the trend doesn't turn out to be their friend.

"Professional stockbrokers are like professional baseball players," Dick says in his Boston accent. "The players who are solid year in and year out are the ones who constantly enhance and practice their craft. They are always perfecting the basics."

The trader who lost out during the oil embargo remained in the business, rebuilding a book of investors, not traders. "He learned the hard way," Dick says with relief. "From then on, he never bought anything but long-term, high-quality stocks. This is how I learned to buy quality stocks and hold onto them for 10 to 20 years."

Today, Dick only buys quality stocks, "particularly when they're out of favor," he adds. "If they beat up major firms, I would consider buying. It's rare that a major company experiencing a tremendous correction doesn't recover.

"One of my favorite times to pick up stock is when a stock sells off significantly, and the institutions dump it at the end of the quarter to get it off their books because they just don't want the name in their portfolio. This may send the stock to long-time lows." He considers the heavy scrutiny portfolio managers get to be a great advantage to him. "They are judged by the short term, quarter by quarter. This is a major disadvantage for them. I'm measured by the very long term."

Generally, Dick defines a long-term hold as one that lasts an entire business cycle, typically three to seven years. "If you buy a great company, regardless of what the economy is doing in the short term, it is likely to work out fine over the long term," he says. He also mentions that it takes discipline to buy when everyone is against you.

Dick calls himself an eclectic contrarian due to his unique ideas and against-the-herd mentality. And because of his investing style, he doesn't measure his performance against indexes because there's no direct relationship. "If we are concentrated in the drugs and banks," he explains, "there's no use in comparing us to an S&P 500 or Dow, or even industry indexes. Additionally, we may move into an entirely new sector if we feel the time is right."

As an example of moving into a new industry group, Dick refers to 1982 when the oil sector was out of vogue. "Oils were an inferior group," he says. "I remember looking at one of the greatest oil companies in the world, which sold at a long-time low with a 10% dividend." He adds: "I'm a great believer in dividend support if you can get it. It's a means of getting paid while you wait for the capital appreciation."

He continues: "With the stock at a low, it was very unlikely that this major oil company was going to cut the dividend. That would be a kiss of death. I said to myself, 'If I buy this stock now, and it does nothing, I'm still getting 10%. How bad could that be?' If the stock appreciates by 10% while you're receiving the dividend, you can start earning some attractive returns."

Acting on his convictions, Dick recommended a great deal of the stock for his clients' accounts, and bought some for himself. Their total returns far outperformed the indexes. "This is a perfect example of how to seek attractive returns without high exposure to risk," he says. "My ideal situation is to buy low-beta, or low-volatility, stocks and still outperform." Dick points out that his clients are often telling him how pleased they are to get attractive returns with minimal risk exposure. "All my customers know my style," he says. "It's worked out very well for them and for me." However, he is quick to point out that just because a stock gets beaten down and the company happens to be a household name doesn't make it a buy. "You still have to do your homework," he says seriously. "When a quality stock tanks, we immediately start our own analysis."

Valuable information comes from his ongoing contact with UBS Warburg analysts and many companies' top-level executives who follow the stock. He notes that it's important to have as many "friends" as possible. "If my research is favorable, and my perception from these contacts is that the sell-off is extreme, then I'll be inclined to buy the stock."

An advantage in evaluating stocks, Dick adds, is a broad and detailed knowledge of the field. "We are knowledgeable in many areas," he says, "and we're very adaptable." He offers two examples. In the mid-1980s, bank stocks were out of favor due to the savings and loan crisis. At that time, he became proficient in the area by researching, studying, and meeting with analysts and bank executives. "After that, people considered me knowledgeable in the banking industry," he says. Consequently, his clients' portfolios that contain the bank stocks have performed very well. In the mid-1990s, utilities were out of favor. "I'm very intrigued with the utility industry. Not only is the yield support attractive for these companies, currently above 6% for a high-quality issue, but there's a tremendous wave of better regulation, along with consolidation in terms of mergers and buyouts. When you can buy low-beta stocks and experience all these positives, things usually work out very well for shareholders," he says. "Utilities aren't the old sleepy utilities they were 20 years ago." He considers certain utilities as solid long-term buys with the added kicker of potential takeovers.

When evaluating companies, Dick says, it all comes down to earnings and management. "I look at companies with strong earnings records, companies with a solid, experienced management team that has vision and can carry the firm's mission." Then he digs deeper into earnings potential, and studies the products. "If it's a drug company, what does their product pipeline look like?" More fundamentals are considered: "How does the price-earnings multiple look? Do they pay a dividend? Are they likely to buy back their own stock? Do the insiders own a lot of the company's stock? What are the prospects for the industry? If it's the drug stocks, it's obvious that the whole world is going to need medical attention."

Although Dick would not rely on technical analysis solely to make a trade, he may utilize UBS Warburg's technical analysts' opinions as a timing device. "If all the fundamentals are in place, I may look at the technicals to try to get the best price," he explains. "I view it as a caddie: if I'm on the golf course and I'm considering a five-iron, I may ask the caddie for his opinion. If he concurs, then that's more of a reason to step up."

In 1997, Dick bought shares in a major telecom company for his clients when it was in its 20s, at a time that it was considered out of favor. "In 1999, it hit the 50s, then the 60s, at which point every analyst on the street was recommending it," he says. "The stock later had an off-quarter, and the stock sank around 15 points, and many analysts changed their opinion to neutral. In my view, if it's a great company and a buy at 60, even if the fundamentals are still intact and it misses one quarter. If it trades down into the mid-40s, it still offers a great deal of value.

Dick is adamant about keeping clients informed in good times and in bad. "It's always easy to call a client when you buy them a stock at 20 and it jumps to 30. But it's much more important for a financial advisor to call a client if a client's stock gets beaten up," he says seriously. "You must explain to clients why their stock is down, and why you think they should sell or continue to hold. It may seem like a difficult call for most advisers, but it has to be done for the benefit of and respect for the client. It also adds to your credibility." He cites the 1999 disaster in Florida when Hurricane Floyd touched ground. "If you owned certain insurance stocks, they probably suffered during this time. But the point is, we can't control the weather, and no one can predict when or where it is going to going to touch down."

He will also consider selling at the end of the year for tax planning. "No matter who you are, every year you're going to have some losers," he says. "I'm always on top of where each account stands year to date with long- and short-term gains and losses. Even if we really love a stock, but it's a loss, we may sell that stock against some gains, then commence new positions later.

This financial advisor prefers to diversify a portfolio with at least 12 to 20 issues, and he may consider some preferred issues as well. A typical portfolio will hold some high-quality bonds: Treasury, corporate, or municipal bonds. All in all, a portfolio may contain 70% equities, 20% bonds, and up to 10% cash. If Dick reduces exposure to equities, it may be lessened to 60%, with 25% in bonds and 15% in cash. "I consider this type of portfolio pretty conservative, especially since the equities are of such high quality," he explains. "But if I make a mistake, I'd rather do it by being too conservative with my client's money." He adds that the cash portion tends to fluctuate the most, he will buy more stock when the time arises, or sell some stock to take money off the table.

While many investors approach Dick about handling their accounts on a discretionary basis, he doesn't believe this is suitable for his business. "I will generally accept discretion only if a client is going away for a prolonged period of time. I like to keep the client informed of everything that's going on in the account as it pertains to trading," he says. "A client needs to understand what is happening, and why. No matter how firmly I believe in a trade, the client probably shouldn't do it if it doesn't make sense to him or her."

"I always treat people the way I would want to be treated," he says as he sits up in his chair to tell a story. "One day there was a TV special on Arnold Palmer. It was called 'Arnold Palmer, the American Legend.' The program pointed how he has been able to maintain his popularity with the public as one of the most popular sports figures in history. Jim McKay, the interviewer, asked him about it. He said, 'Jim, I really don't know what it is. All I can tell you is while growing up, my father taught me a few things. He taught me to be a gentleman, and he taught me to treat people the way I would like to be treated.'

"Although we hear this all the time, very few people in the world really do it. If we all did it, there would be very few problems. In regards to our business, we should ask ourselves: 'What would you expect from your broker?' We are professionals in the business. I try to do the best job possible for my clients, and this includes providing good, sound advice and outstanding service. They are looking to us because they trust us with their life savings. I feel terrible when clients lose money. Of course, we can't call the market and we can't call the stocks, and people understand this. But when they're losing money, you have to put yourself in their shoes and try to handle it in the proper fashion. We do the same thing when they're making money. We are going to try to get some of that money off the table and protect it. Although we're in a business of making fees, if we get to caught up in that, we're not going to do a good job for the customers."

Dick recounts something he learned on the golf course: "The golfers that impressed me the most were the ones who wanted to make our society a better place," he says. "Many were very generous and very proud to be contributing to their community. This has always made a lot of sense to me."

Both Dick and his wife, Ann Marie, feel strongly that if life has been good to you, it's your obligation to give something back. "We teach this to our kids:

If you do well, you must give to those who are less privileged. We point out to them that the way they live is not the way 99% of the population lives,"he says.

"When I was very young, I often saw my grandmother put a quarter in the box at church," he recalls. "That was a big deal to us. My father was incredibly generous with his time and with the small bits of money that he could spare. My mother was always helping people; if someone in the neighborhood was sick, she would make them a pot of soup or a cake. The point is, one should give what they can. While ten dollars might be a great deal of money to one person, someone else might be writing a check for a hundred when a gift of a million dollars wouldn't change their lives. It's also important to give one's time. That's where you can really provide your talents and expertise. This is how we can strengthen a society and help others."

How involved is Dick in the community? He's on the board of Babson College, his alma mater, and the board of the Fenn School in Concord, Massachusetts, where all three of his children have attended. He's also on the boards of the Francis Ouimet Scholarship Fund, which funds the same caddie scholarship that put Dick through college, and the Children's Medical Research Foundation, a nonprofit that serves a hospital based in Dublin, Ireland, and performs worldwide research on children's diseases with doctors all over the world. Additionally, he's involved with the American Island Fund, Catholic Charities, the Multiple Sclerosis Foundation, and a scholarship he endowed in his mother's name at Malden Catholic High School, where he went to school. Ann Marie is on the boards of the Concord Museum and Holy Cross College, and is the former president of the Concord Educational Fund, which assists public schools in the Connollys' neighborhood. She holds these positions in addition to her membership on the board of the private school their children attend. Their teenage sons, Richard, Ryan, and Kevin, are getting an early start with some local nonprofit organizations. The Connollys spend a great deal of time with these community activities, in addition to making generous contributions.

BILL BLOUNT
OUR BEST INVESTMENT: AMERICA

UBS PaineWebber, Inc.
Portland, Oregon

Bill Blount is an all-American man. Walk into his corner office in Portland, Oregon, and you'll feel like you've walked into a Naval commander's control center, with its American flags, UBS PaineWebber and Boy Scout awards, and computer console. Wearing a friendly smile and an American flag pin, Bill will give you a hardy handshake.

It won't take you long to detect his attention to discipline and reverence for freedom. Perhaps these qualities are best attributed to his work during the Korean War, when Bill served for two years as a Task Force Qualified Officer on the USS Essex, one of the era's largest military vessels, which carried 3,000 men and squadrons of airplanes and helicopters. By the time you bid him farewell, his dedication to free enterprise and individualism will have rubbed off on you. You'll also realize the importance of spending less and saving more, so that you can invest in America's future while enhancing your own future financial freedom.

Bill takes pride in his military service, and expresses similar pride in the strictly disciplined investing style he's used for over 40 years. It's the kind of personal strategy that would leave most money managers in awe. Once he gets going, his eyes spark up when he discusses his own investing war stories. Indeed, in the battle for investment returns, Bill is a real hero.

After receiving a Stanford University MBA in 1957, Bill joined Blyth & Company's Portland office. There he pledged to open ten accounts per month and refused to turn down any account, regardless of size. PaineWebber, now UBS PaineWebber, subsequently acquired Blyth in 1980.

When Bill first meets with a prospective client, he states forthrightly: "I want you to understand my basic investment philosophy and how we structure portfolios, because this will influence the direction your account will take." Full disclosure of his investment philosophy and experiences enables him to learn more about potential investors as they discuss their portfolio and expectations. "When I first started in the business, I resolved I'd seek to handle clients' money as my own, while giving consideration to their finances and comfort levels." he says.

Bill also fully explains his basic commitment. "I promise them honesty and integrity in our relationship, and I expect the same from the client. However, communications are on a 'best efforts' basis, and clients are expected to show an interest in their own money." Clients are responsible for contacting him with any changes in their financial situation, and for setting up periodic account reviews."Over time, reviews become less and less frequent as investors have relaxed with very favorable investment experiences," he adds. "Strong markets have assisted my portfolios as well."

Today, Bill's "control center" works with 3,700 accounts, representing 1,500 "families," and in-house assets exceed a billion-and-a-quarter dollars. Recognizing the limitations of a single communicator, Bill initiated a team service approach in 1977. This team includes his daughter, Susan Blount McNiel, David Brauti, Bill's youngest son Kevin, and four assistants. The team conveys Bill's service and message to the client base, thus freeing him to work with clients' portfolios and pursue investment ideas. Bill credits his hard-working team for their communication skills, investment prowess, optimal client retention and flourishing referral network. Of course, the appreciating asset base is also a major contributor.

Bill's batting average rarely slips; if it does, it's usually because he has strayed from his disciplined investment approach. This stock picker adamantly believes that well-run businesses are the creators of wealth. His thoughts on bonds? "There's a great deal of risk for lenders, and their rewards are usually capped," he says. "It's the owners that have the opportunities." He also points out that with inflation rates of 3 to 4%, and taxes eating away a solid portion of any interest or gains, equities are, in his opinion, the best choice for building wealth.

It's ironic, then, that this true-blue stock picker scored one of his biggest hits in the bond market. In the early 1970s, he became interested in railroad bankruptcies."That's when the New York Central Railroad entered bankruptcy," he explains. Bill was more interested in this issue because 70% of the nation's rail traffic either originated or terminated on the New York Penn Central system. "It really came down to this: if you believed in motherhood, brotherhood, apple pie, and the American flag, it had to work out. One's risk was 'how much reward' and 'when.' I started accumulating the 100-year New York Central Railroad First Mortgage gold-backed bonds, which had 5% coupons and a maturity of 2013, at prices of around 12 cents on the dollar." At one point, around 1976, his investment was down 75%! What did he do?"I tripled up and prayed," he says with a smile."I told my wife that if it didn't work out, we could wallpaper our party room with those beautiful certificates!" He bought more at four cents on the dollar.

"In 1980, Congress essentially bailed out Penn Central by 'nationalizing' the system," he says. The investment was subsequently disposed of, netting a profit of 20-fold, with similar results for clients. How did he re-deploy his personal wallpaper now worth $500,000?" The Boy Scouts of America enjoyed a healthy portion. The New York Central experience was a tremendous lesson to me on the so-called 'safety' of fixed-income bonds, as well as the value of patience!"

Bill is a die-hard value investor, one who seeks bargain-priced companies for attractive long-term returns, accompanied by low risk. He scours companies' fundamentals such as earnings, cash flow, capital investment, and book value. To best describe his stock-selection process, it's easiest to consider companies with characteristics he avoids: "labor-intensive, heavily regulated companies that need to run to the bank for their working capital or those that continuously offer new shares to the public; companies that issue too much stock to their executives in addition to excessive compensation; companies with minimal insider ownership; and those domiciled in politically insecure geographic areas."

Although Bill relies on UBS Warburg research for ideas, many are the result of his legwork. He maintains over 160 stocks on his radar, and is an avid reader of numerous financial publications. Many ideas also are gleaned during ordinary life events, from previous investment experience, or through discussions with clients and company executives.

When describing himself as an investor, Bill says, "I like to appraise businesses. Give me an annual report, a research report, and a tour of the company facilities. Then I'll review the data, and look at the problem areas and the opportunities. If the equity meets with our parameters and qualifies on a risk/reward basis, we'll then suggest a position." His clients' portfolios typically have around 30 stocks, including core holdings, many of which he has held since the 1960s. His undervalued "gems" can turn out to be acquisition targets: "At least one or two every couple of years." The Blount Team challenge continues to be the successful placement of funds.

The scores of takeovers that Bill has experienced for himself and his investors are, by nature, the result of the undervalued companies he seeks. He never buys for the purpose of hitting upon a takeover; in fact, most of his takeover hits have occurred after holding an issue for a number of years. "I'm a very patient investor and speculator," he says, "not to be confused with a gambler and stock trader."

Once the idea is identified, Bill recommends a gradual accumulation of shares for his clients and his family accounts. Bill exercises patience when investing. In fact, he feels he is usually early in the game because of his selections of "out-of-favor" issues which have yet to gain or re-gain recognition. He may hold a company on his personal watch list for months prior to purchase.

He sums up his investment life by saying, "I want to help America grow and assist clients in achieving economic freedom. I work to meet my investment objectives, have fun, and provide a helping hand to worthy causes," he explains with pride. "The Boy Scouts of America, for example, work with young men in a very positive framework." Bill has been a Troop Committee Chairman, and his oldest son, Kevin, is an Eagle Scout. "Well-educated young people are the solution to the growth and survival of this country. Investing in family and the education of youth is one of the best uses of money!"

GARY ROSENTHAL
PERFORMANCE...AND PROTECTION

The Rosenthal Group
Prudential Securities Incorporated
New York, New York

Imagine having your portfolio up over 470% in the 33 months between January 1996 and September 1998, and then up another 108% in the 18 months between October 1998 and March 2000. Now imagine missing two major downturns in the market, selling all your stocks at the beginning of a major bear market cycle on March 29, 2000 and buying again after a 50% downturn in the Nasdaq market. Then imagine moving into an all-cash position on June 6, 2001, missing a downturn in the summer and a dramatic sell-off in September.

This track record, audited by a third-party firm, belongs to The Rosenthal Group, a team of three financial advisors with Prudential Securities in New York City. Gary Rosenthal, his son Bret, and their colleague Denis O'Hara use a unique strategy to achieve such stellar results. By managing over $250 million in equity assets, they advise their clients to employ not only different asset categories, but also different methods of managing their portfolios. The senior Rosenthal's investment philosophy is the basis for the group's two distinct money management programs: traditional money management and the group's discretionary Proprietary Analysis & Computer Enhancement trading system, known as PACE.

Gary Rosenthal and his partners are adamant about giving back to their industry. By sharing their success story, they provide a rare glimpse of the secrets behind their successful investment philosophy, as well as their proprietary computer trading application, and reveal what they do to build a book of faithful clients.

The story begins with Gary's past. He has always had a love of numbers, and his desire to invest materialized early.

In the early 1950s, as a 12-year-old paperboy in his hometown of Savannah, Georgia, he was netting a cash flow of $52 a month. "It seemed like all the money in the world to me," Gary says, with a trace of a southern drawl. "My father asked me what I wanted to do with my $52, and I said, 'I want to invest it in the stock market.'" Gary decided to put his money in General Electric, because he felt positive about the company's slogan.

"The GE Theater used to come on every Sunday night at 8:00, and they opened and closed their show with the same phrase: 'Progress is our most important product.'And I said, well, if progress is their most important product, that's where I want to put my money." Gary's father supported his son's decision and took him to a wire house in downtown Savannah to buy all the GE stock he could afford. Shortly thereafter, Gary started following the markets in the papers. "I became fascinated by the Wall Street Journal, the numbers, the stocks, and everything else. That's how I got interested," he recalls.

Gary's interest continued well past his paperboy days. At the University of Georgia he majored in accounting, and went on to earn an MBA from the Columbia Graduate School of Business in June of 1966. By this time, he was well prepared to pursue his lifelong dream: to become an analyst on Wall Street. He soon landed a position as a security analyst with the United States Trust Company and began to develop his own investment style. This involved performing in-depth research with top management and breaking down their balance sheets and income statements.

"Traveling the country, breaking down income statements and balance sheets, and writing 50 page research reports was a marvelous way to begin a career on Wall Street," Gary recalls.

"Accounting is the language of business," Gary explains. "It's not just about numbers, it's a language. Very few people really understand that. When you look at a company's statements, you're looking at hidden secrets that allow superior managements to consistently beat their competition. A skilled eye can unravel those secrets and obtain critical information."

Gary still uses this research centric approach in his work with The Rosenthal Group. He also seeks out change in every aspect of a company, whether it's change in the company's products, the management, or the statements, and he tirelessly examines the fundamentals of the company's industry.

Although Gary still travels the country visiting companies, now they typically come to him. Either way, his efforts are focused on discovering rewarding investment ideas for his clients.

"Research is a twenty-four-hour-a-day, seven-day-a-week process. When my clients ask me how I can work as hard as I do, my answer is simple. If it were work I would not do it. It is a passion. Discovering good investments is like going out early in the morning and entering a forest on a foxhunt with hundreds of other competitors on horseback. The first one that spots the fox is the winner. Beating the competition is what research is all about."

To illustrate his group's methodology, he cites Mercury Interactive. "Several years ago, we met the management of Mercury at a technology conference. We found the top management to be outstanding and the income statement and balance sheet to be excellent. The company had already locked in around 50% of its industry's sales, and the industry was emerging from niche to mainstream. In addition, the company's technology was clearly superior to its competitors, and very few analysts followed the company." The Rosenthal Group built a large position between the prices of $9 and $14 a share. Within two years, the stock increased more than ten-fold, then replaced IBM on a top-ten preferred technology list of a major Wall Street firm.

In 1996, The Rosenthal Group introduced a companion to its traditional money management accounts. This program uses a sophisticated computer-enhanced trading system to manage money. As Gary explains, "As markets have become increasingly institutionalized over the past several years, larger and larger pools of capital have introduced a rising scale of market volatility. Using computer models, institutions rapidly rotate large sums between market sectors seeking short-term gains. This is commonly referred to as 'momentum investing.' This escalating volatility has made the timely buying and selling of stocks more important to portfolio performance than ever before. In order to help harness this volatility for our clients, we developed PACE. The PACE portfolio system smartly combines the group's carefully researched ideas with a sophisticated proprietary computer application to manage money."

The PACE trading and management system incorporates 17 advanced computerized technical tools, each chosen to help identify the flow of funds into and out of individual equities. "PACE essentially pinpoints an entry and exit point for an equity that we love fundamentally," says partner Denis O'Hara.

Protection of capital is one of the primary objectives of the program. The PACE program attempts to cut losses at 10% or less because the group believes 98% of all large losses were originally small losses. "Of course there's no guarantee that we can always accomplish this, but it's our intention to limit our non-profitable transactions to an average of 5% to 7%, and take gains averaging 15% to 30%. This contrasts with most investors' tendency to ride the losers down." Once a position is up more than 15%, the PACE system closely monitors the position for signs of weakness. If our proprietary computer tools begin to detect trouble, the group considers taking money off the table.

"Our performance objectives are also based on the beta," Bret says, referring to the perceived volatility of the stock. "For low-beta stocks, we look for gains of 10% to 15% with a stop loss of 5%, and we'll look for 15% to 30% gains for high beta stocks, with a stop loss of 10%."

Bret points out that the PACE philosophy works optimally when news announcements are absent. "As sophisticated as our technology is, we still can't program our systems to accurately forecast positive or negative news announcements," he jokes. "But the key is to react quickly and decisively once the information is released. Analysts' quarterly earnings expectations for companies are often inaccurate, which can cause overnight share price declines of 50% or more, even for the largest companies. As a result, we rarely hold a position into an earnings release in our PACE program. Remember, our PACE program attempts to protect capital at all times."

The portfolio-management feature of PACE deploys no more than 10% of a client's assets in any single position, thus encouraging diversification. "Technology is key to our success," Bret affirms. "That's why we're continually enhancing our computer technology and are involved in a constant quest to increase our accuracy rate when selecting equities.

"According to an audited report by a top-eight accounting firm, the PACE program has produced returns of over 600% in its five and a half years of existence, beginning on January 1st of 1996," Bret says. "I would say its best attribute is that it shields our assets from downturns in the market. We have incorporated a disciplined stop-loss policy to avoid any major unforeseen downturns.

"For example," he continues, "in the year 2000, the S&P 500, which represents 500 of the largest capitalized stocks, fell around 9%. However, the average stock on the New York Stock Exchange declined about 50% from peak to valley. NASDAQ stocks fared slightly worse, declining roughly 60% from peak to valley. PACE took us out of the market on March 29, at the very beginning of the decline. We then spent roughly six months of the year in money market funds protecting principle during one of the worst bear markets in history. PACE clients ended 2000 in the profit column."

"Our clients take comfort in the fact that we limit their downside exposure," colleague Denis says. "But clients have to get use to this very disciplined approach."

"That's right," Bret responds. "New clients call us frequently to ask why we took losses or gains so quickly. After a few months, they see the results, and they stop calling."

Bret describes one client who initially called constantly, concerned about each stock the group was buying or selling. "One day when the market was tanking, he called us. He was hysterical!" Bret recalls. "I was able to calm his nerves by telling him that PACE took him out of his positions at the first sign of troubles. After that he stopped calling. I called him a month later and asked why we haven't been hearing from him. He said, 'You know, I finally realized what you're doing. And I love it.'"

"When we initiated the program and introduced it to our clients, they all asked us how much of their assets should they place into the PACE program," Gary says. "We recommended 25% to 30% of each client's assets, because we wanted them to diversify their investment style, in addition to the more traditional methods of diversification. And just about everybody agreed to that.

"Several months ago, one client who has been with us for nearly ten years had 25% of his assets in PACE. He called and asked us to increase his PACE allocation to 50% of his assets. He recently asked us to up that to 100%. I asked him why he felt so strongly, especially since our returns were very respectable for his non-PACE managed account. He said, 'Look, I've been investing for 35 years and there's one thing I hate. I hate owning stocks and watching them go down during a deep market correction. With PACE, I don't have to worry about that. In addition, you've proven to me that the PACE program will consistently outperform the market.'"

"This success has enabled us to be the consolidator of our clients' assets," Denis says. "Once they become comfortable with the program and witness the results, they tell us they have no more need for other brokerage accounts—especially the discount brokerages. They are demanding professional money management, and that's what we're providing."

Bret offers an example of the Group's twin investment strategies in action: "In February 1997, we became interested in the networking company Novell. The company, then selling at around $7 a share, came to our attention after it announced a new management team. It was clear to us that this bit of fresh air was exactly what the company needed. We evaluated the company fundamentally. The balance sheet looked strong, and the company was holding about $4 per share in cash. After evaluating the firm's new management team, we decided it was time to meet the players.

"In April we met with the new CEO, Eric Schmidt, formerly chief technology officer for Sun Microsystems and protégé of Scott McNeally, Sun's CEO. Eric was the father of Java, Sun Microsystem's revolutionary computer software language," Gary says. "He impressed us with his insights and ideas, and his vision to change the direction of Novell."

"After calling our clients, we built a major position in our traditionally managed accounts between $7 and $10 per share," Bret adds. "The shares reached $44 around 29 months later, although it suffered many market swings along the way. During this volatile period, we successfully traded the shares in our PACE program numerous times. Furthermore, we sold our last share of Novell at $42 in February of 2000. The stock is now trading under $5. This experience, along with many similar stories in the last 18 months, such as Lucent, Cisco, Nortel Networks, Nokia, Yahoo!, etc., gives us a classic example of the power of actively managing an account versus the traditional approach of merely buying and holding."

"Mercury Interactive and Novell are examples of special situations that are among my favorites, because we can usually beat the rest of the Street," Gary says.

If The Rosenthal Group's traditional money management program has been so successful, why did they decide to augment their practice with a new investment approach?

"In our opinion, a portion of assets should be diversified to a 'style' of investing, in addition to the more traditional definition of diversification in market sectors and number of issues," explains Bret, who developed the computer enhanced trading system in the mid-1990s. "We believe a certain portion of assets should be actively managed with a primary focus on reducing exposure to traumatizing market swings. With this type of investing-style diversification, we believe our clients are able to maintain a more comfortable or stable posture in pursuing long-term investment goals."

This strategy proved itself again during June 2001. At this time, due to its defensive nature, PACE moved its client assets into the security of money-market funds. Although client assets were already down 15.5% for the year as of September 21, Nasdaq was down 43%, S&P 500 was down 26.5%, and the average mutual fund was down around 37%. "This cash position allowed us a sense of conviction that few money managers will have when conditions are sanguine for the redeployment of capital," says Bret confidently.

"Our clients get a multidimensional aspect to investing that they enjoy. It's a very exciting thing for us," says Gary. "I love it. And I've always believed that if you love what you do and have a passion to succeed, you'll find a way to do well. The success will naturally follow. My partners and I are very fortunate that we are able to experience this, while providing the highest level of service for our clients."

JOHN SAFFRO
A PASSION FOR INVESTING

Morgan Stanley
Beverly Hills, California

If financial advisors' success hinged on being an extrovert, professional networker, or expert closer, John Saffro would never have sold his first stock. Meeting John for the first time is like seeing a long-lost friend who is more interested in hearing about you than talking about himself. He's the type to bend over backwards for a friend, or a client, and never tell anybody. He's also the type who would fly to New York to help his daughter pick out a wedding dress. That's when I had the opportunity to meet him.

John has always had a knack for spotting investment ideas. When he was 12, he worked in a grocery store as a "box boy," packing customers' grocery items. One day, while loading the groceries of an older woman, he noticed the latest advancement in soda containers—cans. It occurred to him that with cans, customers would not be forced to leave deposits on their bottles, and then return the bottles to receive their money. With his father's help, he bought shares in a company that was one of the first to put soda in cans. Later, he invested in American Motors because he thought consumers wanted to drive smaller, more economical cars. Both of these investments proved to be winners.

In high school, he learned the art of stock-price movements the old-fashioned way, as a board marker at a securities firm. For four years, he swiftly updated stock quotes by hand on a chalkboard, running back and forth along the long board, as investors sat in chairs watching the price changes. "We had the most recognized issues," he says proudly of the 100 stocks he refreshed. "I learned the ticker symbols awfully fast." He also learned the trading patterns of stocks that would benefit him later in his career.

While attending UCLA, where he participated in the ROTC program to subsidize his education, he continued to work in a brokerage firm. After college, his expectations for serving six months in the Army as a finance officer quickly faded when he was sent to Oklahoma as an artillery officer. Two and a half years later, after supporting the Berlin Crisis, the build-up to the Vietnam War and the Cuban Missile Crisis, he returned to Los Angeles to pursue a career in the securities industry.

John entered the securities business in 1964, when he took a job at a promising Los Angeles office run by two gentlemen with high hopes, Phelps Witter and George Witter. Their establishment eventually served as the predecessor to Morgan Stanley.

The only prospecting John experienced occurred during the first several months of his new career. He contacted everyone he knew who was familiar with his interest in the stock market—people from UCLA, friends and family. He also obtained clients from the departing brokers during the market melt-down due to the oil crisis in the early 1970s.

John never turned down an account and, to this day, never has. Most of his clients initially had accounts valued at $5,000 to $10,000. "During a bad market environment, such as the one I started in, building a book was my only focus," he says. "I would seek undervalued, high-quality companies for a long-term hold. If the shares dipped down precipitously, I would accumulate more shares for my clients." He proudly adds that he has helped create more than 150 millionaires from those small accounts. He's equally proud that he has never lost sleep over a stock he has bought for a client.

When meeting with clients or prospects for the first time, John fully explains his investment philosophy. "If an investor doesn't feel comfortable with my investing process, or if I feel it's not right for them, I tell them to find another advisor, or I recommend one that I feel is better suited for them," he says. The only time John will alter his philosophy for a client is when their objectives change. He will never "fire" a client.

Depending on a client's particular financial situation, when structuring a portfolio, John typically keeps 15% to 20% in cash, 20% to 30% in mutual funds for broad diversification, and, assuming the client is seeking growth, 50% in equities. Within the equities allocation, he will hold between five and eight different stocks. While John rarely sells a stock (he may hold a stock anywhere from five years to "forever"), he may buy several times throughout the year, whether it's a new position or accumulating shares of an existing stock.

Seeking new investment ideas is a never-ending process for John. He likes to identify companies with concepts that make sense to him. He constantly reads research and news items about companies. For every 100 companies that spark his interest, he will closely examine ten. A finer analysis will lead him to invest in one or two, or sometimes none at all. He feels Morgan Stanley's research is one of the best on the street, and he likes to scour various magazines and newspapers.

When he identifies a company that looks attractive, he reviews news stories and comments made by the COO and CFO regarding the future of the company. If they're on target with forecasts three months into the future, it's a plus. If their comments don't hold true, and at the end of the three months these executives concoct excuses, he avoids the company. "If I'm going to invest my client's money in a company, I want to be able to trust the management," he explains. "If, on the other hand, the executives are honest, and consistently offer fair projections, then I can trust the company." The analysis then moves to the next level, the product.

"Typically, I already use the product, or at least I am very familiar with it," he continues. "If the product is good and you would buy it, then it's likely a lot of other people feel the same way. For example, a northern California-based home-supply business entered our area, going head-on with major competition. The company then opened a store in southern California. Few in this part of the state had heard of the company. I walked into the store and was instantly impressed. The store is set up so efficiently that you can walk into this mammoth-sized establishment and get what you want in five minutes." At this point, John maintains contact with the investor relations department and asks to be placed on a mailing list so he can obtain all information that's being written about the company.

John later learned that the company had plans to open up to thirty new stores in California. When he visited the store, he picked up numerous brochures and discount pamphlets. He later sent these items to his clients, and educated them on his research findings. "I asked them to go to the store and report back to me," he says. "Clients soon started calling me back giving the go-ahead to initiate positions."

For three years, the stock hovered around $8 a share. "When the fundamentals improved, we accumulated even more shares," he says. After three years, the concept caught on, and earnings drove the stock up to $30. Another major company later acquired it in the mid-$40 price range.

One controversial stock idea actually resulted in the closing of several clients' accounts. "The company is a biotech company based in San Diego," he explains. "It produces protease inhibitors, which block cells from dividing. This process helps to prevent HIV from spreading." He began buying the stock in the 1990s.

For three straight years, John accumulated positions for his clients in the four-to-six dollar a share level. When the fundamentals improved, he accumulated even more shares. The company had interesting products in the pipeline, so he bought more. Close to four years later, he was still buying more shares for his clients. Unfortunately, his patience outlasted many of his clients'. Several sold out, saying he was crazy for holding a stock that was treading water.

Somewhere near the fourth year, the stock started its move. Within a matter of weeks, it rose to 50, for an average gain of 900% for those patient enough to hold on. John sold most of his positions. A major pharmaceutical company acquired the stock in the mid-1990s for over $100 per share, a whopping 1,900% gain for those clients who held out a bit longer.

Finding an exit point for a stock is typically dependent on several factors, such as John's earnings forecast for the company, and volatility for the issue. In virtually all cases, the stock is held long enough to qualify for long-term capital gains. Price-wise, his objectives are very high "in historical terms," he says.

John sums up his investment process by saying, "With my philosophy, one must invest in companies with a solid future and continue to accumulate and hold those companies over a period of time. If the value of the stock heads south, the fundamentals of that company must be thoroughly examined. If they have not changed, then one must consider accumulating more shares."

John says that this is a philosophy that can't be judged with the increasing short-term volatility in the market.

Lately, this financial advisor has been eyeing the biotech industry. "This is a fascinating area," he says. "It's a volatile area and there are risks involved; you have to look at companies that are developing products you feel offer strong potential for success." He is wary about investing in one-product biotech companies. "I prefer companies with five to ten different products, so if one fails, the others will hopefully be successful. In a one-product company, if one product is unsuccessful, the entire company could fold with it." John has been eyeing several biotech companies and has sent literature to clients to keep them informed of his ideas.

John keeps in constant contact with his clients. "Every new item, every article that is released about a company in which a client is either interested or invested, is mailed to them that day," he says. "If a negative comment is released about a company, I jump on the phone and call the appropriate client."

Fran Germana, who has been John's Sales Assistant since 1985, plays a key role in maintaining close contact with clients. Seated in an office adjacent to John's, complete with a large sliding window for optimal communication, Fran helps John provide regular portfolio reviews, ensures all administration is handled effectively, and helps keep clients well informed. John's son, Chad, is following in his father's footsteps in the securities industry, learning the business from the ground up. By gaining experience in several areas, including operations and research, he will be well positioned to join his father.

John and his wife, Arlene, provide time and financial support to handicapped children at UCLA and Ronald McDonald programs. In 1989 they helped initiate annual fundraisers, which have been very successful for handicapped children. "I'm very fortunate that I'm able to give back to my community both my time and financially," he says. "There's nothing more satisfying than investing in something you truly believe in."

ANDREW A. LANYI
FINDING THE BLUE CHIPS BEFORE WALL STREET DOES

CIBC World Markets
New York, New York

Andrew Lanyi is one of the most illustrious financial advisors in the country, and for good reason. His charisma and his passion for the securities business are equaled only by his highly regarded stock research. I became fascinated as Andrew related many of his lifetime experiences to his investment philosophy. I would be remiss if I failed to share a synopsis of his story, which is detailed in his 1992 book *Confessions of a Stockbroker* (Prentice Hall, 1992.)

In 1944, Andrew spent his nineteenth year in a Hungarian concentration camp with 250 other Hungarian Jews. Their mission was to build a military airport, which they abandoned due to a Russian attack. Suffering and death were both a looming fear and a constant reality.

While passing a nearby town with minimal nourishment and energy, Andrew proposed the bold idea of sneaking into nearby barracks occupied by German troops. He was convinced that with the right excuse, he just might convince an occupant to provide food. Andrew persuaded a comrade who knew a little German to join him. When they entered the building, the charade began. "We came from Bustyahaza. We were building an airport. Any place we can get some food?" his friend asked. They were treated to two medium-sized packages containing meat in aspic and other "delicacies." When they returned to their faction, the two friends shared one package while the others divided up the other one. Two other Jews who were fluent in German tried the trick, and were also rewarded with boxes. One more tried it, and he, too, won the game. The rest of the group did not dare to go. The deception would become too obvious.

Andrew's first lesson was this: "Whenever you do something new, whenever you do something unusual, whenever you do something contrary to the accepted wisdom, you have to be the first to do it. The second one may succeed, the third one may succeed, but there is a major advantage to being the first."

Several days later, while preparing to sleep, Andrew felt he couldn't take imprisonment any longer. Many in the group agreed. He told his friend he had a plan. The idea was to not hide. Rather, he proposed to "walk right into the open" where their presence would be so incredibly blatant, given their branded garb, that it would appear legitimate. They counterfeited a pass bearing a forged Colonel's signature, stating they were under orders to go to a military hospital in Budapest. There was no alternative. To stay with the group would have meant an assured death. Andrew shudders when he thinks of what ultimately became of the rest of the group. Andrew knew that his chances were only slightly better walking through villages with a counterfeited pass, that at any time, they could be gunned down for no reason.

The pair cleverly used their pass when they entered a village to obtain permits from local "judges." Once the judge bought the story, he would provide a pass to the next town, and so on. Ten days, and three village "stays" later, they reached their destination: a village slightly larger than the rest, which was the location of the nearest railroad station. They waited a long hour until the train bound for Budapest arrived. It was past curfew, and anyone could have been shot. They boarded the train, and four days later they arrived in Budapest, where they joined their families. They were the only two who survived the camp.

Andrew shares with me his trusted second lesson: "If you believe in your heart that you're doing the right thing, don't let anything stop you."

His family, having never expected to see him again, greeted Andrew with exhausted enthusiasm. After exchanging their affections, and Andrew telling his remarkable story, they warned him about frequent visits from troops looking for labor camp escapees. He hid in a small cubicle downstairs, alongside two relatives. Several hours later, there was a knock on the front door. "We hear reports that three are people hiding in this basement," the voice said. "The reports say there is a cave somewhere behind the bricks. I will be back." An hour later, Andrew was on the street again. He camped out in a dentist's laboratory, surviving on dried bread and water. Within days, the Germans began withdrawing from Budapest. The war was over.

Several years later, Hungary revolted. The country was fed up with its puppet government. The Russians moved troops and tanks into Andrew's village to stifle the nation's revolt against its government. Andrew and his pregnant wife attempted to escape to Austria, but soldiers caught them at the border. That night they narrowly escaped from the barracks where they were being detained. The next day, they slipped into Austria, where they awaited a visa. From there, the couple immigrated to the United States.

As one can imagine, these experiences had a profound affect on Andrew. He had a new outlook on life. He would pursue his dreams, and nothing would ever stop him.

Once a stage director in Hungary, Andrew tried finding related work in the U.S. "I found that the demand for non-English speaking Hungarian stage directors was quite low," he says.

He interviewed with a mutual-fund company that advertised "no experience necessary." During the interview, a sales manager asked, "Is there any reason why you shouldn't become a successful mutual-fund telephone salesman?" The Hungarian replied, "Only three: I have never sold anything, I don't know what a mutual fund is, and I don't speak English." He got the job anyway.

Seeking business, he targeted local Hungarians, as many as he could find in the telephone book. As his English improved, he expanded his potential client base by cold calling individuals in wealthy New York suburbs. Working ninety hours a week, he slowly expanded his client base. Seeking more opportunity, Andrew moved to a securities firm, where realized he had a knack for picking stocks.

Andrew eventually settled down at CIBC Oppenheimer, now CIBC World Markets, where he runs a distinctive boutique operation. "We try to find very high-quality stocks that you can hold for a very long time," Andrew says, summarizing more than four decades of formula development.

Andrew gets his ideas from many sources. "I generally mark some stocks on the list of the '100 Stocks With Greatest Percent Rise in Earnings,' which is found in *Investor's Business Daily*. I mark companies that I think we should take a look at, because some of them might meet our criteria."

A research assistant provides Andrew with the charts and combs through the "Best Ups" tables in *Investor's Business Daily*, noting those companies that report a "Last Quarter Percent Change" of 30% or more. He skips all the companies that are well known and that sell over $40 or more, claiming that "they've probably already been discovered" or "they obviously don't meet the criteria." Some days there are no companies left, some days there are several. His assistant provides Andrew with a chart for each one, which he reviews and decides whether the company should be investigated further.

"We have a bias," Andrew says. "We prefer to invest in service companies, rather than manufacturing companies. For decades I watched the collapse of even the greatest manufacturing growth stocks. Polaroid, for instance, first rose from near zero to 149, and then in a year and a half, lost 90% of its value. Some of the greatest service companies, on the other hand, seem to continue growing almost without end."

"We look for certain qualities in a company," says Andrew. He normally prefers companies with:

- Protections against fluctuations in the economy: companies that are recession resistant or even counter-cyclical.

- Domination of a niche in an industry: "monopolies or near monopolies."

- An undiscovered or modest following by Wall Street.

- Very fast growth, say increasing sales at an annual 15% rate or over and earnings at 20% or over, year after year.

- A "cookie-cutter" operation: capabilities in one area that can be easily replicated anywhere.

- An ever-growing repeat-order rate.

Andrew cautions that he does not seek the "home runs" but rather, consistently high-performing stocks. "Naturally, not all ideas become winners," he says. "We are dealing in the stocks of companies that we believe are very high quality but still unknown. Our overall investment philosophy is that, as a sensible investor, you should cut your losses and let your profits run."

The team's criteria are so stringent that months can go by before they find a company that meets their standards, and rarely is there a year in which more than three qualify. The analyst will talk directly to a company president, asking him or her a long list of questions. If the company still passes muster, a conference call is arranged, mainly for Andrew's benefit. His goal is to get a general feeling for the quality of the management. In addition to the president, participants in the conference call typically include one or two of his associates, more often than not the financial vice president, and sometimes the chairman.

The team's analysts then request information including the names of suppliers, the names of important clients, and the company's promotional and marketing related printers. The list must be delivered immediately, within a few hours. Why the urgency? "Too many times in the past, while we were taking our own sweet time investigating a company, its price ran up," he says. "That's a luxury we can't afford."

While the information is being delivered, Andrew and his group crunch all the numbers that matter to the team, they then call all the people whose names the company provided to ask them questions about their experience with the company. They continue probing, "Who else do you know is a supplier or customer or has anything else to do with the company?" The team doesn't rely solely on management for the referrals: "We want to get 'referrals' to other people who may see the management from a different angle."

There are very few occasions when Andrew is influenced by technical factors. For example, if he is ready to start recommending a stock, but its chart indicates that the stock is under distribution, he will wait until the selling is over, the stock price turns sideways, and it shows its first upticks. "It's not enough to just buy a good stock. You have to try to recommend it when it starts to act like a good stock," he explains. He never recommends the sale of a stock just because it goes down, and he never suggests doubling or tripling up just because it goes down and looks cheap.

Because Andrew seeks companies that have yet to be discovered, he is often active very early in the game. "Most of the time, the two main factors that move stocks are value and demand. We try to find exceptional value, buy it, and own it until the demand materializes."

Andrew sums up his stock-picking success by saying, "The trick in this business is this: Have more knowledge than others, have more *discipline* than others and have more *patience* than others!"

CHAPTER 14:
CORPORATE PLAN BUSINESS

MARK CURTIS
THINKING DIFFERENT, THINKING HUGE

Mark Curtis
Managing Director—Investments
Consulting Group Director
Salomon Smith Barney
Palo Alto, California

Mark Curtis is a visionary. Standing over six feet tall, with an ever-present smile and a knack for reading minds, Mark is the epitome of an individual motivated by passion for his work. He's quick to provide a tour of his operation, and he proudly introduces each available member of his team. It's clear that he is passionate about the business. He's anxious to discuss the industry trends, and each conversation inevitably leads to a "brainstorming" session. And while many financial advisors struggle to build one strong niche, Mark's business acumen has positioned him at the cusp of many niches, and a leader at many of them. He is a big thinker. He's an even bigger achiever. And he loves sharing ideas so he can see others succeed and progress.

When many financial advisors hear Mark's name, their first question is inevitable: "How were Mark and his team able to introduce so many innovations to the stock-plan industry?" The team is a reference to the Salomon Smith Barney's Curtis Group, comprised of Mark, a Managing Director, and his two partners Karen McDonald, Corporate Client Group Director and John Lopez, Corporate Client Group Director and a team that numbers over 50. Then the next question is, "How are they able to land many of the world's biggest customers?" And as a follow-up, "How are they able to be leaders in so many other business lines as well?"

Mark best explains his ability to capture—and lead—market segments by borrowing a line from Wayne Gretzky: "Most people skate toward where the puck is. I like to think we skate to where it's going." But he feels the real key is a love and passion for the business. And he has plenty of it.

It has also provided him the added edge to persevere. He feels that his love for the business allows him to persevere through its inevitable challenges. He says he's successful not because he's smarter, works harder, or has better sales tactics than other financial advisors. He understands the needs to accept failure as the part of the price of success.

When he applied to Stanford University, the application asked candidates to rank their capabilities in various categories. Mark wrote back, saying that he preferred not to respond specifically to their questions, because he felt they were looking for the wrong information. "I pointed out two things," he begins. "I felt it was irrelevant to rank my raw capabilities up against my peers. I believed they weren't trying to access my capabilities, but the degree to which I would apply my capabilities to achieve my goals. My response was they should be evaluating how applicants would apply themselves to achieve their goals if given the opportunity. I assured them that in this regard I would rate myself very highly versus my peer group."

He was accepted at Stanford, and after completing his undergraduate education, he received his MBA from UCLA. He followed in his father's footsteps by joining the ranks in the securities business. Maybe it's ironic that a visionary like Mark would cite consistency as another key to his achievement. Or maybe it's because he really does see the future. He's been with the same firm since 1981. He's had the same Branch Manager, David Nee, for 20 years. He's still paired with his first love—they were engaged after dating for one week. Mark and his closest friends have been buddies since the seventh grade. He even owns and lives in the same house in which he grew up. He has client relationships that are now entering their third decade. These consistencies extend into his team as well. "Many of my team members have been with me for ten years or more," Mark says. "These long-term relationships provide a wonderful foundation."

Mark's first partner, John Lopez, joined Salomon Smith Barney after college. John is a native of the San Francisco Bay area, having grown up in Los Altos. He worked summers at Salomon Smith Barney as Mark's intern while attending college. He became Mark's partner in 1986. At the time, Mark had only been in the business for four years. John built a business by working on Mark's smaller accounts and then building a client base of small to medium-sized companies.

John targeted individuals that worked at local high-technology companies. Many of these clients had large concentrated positions in their company stock. "I always identified myself as service-oriented when I made the initial call," he explains. "When they heard I was with a brokerage firm, they responded with resistance. I'd ask them what stocks they had positions in. Since I essentially knew they owned stock in their own company, I was prepared to discuss their company's stock, often sharing our research. Since their company stock was quite often their most important equity investment, I looked for ways that I could add value."

Mark initially positioned himself as a consultant to high-net-worth individuals and businesses. "We would position ourselves as the primary financial advisor to individuals, offering them comprehensive wealth-management services. With businesses, we used a similar approach. We'd say, 'We have extensive capabilities in the corporate service area. We would like to show you how you can utilize our services to streamline your procedures or perhaps even completely outsource them to us. You can then devote your resources and attention to your core business.'"

John and Mark continued to develop a market presence with public and pre-IPO companies. In the late 1980s to early 1990s, they faced significant competition from the banks. Until 1987, banks were able to handle cashless option exercises and sales exclusively, lending money with options as collateral to accommodate a same-day sale. In the fourth quarter of 1987, the Federal Reserve allowed securities firms the same flexibility as banks, and the brokerage firms were now in the stock option business.

"Mark saw the stock-option business in its true infancy," Palo Alto Branch Manager David Nee remembers. "If Mark wants to pursue new business, he never does it half-heartedly. In the stock option arena, he focused on various firms that had pioneered these concepts and he proposed buying them outright! He never thinks small," David adds, smiling. "Mark did alter his goals slightly, and then proceeded to recruit strategic members of these firms to move full steam ahead."

"Karen McDonald was the best," Mark says. "She represented the best practices, client relationships, and talent in the business. Karen was the department head in her former firm, and she represented capabilities that we didn't have. This included many great practices at that time: a state-of-the-art way to perform currency conversions, a method for electronic interface with the clients' optionee database, better client service representatives, and more. Karen also brought us to a national level beyond Silicon Valley. Karen McDonald was and is one of the most experienced and highly regarded stock-plan professionals in the industry."

"She has as much experience and knowledge as anyone in the business," John adds. "Karen knows what is right for the client, and she will structure our services to address the clients' needs." John describes his business relationship with Mark and Karen as very synergistic. "Mark is extremely strategic. He is able to position our business to sustain our growth in future years," he says. "He has a tremendous amount of integrity, and presents his ideas with true vision. Mark a great presenter, and is both extremely professional and knowledgeable."

John is the tactical one who is able to execute and handle day-to-day issues. His duties range from dealing with large transactional issues to working with company executives. He is generally more market-driven than the other partners.

Mark's vision, John's business-development acumen, and Karen's experience, has allowed the triad to shape the stock-plan business.

The pursuit would also benefit legions of other financial advisors. The Corporate Client Group significantly aided Shearson Lehman Brothers, a predecessor to Salomon Smith Barney, in constructing what is now considered the strongest corporate-benefits service on the Street. The firm's infrastructure currently includes an entire department, founded in 1996, dedicated to what was initially their collective vision.

Mark's team is one of the largest corporate services teams led by financial advisors in the industry. With Mark, John, and Karen at the helm, over 50 members maintain relationships and handle the influx of new business. The team's company roster currently includes well over 100 companies, many of which are Fortune 500 companies, and hundreds of thousands of plan participants.

John describes the team's secret to their full-service capability as: "Quality service and execution. We are capable of providing this through a combination of technology and an experienced client-driven team. Few can match our high level of commitment or experience."

The Palo Alto-based team drives the service, but partners with other teams in various locations around the country provide local support to both the corporate client and their employees. These locations include Detroit, Toms River, Portland, Seattle, Southern California and New York. At the Palo Alto office, there is never a dull moment.

While spending a day with Mark and his team, I witnessed an impressive operation. The team seems more like a start-up, with strong revenue growth and players recruited from other organizations. It constantly appears as if every individual is working on a highly urgent project with a sense of purpose.

Mark likens the growth of the team to a professional sports team. "We are in enough different businesses now, that it's similar to drafting players," he says. "You draft the best athlete and you figure out who plays what position later. At some point, you just hope that everyone doesn't want to play the same position.

"Our team is essentially an example of one plus one equals four," Mark continues. "And every individual is a key component to our overall success. Even though someone may just represent one part of the our operations, they can have a dramatic effect on our entire business."

Mark is a big proponent of incentive-based compensation, giving each member of the team a piece of the overall revenue. "It's important for people to feel like they're an owner of the business, and that they can affect our level of success. Our success is the product of our collective hard work.

"The incentive that we use to reward each member of the team leads to innovation, and high responsiveness to our clients' evolving needs," Mark says. "This has been a critical component of our success." This reasoning is the basis of many industry-wide innovations that the Group has developed in response to customer needs.

Examples of their innovations include their role as the first group in the industry to electronically interface with clients' databases, in 1989. Another example takes place in 1991 when a client, a major high-technology company in Northern California, mentioned to Mark the benefits of having a voice-response system for their 401(k) plan. Mark and the client flew to New York. Shortly thereafter, the team introduced the industry's first interactive voice-activated response system for clients' information inquiries, real-time quotes and real-time execution of employee transactions in the stock plan industry. "This resulted in a quicker and more efficient process for the employee, and off-loaded many of the employee inquiries from the company," he says.

Several years later, another major technology company requested a more streamlined option exercise process. The team worked to address the regulatory issues necessary to accommodate the clients' needs and virtually eliminate the paper flow. Most recently, a major software firm provided significant input by beta testing the firm's stock plan website capabilities.

One of the benefits of this team is that every client has access to an appropriate team member. "Clients don't want to get voice mail, or even an 'I'll have someone get back to you,'" Mark says. "That's why we attempt to have multiple contact people for every client."

Mark even makes it a policy to have two Group members participate in client meetings. "This way, they build relationships with more than just one person, and the back-up person is familiar with the client," Mark says. "I believe that when clients evaluate their financial advisors, they primarily base their review on the relationship. Everything else is second to that."

Corporate clients have at least one dedicated team member to help employees with the reinvestment of their stock proceeds. Others are responsible for various client services, including cashiering, fixed-income, cash, knowledge in rule-144 stock, hedging strategies, foreign exchange needs, and asset management services.

Salomon Smith Barney's Palo Alto-based Corporate Client Group has won the business of many of the world's largest companies largely based on the combination of their experience, capabilities, and reputation. "We handle the accounts for many of the company's employees," John says. "Some of them are high-net-worth individuals, and some are newer employees. Regardless, we attempt to provide them all with great service. You never know who might have the best connection within the company to earn more business, or who might be going to be the next hot start-up."

Mark is currently positioning the Group for what he believes is an imminent convergence. "Aggregation of accounts, or one-stop shopping, will continue to be significant trend in the future," he begins. "The advent of new technologies will change the expectations and demands a client has for us. The advice quotient will not change, but what will change is the expectation that we can make it easier to manage their financial lives. To maintain a leading edge, we will have to provide a platform that aggregates their various accounts at one spot, even if it's not from a proprietary source.

"This convergence will occur among all financial-services-related professionals: financial planners, lawyers, accountants, bankers and others. Imagine your accountant, your broker and your banker having on-line access to your personal financial web site. Imagine the value equation: our collective abilities to provide more timely and comprehensive advice to clients, while at the same time utilizing technology to reduce a large portion of costs associated with delivering that advice."

Mark senses that this trend will create more strategic partnerships. "I think it will become a requirement for the CPAs, banks and others in the financial industry seeking to broaden their business," Mark says. "And for the brokerage firms that want greater distribution, it could be enabled via strategic alliances." He continues to explain the challenges these parties will face as they pursue additional revenues. "Will bankers or CPAs really want to develop sophisticated asset-allocation strategies? What about all the compliance issues? And if they decide they want to be a money manager, the basic nature of their core client relationship will shift in a very substantial way.

"If these parties seek to build their own capabilities, as well as their own brand which they'll need to establish credibility, it's going to be expensive and will experience some obvious delays in market. Joint ventures are the best way to go for them." Mark feels that full-service firms like Salomon Smith Barney are most likely to form these strategic relationships.

Mark underscores that it would be a mistake to ever de-emphasize high-net-worth individuals. "Our high-net-worth clients see tremendous value in outsourcing their financial-management requirements to us, and when we do well for them, they tend to refer other business to us."

The same concept that has worked well for the high-net-worth market has provided a blueprint for the group's success in the corporate marketplace. "We use the same consulting approach that we use with high-net-worth individuals." Mark adds, "We feel we can really add a tremendous amount of value in helping them manage their business more efficiently."

For example, a start-up company may need up to ten outside vendor relationships in place to support their corporate infrastructure. "By outsourcing these critical tasks to us," Mark says, "we can become the business enterprise's consultants of choice in matters of retirement-plan management, cash management, stock plans and more."

He also sees growing corporate emphasis in the utilization of deferred compensation plans. "I have read that in the next ten years, there will be more assets in deferred compensation plans than 401(k) plans. From a competitive market standpoint, how much competition is there in the 401(k) area? How much competition is there in deferred compensation?" Mark explains that this might be a tremendous new marketing opportunity. "You don't have to be a great a salesperson if the market opportunity is that great," he reasons.

Mark points to the downsizing of America's biggest companies which has occurred, with the outsourcing of various functions to outside companies, as a significant trend over the last ten years. "We have benefited from this trend significantly. We also realize that many of our clients may experience career risk from the choice of outside vendors. We are very sensitive and respectful of that issue. This is why it's imperative that we know how the various issues interrelate: How employee communications issues might relate to stock plans, which relate to deferred comp, and so on. Furthermore, these companies shouldn't have to add additional staff just manage our relationship."

Mark feels strongly about the benefits of employee ownership and believes that this domestic trend will become a global one as well. "It's exciting to see international companies set up incentive-based compensation plans."He has also participated in this movement through the time he gives to industry associations. Mark was a founding board member of the Global Equity Organization (GEO). GEO is a non-profit association that unites leaders within the equity-based employee compensation arena. These are individuals dedicated to encouraging and promoting the highest standards of professionalism and administration within equity-share plans throughout the world. The organization provides an open forum for exchange among its members, whereby communications are open, regardless of position or affiliation. "This is a global trend, and this organization is at the forefront to help ensure the best practices," he says.

Mark believes that success is partially measured by what you give back to the industry, as well as the community in general. "In reality, the more you give to your industry and the community, the more you will be rewarded for it," he says. "If nothing else, giving seems to re-energize you, especially if you're helping out within your own industry. By sharing your own ideas and thoughts, it can help to reconfirm your own approach with others who are familiar with the business."

Recently, Mark and his team spent considerable time preparing a response to a request for proposal from a large corporation. In the end, the deal went to a competitor. When Mark heard the news, he called the winning consultant and congratulated him. "He was shocked to hear from me," Mark says. "As much as I hate to lose, I was genuinely happy for him, and I believe that the client will be well served." Still, to this day, he has never received a similar call. "I don't understand why others don't feel the same way," he says in a serious, yet surprised voice.

There are few who are as accepting of failure as Mark."I have never been afraid of failure. It's not because I always believed I was would succeed. It is because our business almost requires a lot of failure to succeed," he says. He compares this to cold calling, where a financial advisor will statistically have to make many calls to open a new account. Using Mark's logic, more "no's" will inevitably lead to more "yes's.""When I look at my achievements, I look at the amount of failure that it took to get here. I strongly believe that success partly comes from the acceptance of our willingness to fail."

Mark cautions that using this line of thinking requires one to calculate the downside, or pain factor, of failure."I would never recommend that someone pursue anything if the downside of failure is greater than the reward of succeeding," he says. When he's coaching his children's basketball team or offering advice to his kids about competition, he tells them that there can be multiple winners."There's the winner of the game, but anyone who tries their hardest and gives it their best shot is never a loser. Eventually, or inevitably, that person is and will be a winner."

Mark recounts another vision he has for the future."I expect to be in this business forever. My father worked right up to his last year, at age 77,"he says.

"I hope they will never make me retire. This is what I do and love. Plus, I hope to see my sons succeed in this business." Mark then ventures to guess what the business will look like at that point in time, and how he's going to position his business. "R.J., fifteen years from now we'll be…" he begins with a smile.

Sigmund Munster
The Complete Package

Morgan Stanley
Columbus, Ohio

See related section:
Building Loyalty and Relationships: Relationships, Relationships, Relationships

Like many successful financial advisors, Sigmund "Sig" Munster is engaged in the lucrative 401(k) business. He's selling the same product his competition sells. A company may not want to go to the trouble of transferring the plan it already has to a new provider. So the question is: What can Sig offer when selling 401(k) programs that will separate him from the rest of the field? As in so many success stories, the answer is service, but for Sig, service of a particular kind. "With 401(k) business," he says, "one of the keys to service is education."

"As obvious as this may seem," he explains, "many of our competitors try to skip the education part. I suppose it's a combination of not having the experience to educate their clients and employees, and a lack of time to do it properly. But this is an important ingredient that can't be left out of the recipe. To omit it would be like leaving out the yeast when you bake a loaf of bread. The right way to do the job is to make sure that all the participants understand how the plan works. Believe me, this is time-consuming. It requires going to the client's site and conducting group sessions for the employees. It also means meeting with individuals on a one-to-one basis.

"Often, it's a matter of assisting participants with the investment selection and tailor-making an individual's plan to help meet his or her personal needs. Then there's a lot of detail work because there are a lot of forms and applications to complete. But you've got to do it right, or you're going to have an unhappy client."

Much of the detail work is at the administration end of the business. Here, there's considerable paperwork to switch a company with an existing 401(k) plan over to a Morgan Stanley account. "We have home office people who focus in these conversions," Sig says. "It's vital to make sure that the company's data runs smoothly from their computer to our computer. When it comes to things like payroll deductions, for instance, there can be no room for error."

Sig and his team have been involved in the development of the 401(k) business at Morgan Stanley from the beginning. They have been instrumental in helping to shape the program. "We built this from the ground up, through extensive research and analysis of what our customers want most from a 401(k) plan," Sig says. "That's why we can offer a custom-designed, hassle-free program that fits the needs of each company we prospect.

"Once we set up a 401(k) plan, that's just the beginning. We're continually helping clients complete required forms, and these forms are always being updated. We take pride in doing this sort of paperwork in an orderly fashion, always making sure everything is properly completed. We do it all. The complete package."

Sig's son, Greg, a Financial Advisor and partner, adds: "The client is number one. And when we work with our clients, it's one client at a time. Each client is very unique to us, with his or her own goals and objectives."

Sig emphasizes that it takes a team effort to implement a 401(k) plan. His team consists of his son, Greg, long-time associates Henry Ricter and Mike Mahle, and two secretaries. The financial advisors work as a partnership. Each have a percentage of ownership, similar to the way many law firms operate. Because everyone has a vested interest in providing superior service to 401(k) clients, the team functions with clocklike precision.

Similar to how he built his traditional clientele of individual investors, the lion's share of Sig's 401(k) business also comes from satisfied clients and their referrals. Many clients who invested with Sig in years past have prospered, and now own or operate successful enterprises. Pleased with the way their personal accounts are handled, they approach his team to implement their pension plans. Of course, Sig and his partners aren't shy about soliciting their clients for business. "With the number of clients we service," he explains, "there's a reservoir of leads for us to call on that will keep us busy for years. It's just a matter of calling them up and saying, 'We've done a pretty good job for you,' and waiting for him to agree. Then, I'll add, 'I'd like to talk to you about your company's 401(k) plan. When's a convenient time for me to come out to see you?'"

Sig's son, Greg, says, "We ask everyone we do business with for leads. It's not only the owners and heads of companies that we ask. Referrals from employees of companies have also been very beneficial to us."

As soon as the team makes contact with the head of human resources or whoever is responsible for this benefit, the team sets up a meeting. "Once we get in the door for a presentation," says Sig, "we can provide pretty compelling reasons why their company and employees will benefit from transferring their plan to us."

One of the first questions Sig and Greg ask a prospect is: "Are you happy with your provider?" Greg says, "If their provider can't offer all the services we've got under one roof, including education, then we ask them to give us due consideration. 'Look at our results,' we'll say. 'We have a variety of quality mutual funds from which to choose, and you're not limited to just our funds. You will have access to a variety of funds.'"

"It's important that they know they have choices," Sig adds. "Many providers can't offer choices. With us, we have relationships with a number of outside mutual funds companies or other providers. We can even give access to individual money managers, not just mutual funds. We have a very compelling story."

As many financial advisors realize, it's hard to get a company to change providers, especially if they have been satisfied with their current provider for years. "The biggest challenge is getting through the conversion process," Sig says. "In fact, Greg is currently undergoing two conversions.

"Companies consider conversions to be a real headache," Sig continues. "If we hadn't done it so many times, it would be a headache for us, too. We just have it down to a science; we've practically perfected the process. We make it so easy for a prospect, that if there are any long-term benefits at all, it's worth it. The key is to ensure that it's absolutely the right decision for the client and the participants. If you do the best thing for a client, and the best thing for the participants, down the road everybody's going to be happy."

With all the corporate retirement plans Sig and his team recruit, with hundreds of thousands of participants, how are they able to maintain a high level of individual service? "When a 401(k) customer needs help immediately, no matter where they are in the country, and even if someone on my team can't be there fast enough to provide this service, we'll have someone there from one of our local branch offices ASAP," Sig says. He notes that the older, more established firms, such as the fund companies, don't have the people in the field to service clients' needs. "This is probably the most needed aspect of the service," he says.

Sig also mentions that he completes the entire package by providing high-quality back-office support, which ensures that all paperwork is completed and updated, and is always in compliance with legal requirements. "This can save clients money in legal fees, and other related fees," he adds.

When asked to sum up the reasons why so many companies have transferred their corporate plans to the team, Sig is quick to offer the following list of advantages and services it can offer:

- A custom-designed employee communications program aimed at building awareness of the importance of saving for retirement, educating participants on the various investment options, and motivating them to remain active retirement savers

- Dedication to Retirement Planning, through specialists who can educate the plan's participants, assist them with investment selection, and guide them through the details of the plan

- A single source for investment, record-keeping, compliance, and communication services that minimizes day-to-day involvement in plan administration

- A flexible, goal-oriented approach to investing, based on careful analysis of the plans' employees' needs and level of investment sophistication

- A broad choice of investment options, including dozens of outside funds, as well as a self-directed brokerage option for active investors

- State-of-the-art systems technologies that reduce paperwork and maximize efficiency

- Seamless integration with the plans' payroll service providers

- Flexible, convenient, automated account access either over the phone or on the Internet

The team recently earned a large Columbus-based 401(k) plan after they were able to meet with various departments within the firm to make the sale. "In the end, we won the plan because our costs were cheaper and they were thrilled with our education program," Sig says. "Previously, they were being serviced by one single individual in Columbus. Our story is so compelling that as long as we can get our foot in the door, we can make the sale.

"We offer a complete package."